Policy Passages

Policy Passages

Career Choices for Policy Wonks

Edited by
Howard J. Wiarda

With contributions by

Carolyn Blackwell
Steve D. Boilard
Steven Bosacker
John Brigham
Alfred G. Cuzán
Lowell R. Fleischer
Elizabeth D. Gibbons
Melvin A. Goodman
Margaret Daly Hayes
Victor C. Johnson
Thomas E. Mann

Joseph S. Nye, Jr.
Norman Ornstein
Thomas Orum
Janine T. Perfit
Susan Kaufman Purcell
William D. Rogers
Rebecca Root
William Schneider
Donna E. Shalala
K. Larry Storrs
Howard J. Wiarda

PRAEGER

Westport, Connecticut
London

Library of Congress Cataloging-in-Publication Data

Policy passages : career choices for policy wonks / edited by Howard J. Wiarda.
    p. cm.
    Includes bibliographical references and index.
    ISBN 0-275-97528-2 (alk. paper)—ISBN 0-275-97529-0 (pbk. : alk. paper)
    1. Policy science—Vocational guidance—United States. I. Wiarda, Howard J., 1939–
H97.P6488 2002
320'.6'02373—dc21   2002070904

British Library Cataloguing in Publication Data is available.

Library of Congress Catalog Card Number: 2002070904
ISBN: 0-275-97528-2
    0-275-97529-0 (pbk.)

First published in 2002

Praeger Publishers, 88 Post Road West, Westport, CT 06881
An imprint of Greenwood Publishing Group, Inc.
www.praeger.com

Printed in the United States of America

The paper used in this book complies with the
Permanent Paper Standard issued by the National
Information Standards Organization (Z39.48-1984)

10 9 8 7 6 5 4 3 2 1

Contents

III. Life as a Policy Wonk

IV. Expanding Access and Influence

V. Conclusions

Introduction:
Pursuing Careers in Public Policy

Howard J. Wiarda

Many of us who enter the political science or public policy fields do so because we want to influence the policy process as well as study it. We recognize, of course, that we need to acquire knowledge and expertise in our field but we also want to move the policy process along, and to translate our best and noblest ideas and ideals into good policy. As young people just beginning our careers, that is one of the main reasons to study political science.

To date, however, there is no book that tells us how to do that, how to get started, how to influence policy, what career options are open at different points in our lives, and what lifestyle and even lifetime consequences follow from the career, graduate school, or law school options that we choose. There are dozens of self-help books for young people and seemingly endless brochures that describe internships or provide addresses and phone numbers of Washington-based think tanks, government agencies, and congressional committees. But there's no book that describes what it's like to have a career in these policy-making agencies, what you actually do when you work on policy issues, or how and in what positions you go about influencing the policy process. That is what this book seeks to provide.

Our title is a takeoff on the title of writer/journalist Gail Sheehy's provocative best-seller of a few years back, *Passages*. Whereas Ms. Sheehy analyzes the age passages we go through in life (20s, 30s, etc.), this book focuses on policy passages: the key choices that we face at different stages of our lives—particularly as young people—and the consequences of the career choices that we make. These issues have acquired particular poignancy in recent times as careers have become more uncertain, jobs less secure, and as many people struggle to balance career, family, and other obligations.

Here is the dilemma. Many young people between the ages of eighteen and twenty-two are facing the first big, important, long-term choices of their lives: what to major in or what combination of courses, certificates, and degrees to put together; whether to stop at the B.A. degree (and then what?); whether to get a job, try for an internship, or go on for a law degree or an M.A. or Ph.D. This is the first critical policy "passage" in their lives. Many of these students are interested in policy careers but they usually know almost nothing about what those careers are like, how much and what kind of education is necessary, what it's like to work in the White House or on Capitol Hill, and how far they can go and in which directions if they opt for a policy career. Yet it has been our experience that many of these decisions are made in the dark, with insufficient knowledge and often bad advice. Our book seeks to remedy that situation.

A second "passage" occurs a few years later (it often seems like a lifetime!), in the mid-to-late twenties, after you have gained some experience or earned an M.A., a law degree, or a Ph.D. At this stage, you must decide what career options are open, how these differ from the options open to someone with only a B.A., and whether you're interested in government service or a public policy career if, to go directly into government from school or try to establish a private career and reputation first in law, business, research, or teaching, and then go into public service. Or perhaps, if you have a job in Washington or in state or local government directly out of college, you've discovered by this stage there's a glass ceiling above which, without more education, you cannot go, and so in your mid-to-late-twenties you decide to go back to school, a difficult step if you've been earning a salary, have a car and, your own apartment, and are preparing to become a "poor, struggling" student again.

A third policy "passage," we have found, occurs around ages 35 to 40. This is not quite a "mid-life crisis" yet, but let's face it, you are getting up there. You may still be floundering, or perhaps happily settled but still "itchy" in your present career, or maybe you've decided you made a mistake early on and a career shift is in order. You may feel dissatisfied, want to do more or go higher, want an alternative lifestyle and a different career, more education, or perhaps pursue the career you wanted at age twenty, but for a variety of reasons were unable to follow. How then do you go about switching careers in mid-life? Is accomplishment in one career transferable to another one? How do you shift at this age from being a young lawyer or scholar to being a policy influential—or perhaps vice versa?

The fourth policy "passage" we have identified comes in the fifties. By this point our policy wonk may have already had a successful career and be eligible for early retirement. Should you take the early retirement, do you want to be "put out to pasture" this early, or are other possible policy-relevant career options open? How, at this stage, do you make the transition, for example, from a career in foreign affairs, politics, the armed forces, or teaching and research to a career as a public policy-oriented foundation executive, a decision maker at a non-governmental organization (NGO), or perhaps the administrator of an international studies or public policy program at a college or university. At this age, career policy wonks often have a difficult (but by no means impossible) time adjusting back to the life of a modern university; on the other hand, if you're an academic in your mid-fifties and have never been in government before, it may be a difficult (but not impossible) task, at this stage, to make the adjustment to a government career.

This book is designed to inform young and maybe not-quite-so-young political science and public policy students about career options in politics and policy making. It does so by focusing on the real-life career experiences of policy makers with political science backgrounds, as well as political scientists who go in and out ("in'n'outers" in Washington terms) of government service in varying capacities and at different stages of their careers. A great variety of persons of diverse backgrounds, age, race, gender, and career tracks are included in this book.

It has been our experience, after many years of listening to, talking with, and advising college and university-age people (including our own college-age children) that they often lack the basic information to make intelligent decisions about careers and career patterns. Usually their peers, parents, college counselors, or faculty advisors are not well informed about most policy careers, what's necessary to qualify for them, or what, often lifetime, implications follow from the choices made. If I opt to stop my education at the B.A. level, then what are the possibilities open to me and what are the limits or "glass ceilings" on my career? Should I try to get a law degree; an M.A. (Master of Arts), M.P.A. (Master of Public Administration), or M.P.P. (Master of Public Policy) in a good public policy program; or possibly aim to get a Ph.D? How and in what areas do these advanced degrees improve career opportunities?

Another important question is whether I should enter public service immediately upon completion of school or first establish a reputation in another career (law, scholarship, journalism, for example) and then use that as a stepping-stone to enter public service but, hopefully, at a higher level? If I'm interested in being a policy wonk, whether at the local, state, or national level, should I try to do so at age 21, 25, or 40? These are often not easy questions to answer, but let us provide one example—with numerous others supplied later in the book. At the Department of State, for instance, it used to be that the entering age of young FSOs (Foreign Service Officers) was in the early twenties, often directly out of college. Now, the average age of beginning FSOs is twenty-seven or twenty-eight, almost all of whom have an advanced degree (master's or law degree; a Ph.D. is less valued in the State Department), foreign-language speaking ability, and two to three years experience abroad with a private business, Peace Corps, or in some other capacity. So at State (and elsewhere in the federal government) the average age of new policy makers is going up and their level of training and experience is increasing as well.

"If I opt for a career as a policy wonk," my students ask, "am I committed to stay with it forever? What if I get tired of it and want to change, am I locked in?" Emphatically not, our contributors say. In fact, one of the most significant findings of our survey is how often and how readily policy wonks change jobs. Most of our contributors have had three, four, five, or more careers in their lifetimes, often going back and forth between academia, think tanks, government work, politics, the private sectors, foundations, and so on. Some of these are "in'n'outers" who regularly, in the famous Washington "revolving door" process, teach or work for private companies for a time, then go into government for a time, then return to teaching, writing, the private sector, then back to government again, and so on. Others stay with the same issues or area (human rights, Latin America) but may work for four to five different organizations in the course of a career. Still others work in public policy for a time and then get out permanently—or are "retired" by the voters. The paths and patterns are immensely varied; in future generations, as job mobility likely increases, the number of job and career changes that people make is likely to increase even more.

This book seeks to provide answers to the career questions posed here. It does so by examining the career patterns of persons who have made or are making all these choices, who have gone through or are presently going through these "passages." It brings together the life histories of policy makers of different ages, different careers, and in different policy positions. Lawyers, academics, interns, defense officials, foreign service officers, congressional aides, career public servants, staff assistants, state and local government officials, United Nations administrators, lobbyists, and many others all make an appearance in these pages. The variety of points of view and career paths is astounding.

Each contributor, representing a great variety of careers, ages, backgrounds, and professions, has been asked to analyze his or her career, the options open at different stages, and the lifestyle and career implications of decisions made early in life. Not all career options and contingencies can be presented, of course, but certainly the major ones are here. And, after all, there is no one magic formula; as our contributors' testimonies certainly reveal, we all have to find our own niche, our own way, often by trial and error. Indeed, one of the striking themes that comes through loud and clear from a number of our contributors is—once you're prepared and have the right credentials—how often luck, serendipity, and just being in the right place at the right time plays a role.

To facilitate thinking about alternative career options and possibilities, our authors have been asked to follow, as much as possible, a common outline. They have been asked to analyze and ruminate about their own careers, the agencies where they've worked, both the paths taken and the paths not taken, and the consequences that followed from these choices. For example, we ask each author to provide a brief autobiographical statement concerning his or her background—without it turning into an uninteresting ego trip. Then we ask them about early career decisions in college: their choice of a major, how they became interested in their particular career goals, what their thinking was about graduate or law school, and what they decided: first, at ages 18–22, then at ages 24–28 (presumably, if they had continued their education), and later in life.

Next, we asked them to tell us about their early careers: their experiences, if they were happy with the choices they made, if they'd considered other options and when? Some of our contributors were so happy with their careers that they stayed with them, others shifted jobs in their late twenties or thirties, still others decided their early experiences were valuable but, usually with only a B.A., found a glass ceiling held them back from advancing, and were determined to go back to school for more education. We asked our older authors if they contemplated a career shift around ages 35–40, about sticking with their original careers, or exploring other options in their forties. Don't forget that even for 55-year-olds, life isn't over. Indeed, we found career shifts in every age as people contemplated whether they should keep going, change jobs, or take early retirement.

This is not just the usual "telephone book" of career options and Washington addresses found on your college counselor's desk—useful though that is. Rather, it is a living, breathing discussion by real people of their career goals and dreams, their accomplishments and disappointments, of good steps, missteps, and missed steps. Every one of our contributors has actually lived the life that she or he describes, has firsthand knowledge and experiences in the careers and agencies described here, knows the policy arena intimately and personally, and is able to describe vividly what it's like to have a career in the State Department, CIA, the think tanks, Congress, and other policy-relevant institutions. Is the work exciting or boring (the former, almost all our contributors agree), creative or bureaucratic (a little of both—but that's true in all jobs), worthwhile or not (emphatically, YES). Indeed, almost all our contributors agree that their public-policy experiences were among the high points of their lives.

Then, there is the question of education: how much education should one get, what degrees, and when? What's the best way to prepare for a policy career, to get started, to wedge open the door? Almost uniformly our contributors advise: get an internship, go to Washington, work on a campaign, get as much education as possible. For these are tough career choices to make, and they can best be made by listening to people, of a variety of ages, who've already gone, or are presently going through, the process, who have a wealth of experience, who know what it's like from inside the system.

The book explores some fascinating and innovative modern themes. One of these is whether women's policy career patterns are significantly different from those of men: more uncertain, often interrupted because of family obligations, or not. Do minorities and naturalized citizens, in this increasingly multicultural society, follow the same career patterns or do they have added barriers to overcome? And how are careers shifting: from the public to more private sector activities; from national to state, local, and urban issues; from the State and Defense Departments during the cold war to (in this age of globalization) the more economic departments like commerce, treasury, and the office of the trade representative? As issues such as the environment, health care, and education come to the fore, do jobs and opportunities increase in the agencies responsible for these issues as our priorities change?

In this volume we have contributors representing not only a variety of age levels (our "passages"), but also a diversity of ethnic and racial backgrounds. Men and women are equally represented. There are lawyers, diplomats, cabinet officials, congressional staffers, CIA and military officials, governors' aides, professors, graduate students, denizens of the think tanks, UN officials, media experts, and a great variety of others. All write from a personal perspective about their careers, why they chose the careers they did, what they actually do in their various jobs, and the opportunities as well as missteps along the way.

We believe there is a crying need for such a volume. There is nothing comparable in the literature. For this is not just a manual of names and addresses but a series of personal statements, life histories, career options, hard choices, forks in the road, and the lifelong results of the career choices all of us are called on to make. Students, parents, college counselors, advisors, and anyone who is contemplating a career in public policy will want to read this book. It is aimed mainly at those, students and others, who are just beginning their careers; but those who are contemplating a career switch or finding their present positions disappointing should peruse the book as well. There is much useful information here for policy wonks of all ages.

A LOOK AHEAD

Twenty or thirty years ago it was still possible, with only a bachelor's degree, to contemplate a rewarding career in Washington policy making. By now, however, that possibility is quickly disappearing; in virtually every agency we sampled, we found that a master's has become almost required as an entry-level degree. In some cases (for example, congressional staff, the State Department) we found that the master's degree is really all you need to move ahead and have a rewarding career, but in many other agencies, think tanks, and so forth, a Ph.D. or law degree is often necessary to move up to higher levels. In other words, in these latter agencies a master's degree may get you your first job but after a couple of years as a research assistant, you may discover a glass ceiling and that a more advanced degree is necessary to go to the top. That discovery helps explain a second career passage and why a large proportion of graduate and law school students in the Washington-area universities consists of people in their late twenties or thirties who are already working in public policy jobs but find they need more education and more training to move ahead.

Our book, therefore, begins with contributions from persons who stopped at the bachelor's or master's degree and the career options—and limits—open to them. We begin with a brief biographical statement from Carolyn Blackwell who received her bachelor's degree from Wheaton College in Massachusetts. Ms. Blackwell began her Washington career working in the development or fund-raising office of one of Washington's major think tanks, then moved up in that same think tank as a research/administrative assistant to one of its senior scholars. She thoroughly enjoyed that work for four or five years and also worked for the Montgomery County (a Washington suburb) Planning Commission but then, recognizing that she could not rise any higher, went back to graduate school in urban planning.

A similar story is told by our second contributor, Janine Perfit. Ms. Perfit came to Washington directly out of college, worked for a time at a think tank, the Center for Strategic and International Studies, then got another think tank job as a research assistant at the American Enterprise Institute for Public Policy Research (AEI), and almost immediately began studying for her master's degree at Georgetown University while working at the same time. Her employer encouraged her graduate school career by providing for flexible hours. Finishing the master's, Ms. Perfit stayed on at AEI for a time with greater responsibilities, before undertaking a career passage of her own to successful careers as a program director at the International Republican Institute and, later, the Inter-American Development Bank.

Our next contributor, Steven Bosacker, has had a very interesting career. He was active in politics in college and, on that basis, was invited to join the staff of Congressman Tim Penny of Minnesota. Mr. Bosacker enjoyed his career as a congressional staffer immensely, eventually reaching the position of chief of staff. But over time he, too, decided to go back to school and get a master's in public administration (MPA). He then worked as staff director for the board of regents at the University of Minnesota, but could not resist returning to a high public policy position as Chief of Staff to Governor Jesse Ventura, responsible for 50,000 employees.

The next main section of our book relates the stories of persons who did go on for advanced degrees right away, went directly from undergraduate college to law or graduate school, and, building on their academic training, enjoyed high-level careers in public policy—or perhaps went back and forth between public service and other kinds of rewarding careers. In this section we begin to see one of the most interesting findings that emerges from the book: in general, the higher the level of education one has, the more options and possibilities one has in a policy career. Some persons, we have already seen, can have rewarding careers with only a bachelor's or master's degree; but it is also the case that for a person interested in public policy, a law degree, or Ph.D. often gives you both more opportunities and more options in your career.

We begin this section with a contribution from prominent public law professor John Brigham. Prof. Brigham was a student activist at Berkeley in the 1960s, and informs us that he still has that Berkeley activism as part of his value system. Prof. Brigham has been involved in numerous public policy issues but for his career has chosen to remain in academia. He makes the interesting comment that he seeks to influence public policy indirectly through his research, teaching, and the many students he has had who have gone on to law, judgeships, and other policy careers. A professorship also gives one enormous amounts of time and freedom to pursue issues in depth and independently, which is rarely true in public service.

A second essay in this section comes from Lowell Fleischer. Dr. Fleischer also received his Ph.D. in political science, took the Foreign Service exam while still in graduate school, and opted for a career with the Department of State as a Foreign Service Officer. His has been an exciting and rewarding career at embassies in Eastern Europe and Latin America as well as at the State Department in Washington, D.C.

The third essay is by Prof. Joseph Nye, who is presently Dean of the Kennedy School of Government at Harvard University. Dr. Nye has had a fascinating career as a teacher, author, and government official. He has occupied several high-level government positions and is known as an "in'n'outer": one who goes into government for a time, then returns to teaching and research, then back to government in a different agency and at a higher level, back again to teaching and writing, and so on. It makes for a varied and interesting career but is sometimes a little hard on moving expenses and on children and families who need to change schools, friends, and addresses frequently.

The next chapter is by Susan Kaufman Purcell. She is another "in'n'outer" and has had a marvelous career as a teacher, writer, government official, research institute scholar, and overall policy influential. In other words, she is one of those who, when she writes something about foreign affairs, people sit up, take notice, and actually read it. But like other "in'n'outers" such comings and goings between several careers can sometimes be disruptive and lead to a lack of permanence in any one single position.

The last statement in this section is by Attorney William Rogers. Mr. Rogers was a political science major as an undergraduate and opted for law school over graduate school. He has practiced law at various times in his career but he has always had a strong interest in public policy and has served in government in a variety of capacities. Mr. Rogers is a partner in the big Washington law firm of Arnold & Porter and is widely thought of as a consummate Washington "insider." When he wants to get something done, he knows what phone numbers to call, whom to reach, and how to wheel and deal, how to make the wheels of government turn—and his phone calls are always returned at the highest levels of the U.S. government. If you opt for a career in law but want also to be a policy influential, Biu Rogers would be an excellent role model.

The next section of the book tells about life as a policy wonk at a variety of levels and in a diversity of careers. In the first chapter Steve Boilard, a Californian, discusses his career and the work he does as a policy researcher working for the state legislature in Sacramento. Next Elizabeth Gibbons, a Smith College graduate who went on to get a master's degree at Columbia University, talks about her career as an international civil servant working with the United Nations Children's Fund (UNICEF) on humanitarian relief programs in Africa, Haiti, and Central America. The editor of this volume follows with a chapter on Washington think tanks, what these institutions do and how they influence policy, with some hints about obtaining internships, positions as research assistants, and senior scholar positions.

In the next chapter, K. Larry Storrs tells about how his career as a missionary, graduate student, and young academic led him to satisfying work as a researcher with the Congressional Research Service (CRS), which serves as Congress's research arm. Our next contributor, Victor Johnson, had a similarly rewarding career with the Congress, serving first as a congressional aide and then moving up to chief of staff of an important congressional foreign affairs subcommittee during a time of particularly controversial policy. Later, under President Clinton, Johnson moved over to the executive branch serving as regional director of the Peace Corps.

The media has become increasingly important in American politics; people now get their information more from television than from any other source. So here we devote considerable attention both to the media and to the important issue of how politicians and others deal with the media. We begin with a chapter by Norman Ornstein who, in addition to holding forth at one of Washington's major think tanks (AEI), is known as Washington's leading "quotemeister." Ornstein spends an enormous amount of time on the telephone providing political background and information to journalists; he is rewarded by being designated by the *Washington Post* as "the most quoted person in Washington."

Next comes an essay by Thomas E. Mann. Mann is Ornstein's counterpart (and good friend) at another think tank, the Brookings Institution. Over the years the two have collaborated on a great variety of Washington programs sponsored jointly by AEI and Brookings, to provide policy orientation for freshman congressmen, to train journalists on foreign policy analysis, and most recently to provide insights on how the leading presidential candidates would actually govern, as distinct from campaigning. Both Mann and Ornstein are professional political scientists who have parlayed their graduate training into full-time careers, with Mann serving as executive director of the American Political Science Association before moving to Brookings as director of studies.

Another contributor with extensive executive branch experience is Melvin Goodman who for many years worked as an analyst for the CIA on Soviet affairs, and later had a second career with the Department of Defense. Goodman's essay deals with some controversial issues that all would-be policy wonks must weigh carefully: how much of your own life and integrity must you give up for the sake of the agency you work for, what if your employer politicizes the analysis you provide and distorts it for partisan purposes, and what happens when your own values conflict with those of your employer?

Another professional political scientist is well-known CNN television political commentator William Schneider. Like so many of our contributors, Bill Schneider has had a varied career as a teacher, think tank scholar, writer, and now television star. Watch Bill carefully the next time you see him on CNN: his genius is to take complex political science concepts, techniques, polling, and analysis and put them in laymen's terms that the general viewing public can understand. He recounts his career and tells what it's like to be CNN's chief political commentator. Next time you see Bill on television, ask yourself if your understanding of what he's talking about derived from your taking Poli Sci 101!

Our next section deals with issues of expanding access, opportunities, and influence. In the first essay of this section, Margaret Daly Hayes tells the story of her career and deals with the issue of women in public policy. The question is: Do women have special barriers that they must overcome to pursue careers in public policy and in moving up the career ladder? The answer seems to be, even in the twenty-first century, yes. Take the case of Dr. Hayes herself. In many respects she has had a marvelous career, working for Johns Hopkins University, the Senate Foreign Relations Committee, as a lobbyist in the private business sector for the Department of Navy, and recently as the director of a Defense Department training center. But she has also taken time out to have a family and to spend precious quality time with her family. So being a professional woman in Washington policy making offers marvelous opportunities but it also implies occasional barriers to a woman's advancement as well as difficult tradeoffs—not necessarily insurmountable—between professional and family life. Dr. Hayes has surmounted these obstacles with grace and good humor, but not everyone can be as fortunate as she.

In the next chapter we wrestle with the complex issue of race and careers in public policy. Our contributor is Dr. Thomas Orum, an African American from Detroit, who has had a distinguished career as a scholar and diplomat. Dr. Orum joined the Foreign Service while still a graduate student and served in such countries as Brazil, Portugal, Nicaragua, and Guinea-Bissau as well as the Sinai. His chapter tells the tale of his exciting adventures abroad, but it also wrestles with the complex issues of race, racism, and affirmative action globally and within the Department of State. His views on all these issues are nuanced, insightful, and perhaps controversial.

The final chapter in this section deals with the issue of how foreign-born political scientists adjust to American politics and policy making. The answer, according to our contributor Alfred G. Cuzán is: Quite well, with some difficulties, thank you. Of course, it varies according to nationality, race, language skills, training, and other factors, and to do full justice to the subject we would need a far larger "sample" and number of contributors than is possible to include in this volume. But our purpose here is not to present a definitive scientific study, only to offer some illustrative case studies. And Cuzán does that admirably, telling us how and when he came to the United States, how he learned English, his political science background in undergraduate and graduate school, and his career both as a political scientist and as a policy-engaged citizen, involved in the hot issues of academic politics and U.S. foreign policy.

The final section contains two chapters. The first, a sparkling and fun presentation entitled "How to Be a Public Policy Manager in Washington," is by former Secretary of Health and Human Services (HHS) Donna Shalala. Dr. Shalala had a distinguished career first as an academic political scientist, next moved into university administration and became provost of the University of Wisconsin, then was tapped by President Clinton to be his secretary of HHS, and next returned to academia as president of the University of Miami. She was widely recognized as one of Clinton's most effective cabinet secretaries. But while occupying these high positions, Prof. Shalala has not forgotten her political science roots: the chapter included here is the edited transcript of the Pi Sigma Alpha (the political science honorary) lecture she presented at a meeting of the American Political Science Association.

Following Secretary Shalala's presentation, the editor of this volume sums up the lessons learned from all our contributors and offers comments and some advice to future policy wonks poised to begin their "passage" into the exciting area of public policy.

Part I

Stopping at the Bachelor's or Master's Degrees

1

Storming Washington—
and Returning to Graduate School

Carolyn Blackwell

INTRODUCTION

The question I want to address in this chapter is when the best time is to return to graduate school. My response is biased by my own experience. Having worked for several years, it may be no surprise that I would advocate that approach. I'm writing this while immersed in my first year of graduate school where there are students of all ages and levels of experience. This gives me the enlightened position of seeing all sides of the debate. I'll go into this more later, but I would say judging from my classmates, those who are best prepared for and interested in the program are those with more direct work experience.

To provide a little bit of a personal background, I am 29 years old and am currently in a two-year master's program in urban planning at the University of Pennsylvania. I received a B.A. in international relations from Wheaton College in Massachusetts in 1992. My interest in international policy (and inability to get a job in New York) landed me in Washington, D.C., where I worked for a non-profit think tank and, later, in a position with a local government office.

Many factors motivated my decision to return to graduate school in urban planning: an intense interest in the subject, a plateau in learning and responsibilities at work, and maturity. In truth, my career would be a dead end unless I received an advanced degree. However, for years I was stumped when it came to what program to pursue. I am one of those people who is fascinated by so many things that I don't know what to choose. I'd been agonizing with indecision when it came to graduate school—sure that every program would interest me but none would totally satisfy me. That is until the day a friend told me a story that inspired a latent passion in me. The story was about the construction of a new highway, which cut off access to a thriving community. As a result, everyone who could afford to moved. The rest remained in squalor—no access to jobs, virtually no stores, and decrepit housing. I couldn't believe that such poor planning could have such dire effects. Why this story touched me so deeply and motivated me to get my master's degree in urban planning still mystifies me. Up until that point, I'd been working for a number of years on international trade policy issues—a far cry from urban planning.

But let me get right to the debate. Is it best to return to graduate school immediately after college, a couple of years later, or more? I stand firmly in my opinion that it depends. Certainly students shouldn't consider graduate school without some meaningful work experience; but maturity and solid goals are added bonuses—and both extremely personal. My advice would depend on a number of different factors. It depends on how well you prepared yourself in college for the workplace, how goal oriented you are, and how motivated you are to achieve your goals. In the policy profession, it is increasingly necessary to have a master's degree. The field is both highly competitive and requires thorough knowledge and understanding of complex issues. Knowing that graduate school is the inevitable outcome, the questions become when to go and to which program. I put it off until I was very ready to go back to school. Time can help a person better understand important personal goals and interests, which will make graduate school more fulfilling. Timing is an important consideration. Ask yourself if you are excited by what you're doing, if you are being challenged, and what would help you achieve your goals or do your job better. In the policy world, at some point, the answer will lead you back to school.

BUILDING THE FOUNDATION

Undergrads should take full advantage of the great internships available during the Summer and throughout the semester. At no other time will a person have the chance to experiment with so many different career tracks. Not only does this help students establish the foundation of their careers, but it also gives them greater insight into the professional world, which, in turn, helps them better establish their goals. Internship experience is a major component in the ability to succeed at work and, later, in school. People who seek out opportunities through internships will have many more doors open to them than those who don't. Take me, for example.

During the summer between my sophomore and junior years, I interned at a private, nonprofit, disaster-relief organization called AmeriCares. The mission of the organization is to provide critical medical supplies to areas struck by natural disasters, war, or famine. It functions solely on donated goods from aspirin to chartered

planes. The internship was a great opportunity for me to see how an office func-
tioned while exploring my idealistic interests in saving the world from disasters. I
began my internship with the mentally sapping task of organizing files, but ultimately
I became responsible for obtaining donations, writing letters to members of Congress, and loading planes destined to Iran, Ethiopia, and Russia. The projects raised
my consciousness of the indirect effects of war and authoritarianism, both of which
denied citizens the urgent medical care and food needed to survive. The internship
also gave me my first look at the challenges in undertaking these projects.

TAKING THE FIRST STEP

After college, I hoped to work on international economic development issues
for the private sector. Upon graduation, however, I had one internship, one foreign language, and one leadership role under my belt in a world where graduating students increasingly had many of each. The challenge that I was going to face
in obtaining my first job with my limited skills became obvious in my first interview. Human resource officers have a knack for displaying the stack of several
hundred resumes that describe people who are much more qualified than you. In
this particular interview, I was advised either to go back to school or take an unpaid
internship. I pursued a third option, which was to aggressively seek a job and sell
the employers on my potential.

More than anything, I knew that I was not ready to return to school. Not only
had I just emerged from four difficult years, but I also had no idea where I would
want to apply myself should I proceed toward academia. As I was desperate for
money, an unpaid internship seemed like an unrealistic option. (I have since observed
many interns take on paying jobs at night to help pay the bills until the internship
yields a paycheck.) Furthermore, I was very anxious to begin my career so that I
could better understand what it was that I enjoyed about the public policy profession.

While my career choices were few, due to my lack of experience and limited
education, my options still seemed numerous. A career in public policy could lead
to any number of jobs, including those in legal, political, business, or research offices.
I was most attracted to the world of research institutions because of the typically
broad array of subjects covered, the high caliber of analysts, and the opportunity
to be introduced to policy issues by the world's best-known scholars. The jobs available to college graduates in a think tank are essentially administrative, with the
exception of minimal research responsibilities—that is until he or she proves capable in other areas. In comparison, graduates with a master's degree fill both administrative and research positions. Because a position in a think tank is highly
competitive, those with higher degrees often fill entry-level, administrative positions in the hope of moving quickly into a research position. For example, a Ph.D.
candidate in international relations also sought the position I was after, which was
originally listed as administrative assistant.

My first invitation for an interview came from the Center for Strategic and International Studies (CSIS). The position was in the development office and the responsibilities included coordinating conferences and maintaining the membership of a group that included CEOs only from Fortune 500 companies. To me, this was obviously going to be a great opportunity to gain exposure to some of the highest-level policy makers and business leaders, as well as to learn the primary issues facing the business community. While it was clearly a departure from my interests in developing countries, I saw this job as a chance to get my feet wet as well as in the door.

As it turned out, my main responsibility in my new job was to organize the Center's thirtieth anniversary celebration. This was to be an elegant three-day gala with a number of well-known speakers and five-hundred accomplished guests. I spent my days writing letters, rewriting agendas, maintaining a database, photocopying, attending planning meetings, and sending out mass mailings. While this was not what I had in mind for myself, the experience I gained from this conference was essential to learning how to carry out very typical professional duties. In fact, in subsequent interviews, people often expressed interest when noting my event-management skills. It was not necessary, however, for me to have a master's degree to accomplish these tasks.

Early on it was clear that I would not have any research responsibilities in this position. Because I did not want to remain in an administrative position, I began to think about other opportunities about six months into the job. My preference was to stay within CSIS and move to a more research-oriented position. Shortly thereafter, a position for an administrative assistant to one of the world's leading economists became available. The position was working for a former professor of economics and long time State Department official. Because of his many years in an academic institution, I overlooked the administrative aspects of the job and felt certain that this former professor would very likely require research assistance. I was right. He was very sensitive to my interest in learning from him and was persuaded by my persistent reminders of my ability to assist with his research. The work he required was challenging and, at times, pushed me beyond what I knew how to do.

It is at this point that I feel the debate begins on whether one should have a master's degree. I was conducting research and analysis for very high-level audiences, and met frequently with policy experts. Would I have been better at my job with a master's degree? Probably. But it did not prevent me from learning the proper analytical tools and research methods necessary to do the job right. Many people would say that one learns more on the job than one would learn in school. While I cannot validate this statement, it is true that in an office, the amount that one can learn by reading everything that comes by one's desk will certainly provide an excellent education. For this reason, I felt that working in an environment with highly capable people and an infinite flow of information would best suit my professional development while I was determining where my ultimate path would lead me.

My goals in this position included not only absorbing information, but also developing contacts and building professional and technical skills. This certainly came true.

Corporations, government offices, and private institutions frequently approached my boss to conduct analysis of current international trends. I performed research for many of these projects. They included analysis of the Latin American petroleum industry, competition in the agricultural industry between the United States and Latin America, migration from Mexico to the United States, and U.S. unilateral economic sanctions. The research was rigorous and required a significant amount of investigation and analysis. In addition to research, I was able to work with a number of knowledgeable people on these projects, including members of Congress and their staff, industry leaders, and senior government officials.

Day to day, however, I was never without administrative responsibilities. This is a common feature in think tanks. On a project that involved mailing publications to 1,300 people, I sustained great injuries from eight paper cuts. CSIS, like most other research institutions, has small programs each with its own financial backing and limited resources, which are large enough to support only the essential staff—typically a scholar and a research assistant (with either a bachelor's or master's degree). The research assistant is required to wear multiple hats: secretary, analyst, editor, project manager, and creator of presentations. There are no limits to what one can accomplish in that position. The accomplishments depend solely on personal motivation. The limits are strictly bureaucratic and prohibit employees from those higher-paying positions that have more prestige, but they typically do not prevent someone from taking on great projects that may lead to publishing an article or managing a project.

The structure of a think tank encourages young people to leave after a short time. The pay is lousy and promotions are rare. Most junior staff members get itchy to leave in less than two years, but the average tenure among this group is about three years. Frankly, this structure is highly beneficial to both the institution and the individual. It maintains a consistent level of young, talented, highly motivated people in the institution at the junior level. It also encourages them to broaden their experiences by going back to school, analyzing policy from inside government, or experiencing the impact of policy from the business perspective. On the other hand, a CSIS scholar pointed out how it seems that just when the junior staff members have risen to their potential, they find a better-paying job in another institution.

MAKING THE NEXT MOVE

When it came time for me to leave CSIS, I was still unsure what job I wanted to pursue. I explored my interests by attending conferences, taking classes at nearby schools, and applying for a variety of jobs. My experience at CSIS made my resume look impressive, yet I still lacked specific expertise that many employers sought. (When the private economy is strong, the junior staff at CSIS has no trouble finding high-paying, private sector jobs, particularly in consulting.) If I were to remain in the policy arena, it seemed increasingly critical that I pursue a master's degree. This is much less true for those who transition into a job in business.

Many of my young colleagues left CSIS after two or three years for graduate school in either business or law. Both degrees were considered more practical than getting a degree in international relations or public policy. Applicants hoped that a business or law degree would teach them the technical aspects of international relations from either the business or legislative perspective. Many of these people still intended to apply their degrees to positions in the government or in think tanks, while others are lulled by the high-paying jobs in private industry.

Among the best assets of Washington are the many nearby universities, which offer classes on virtually any subject. I considered business and law schools, but ultimately I was drawn to a class I took at the University of Virginia in urban planning. My interests in international relations remained keen, but like my colleagues, I wanted to work toward a field that seemed more tangible. Urban planning combines economics, public policy, and design, and the effects of planning are felt both locally and globally. One of the leading issues facing urban planning is globalization—planners are positioning cities to better compete on an international scale. I saw this as an opportunity to combine my interests in international relations with my desire to affect real change.

I decided to spend the year before graduate school learning the fundamentals of planning in a local government office. At the Montgomery County Department of Parks and Planning in Maryland, I conducted research on a number of important issues facing the county including economic development, affordable housing, and immigration trends. The skills and knowledge that I acquired during my short tenure were the most helpful in preparing me for graduate school. I was fortunate to be working with a staff who was eager to expose me to as much as possible—a very unusual occurrence. They'd invite me to all the meetings where they thought I'd learn something, copied interesting articles, and introduced me to anyone involved in planning. After this fortunate experience, I realized how important (and lucky) it is to work for people who take an interest in your professional development. I'm very happy that I worked in the field for a year before going into an urban planning program. While I still had a lot to learn, I was exposed to a lot of important planning issues—such as the procedure of initiating and completing a task, and the biases of the various players in planning. Not only is it important to work in the field of intended study, but also I would strongly urge those who are interested in public policy to work within the government to understand how it operates. I doubt that an outsider would be able to understand the political process as well as someone who has worked within the government.

Interestingly, almost all of my colleagues in the government had master's degrees. Montgomery County's reputation in city planning is nationally renowned for its progressiveness and innovation; perhaps this has something to do with its highly educated workforce. Those who had master's degrees were better able to get promotions, more responsibilities, and higher pay than those who stopped at the undergraduate level. Like my experience at CSIS, I would have been met with a glass ceiling had I not already decided to pursue an advanced degree.

BACK TO SCHOOL

So here I was, twenty-seven years old and cramming for the GRE. My time to do the grueling application process had finally come. Choosing a graduate school is a very difficult process and requires talking to professionals, current students, and professors. My goal was to attend a university that offered the best in teaching, the most modern planning tools and techniques, and a high student caliber. Sources of information often can be biased, which perhaps makes the decision that much harder. Choosing the best school usually comes down to deciding which one offers the best opportunities when a student graduates. Among all of the schools I was considering, the University of Pennsylvania offered the best in teaching, innovation, and exposure. The program features highly acclaimed professors, hosts frequent guest lecturers by leading practitioners, and offers classes in any of its schools.

The average age of my classmates is around twenty-five. Most of the students have a few years of experience. A couple of people have come straight out of college, but they have had several planning internships. Almost all of my classmates have identified their goals and targeted their interests to the available classes and internships. Some students, however, came to graduate school not knowing what they wanted to do, but thought that getting a graduate degree would help them figure it out. That's an expensive waste of time, in my opinion. It's always a good idea to take classes in subjects that are personally intriguing—but to spend two years and thousands of dollars only puts off the inevitable decision. These are the people who will get the least out of the program and who offer the least to their classmates. Graduate school is not a place to pass time while one tries to determine career options. If students are unfocused in graduate school, they will not learn as much as their classmates and, more importantly, will not understand the application of their newly acquired knowledge. If boredom or indecision were the problem, I would urge that person to try different jobs and hope that his or her interests become clearer. While graduate school is a necessary and worthwhile investment, practical learning takes place more on the job than it does in an academic environment.

Even with my years of work experience and graduate school education, there are still challenges ahead. Because I intend to seek a position at a more senior level when I graduate, I expect to face obstacles due to my limited planning and managerial experience. I hope to offset this by getting relevant internship experience and building connections in the planning field. Having been on the hiring end, I know that experience is essential, a strong education is very important, and a personality that compliments that of one's future boss is critical. I will have locked in the first two, and I keep my fingers crossed on the last one.

CONCLUSION

What is the moral of the story?

- Do not rush the decision to attend graduate school.
- Work experience is key to becoming valuable at any job or graduate program.
- Exploring your interests by holding different jobs or by attending classes and lectures only helps to develop a deeper understanding of your goals.
- Making a choice does not lock you into a career, but consider your choices carefully.
- Don't get stuck in an unsupportive job or in one that offers little in the way of learning.
- Interested in public policy? Know that graduate school is inevitable; find out what is most compelling personally; and work for the government for at least one year.
- Find a graduate program that is personally enriching and offers the best opportunities after completion.

2

Coming to Washington to Earn an M.A. and a Career

Janine T. Perfit

Growing up in one of those not so famous "bedroom communities" of post–World War II Long Island did not lend itself to even a hint of life after high school. The daughter of a milkman and a homemaker (now referred to as a stay-at-home mom), my earliest influence was an immigrant grandmother who was fluent in French, English, and Spanish. With her prodding, I became a pen pal to her brother living in Paris, corresponding frequently in both Spanish and French, always under her watchful eye. Uncle André was fluent. I was not. Over time, however, I developed a knack for languages.

So when the time came to graduate from high school, choose a college, and leave home, I found I had not much more to cling to other than my fascination and facility with foreign languages and interest in foreign policy. College selection in the mid-1970s was based on two criteria: financial aid and moving far enough away from home so your parents couldn't drop by for a visit without first making hotel reservations. Like many of my friends, I limited my search to upstate New York and focused on purely liberal arts colleges. After a whirlwind tour of several schools that were located at least 350 miles from home, I chose the one that was the least known but offered the greatest monetary incentive to attend.

Eisenhower College, situated at the top of the Finger Lakes region in Seneca Falls, New York, was founded in 1968 as a living memorial to the former general turned peace time president. A liberal arts school originally built for fifteen-hundred students, its enrollment never rose above six hundred before it was forced to shut its doors in 1983.

The isolation of Eisenhower College in upstate New York served to shield me from national trends that pointed to technological and scientific careers as the wave of the future. I forged ahead with a major in Spanish and a minor in French, while also delving deeply into the "world studies program" that placed emphasis on comparative politics and international relations. Life after college did not enter into my plans until just a few months before graduation. Then the burning question was, "What are you going to *do* with a major in foreign languages?" More years in school seemed a daunting task and teaching languages to elementary school children was not what I had in mind either. As the deadlines for applications to graduate school approached, a rather offhanded suggestion from my French teacher opened the way for what would soon be known as a "career choice." "Why not get a master's degree in international relations emphasizing Latin American studies?" (Soon thereafter I realized how noble she had been in making this suggestion, knowing full well that Latin American studies would force me to further pursue my Spanish language skills while letting my French fall by the wayside.)

Never mind that no one in 1979 could find Latin America on a map, I applied to one program and was accepted into one program: Latin American Studies (LASP) at Georgetown University. Although the two-year master's degree program was grounded heavily in political science and economics, I was allowed to enroll based mostly on my strong language skills. I spent most of the first year playing catch up to the other students who had come to Georgetown with a broader political science background.

Working the first four months of graduate school at Yogi's Yogurt led me to think that there had to be something more to international studies than shakes and fruit toppings. The day I met with my advisor to talk about internship possibilities was the exact day he had received notice of an opening in the Latin American program at the Center for Strategic and International Studies. The well-known research organization, affiliated at the time with Georgetown University and known to Washington insiders simply as CSIS, held the generic identification of being "a hard-line think tank."

I was hired on the spot as a research assistant to the Director of the Latin American Studies Program. My duties were varied and ranged from the mundane (envelope stuffing) to the miraculous (arranging meetings between foreign heads of state and my boss). This first big break in my career also happened to coincide with an election year. In 1980, most professional staffs in Washington's think tanks (conservative and liberal) dedicated themselves to writing policy positions and prescriptions for the next president of the United States (Republican or Democrat).

Learning the ropes of how to be a foreign policy maker in this atmosphere charged with campaign rhetoric and very differing views on what America's policy should be toward other nations, provided me with a rich experience that most people don't benefit from in their first years on the job. I learned the basic importance of many things that have stayed with me throughout my career. While most might seem obvious, they are the keys to shoring up your image as a reliable, responsible, and hard-working employee:

1. Do even the most boring tasks well. Everyone has to prove themselves worthy of greater responsibilities by photocopying mass quantities of documents. Nothing makes a greater impression on a superior like a document that has been photocopied correctly.
2. Get to know your bosses' contacts. Make them part of your network of contacts. The more people you know in the field, the greater your influence will be when the need arises to know "people in high places." Avoid making enemies.
3. Keep up with the issues. The policy community jumps from theme to theme depending on which way the political winds are blowing. It is essential to keep up with the rapid changes in issues, personnel, foreign leaders, and policy debates.

The November 1980 elections brought a change to my job situation. Even before Ronald Reagan was elected president, my boss, with me in tow, took a position as Director of the Center for Hemispheric Studies at the American Enterprise Institute for Public Policy Research. (Another conservative think tank, known simply as AEI.) My duties as research assistant were much the same as they had been at CSIS, a little bit of everything. But this time I had a much deeper understanding of how Washington figured into foreign policy making *and* I had the beginning of a very impressive Rolodex of contacts in the policy community.

My graduation from Georgetown coincided with the Reagan Revolution that swept many think tank professionals into government office, which included my bosses at AEI. Two new bosses, both academics and neither with Washington experience, were hired to take policy making away from the politicians and return it to the researchers. Together, we embarked on a long-term program of conferences, publications, and an extensive research agenda.

In an informal survey of my classmates from Georgetown, I learned that a very small percentage of my fellow graduates in 1981 had found work "in the field." Some had found work in the tourism industry or in the banking sector, but many had opted to continue toward a Ph.D. in economics, political science, international business, or history with the hope that the job market for Latin American or foreign policy experts would open up a few years hence. I knew I had been fortunate to get those two think tank jobs prior to graduation and vowed to work diligently in order to keep what I had. The important thing was to climb the career ladder with my master's in had thus avoiding the need to earn a higher degree and spend any more years in school.

The work at AEI was interesting and provided regular contact with a wide array of policy makers, both U.S. and foreign. Washington proved the perfect place to experience firsthand the crafting of "U.S. policy toward Latin America." As issues of waning dictatorships and nascent democracies loomed large on the horizon, I found myself in the center of the world of policy makers who were working by trial and error to redefine U.S.–Latin American relations. By the end of six years at AEI, I felt reassured that I did not need to pursue a higher degree to advance my career. The realization dawned on me that the need for a Ph.D. had been replaced by the vast experience I had gained working in the policy community, the extensive numbers and types of contacts I had made, and the knowledge I had gained about how the "real world" worked.

As the Reagan Revolution began to wind down, AEI found itself faced with a shrinking budget and limited resources to support the large numbers of staff who were leaving government positions and coming "home" again. In 1986, I was among the more than one-third of the staff who were let go from AEI's employ due to a "reduction in force."

My unemployment did not last long. As I looked to take the next step up the career ladder, I took to heart all the lessons I learned working in the policy making community: do a good job, collect and care for your contacts, pay attention to issues. I knew these lessons would help me make a lateral move, but I wanted something more: I wanted to have a job that would require me to travel so I could see what it was that I had been researching all those years.

The National Republican Institute for International Affairs (later changed to International Republican Institute or IRI) was the perfect opportunity for me to advance my career, use all I had learned about policy making, call in help from my contacts, *and* travel to the region. A Washington-based non-governmental organization (NGO), loosely supported by the Republican Party, IRI was established in 1984 to strengthen the role of political parties and other institutions as "key actors" in advancing democracy worldwide. It was part of a network of agencies, including the National Endowment for Democracy and the National Democratic Institute for International Affairs, created by Congress to support democratic movements abroad. I was hired (with the help of an influential board member) as a program officer. During 1987–1990 I was unofficially dubbed the "Program Officer for Non-Democratic Countries."

My portfolio included several low-visibility, but high-risk programs in Chile, Nicaragua, Mexico, and Cuba. I worked with many courageous people in these countries who were willing to accept U.S. technical and financial assistance to expand the limits of political rights, fair electoral contests, and democratic participation. The work was fascinating, I became much more fluent in Spanish, and the travel (although not to Cuba) was extensive. I spent nearly a third of each year traveling to more than twenty countries of the region. It was the right moment to be working in Latin America in the field of democratic institution building. I was actively putting into practice some of the policies I had spent so many years researching. I could not have mapped out a better path for my career.

While fending off questions from family and close friends ("What do you do for a living? Work for the CIA?"), I learned new things firsthand about Latin America and about foreign policy making. I learned of the rich cultures, the socioeconomic realities, the historical sensitivities in relations with the United States, and the passion for politics. In the course of experiencing Latin America first hand, I often wondered how I was perceived, not only as an American but also as a woman.

As an American, I was welcomed more often than not. In the fight for democratic freedoms, America is seen as a good model, and assistance (technical, but more important, financial) was welcome. As a woman, it seemed that although the Latin culture may differ sharply from the U.S. in its treatment of women, there has been a general understanding in Latin America of the advances women in America have made since the 1970s. Therefore, as an American professional woman, I was welcomed into Latin society and the political arena. Unfortunately, my female Latin counterparts may have to wait twenty more years before that same privilege is afforded to them.

As the region moved from democratic transition to consolidation, I was named Director for Latin America and the Caribbean at IRI. With a small staff and a modest budget, I oversaw programs to strengthen NGOs, political parties, and other democratic institutions in a dozen countries. Soon I was asked to extend my expertise in transitional countries to visit countries in Eastern Europe and the former Soviet Union. While working in these areas, I longed to return to Latin America and the culture that I knew; democratic transitions may be similar, but cultures are not.

Twelve years climbing up the career ladder had fulfilled my professional life but left my personal life lacking. Deadlines, travel, strategic planning, endless meetings, quarterly reports, and needy grantees all had to take a backseat when, in 1992, I was married. It took some time to realize that my career would not be hindered by my marriage, but that a supportive husband actually enhanced my professional capabilities. Of course there are tradeoffs, but I have learned that marriages are built on respect for each other and that is a solid foundation from which to build a successful career. In the long run, my career achievements have been more satisfying since I have had an encouraging husband with whom to share them.

Working in the field of international political development, it should never surprise me that my career has been intricately intertwined with domestic politics. In 1994, I joined nearly half the staff at IRI who either resigned or was let go due to a change in the organization's political leadership. I left with eight years of field experience and my multinational contact list intact.

An opportunity arose almost immediately. The Inter-American Development Bank (IDB), located just one block from the IRI offices, had an emerging program focusing on the state and civil society. I never knew much about the work of international financial institutions and the bank's monolithic headquarters building always seemed to be less than inviting to outsiders. Days after my separation from IRI, I attended a conference at the IDB that launched the new initiative. My understanding was that this was work in the field of democratic development under a title that was more politically correct for the bank's member countries. I set my sights on being hired by the newly founded State and Civil Society Unit.

Once again, my extensive network of contacts served me well. I used the good offices of several Latin American colleagues, both in government and in NGOs, to support my candidacy. I also gained the endorsement of Washington-based contacts, Democrats as well as Republicans. Having the right supporters pulling for me at the right time was a winning combination. I was hired as a consultant to the State and Civil Society Unit of the IDB in 1995.

While my experience in democratic development, NGOs, and institution building was a solid background for the career ahead, nothing could have prepared me for the challenges posed by the IDB. The bank is a multinational lending institution. It is not a think tank, and it is not an NGO. It works to serve its clients, which are the twenty-six borrowing member countries of Latin America and the Caribbean. Serving the governments is much more demanding than serving NGOs. Working with twenty-six bureaucracies (and as many cultures) is equally challenging, and making million-dollar low-interest loans is much more difficult than making small, non-reimbursable grants.

Working at the IDB is like traveling to Latin America without getting on an airplane. The halls are teeming with representatives from the "borrowing member" countries, the "C and D" countries (the poorest of the region), and the "extra-regional" countries, among others. It is exciting to be in a place where meetings are conducted in a wide variety of accents. Everyone is speaking Spanish, but you have to adjust your hearing to understand a heated debate between an Argentine, a Nicaraguan, a Brazilian, and an American just trying to keep up. Lest you commit a grave political error, you must identify the nationalities sitting around the table early on. For example, when discussing border disputes, it is wise not to invite two neighboring countries to participate at the same time. A mini-dispute will inevitably arise, often causing more tension in the hallways than in the region where the border is located.

My work at the IDB is in an area commonly referred to as "governance." It includes projects focusing on modernization of the state and strengthening civil society (formerly called NGOs). It is what we used to refer to as strengthening democratic institutions, without hinting that perhaps these institutions may be weak, and thus, still need to be strengthened.

When designing projects in these areas, I constantly must remind myself that these are political issues. Yet the IDB is a development bank, dedicated to the social and economic development of Latin America and the Caribbean. "Politics," narrowly defined, is not supposed to be taken into account in making bank decisions, yet politics is everywhere. Special care must be taken to frame political projects so they are seen as necessary only within the socioeconomic context.

Recently it occurred to me that after twenty years of building a career dedicated to developing democracy, the situation in Latin America should have reached a point where democracy was stable, and I would have to look elsewhere for a job. But those years have served to show me, and all persons working in the area of democratic development, that it is not time to change our career paths. Democracy in Latin America and other regions has come a long way. There have been vast transitions and strong consolidations, but new challenges have arisen that desperately need our attention.

Latin American democracies are struggling to overcome the devastating effects of narcotrafficking, corruption, bloated state bureaucracies, threats to citizen security, limited participation from citizens, voter apathy, and rejuvenated dictatorships. These challenges bring the job of building democracy to a new and different level than the kind of projects I worked on in the early years of my career. It is no longer sufficient to simply offer good advice backed up by convertible currency. These are complex issues that require the donor community to work as partners with the public and private sector and the citizens of Latin America.

A special bonus that comes with working at the IDB is the family-friendly culture. Latins have families, love families, and support family life. This culture manifests itself in bank attitudes and schedules. Flexibility is more widely practiced than in most U.S. businesses and government offices. Realizing this early on, my husband and I found the perfect opportunity to start a family. We found that where travel, meetings, and deadlines always had intervened before, the bank offers a much more flexible atmosphere that, in turn, helps us raise our child. I found the time for maternity leave, as well as the opportunity to adjust my priorities. So many years of putting democratic development ahead of all other goals ceded way for the first time in my career to put child development at the top of the list. As with marriage, I soon found that being a career woman and a mother has strengthened my professional capabilities. Every day at work I better appreciate the new found personal attributes that motherhood has bestowed upon me: exercising extreme patience, juggling numerous tasks at once, and functioning efficiently on fewer than the recommended hours of sleep.

Of course, decisions about when to have children and how many children to have are very personal and must be weighed very carefully. Yet, despite carefully made choices, it must always be kept in mind that not everything can turn out perfect. Delays in having children bring certain costs and raising children means making tradeoffs. Career mothers know this better than anyone, although for many of us the truths do not become evident until after life-altering decisions are made.

From a personal point of view, I rarely contemplated taking time off from my career for marriage and family. I know colleagues who have done that and have seen how extremely difficult is it for them to reenter the job market. It is particularly evident in Washington where "out of sight, out of mind" rings true. Women who opt to take themselves out of the field for an extended period of time are, to be perfectly blunt, forgotten. I always felt I had dedicated too much to my career to let that happen to me in mid-climb.

Having made it through many of the tough choices now, my biggest concern is what my four-year-old son will tell his classmates when the time comes to explain what mommy does at work. The answer will be something like this: "She works at a bank, so she must be a bank teller."

I enjoy working at the IDB. It is a fine place to be at this point in my career. It is interesting, challenging, family-friendly, and abounds with the Latin culture I have grown to enjoy. I have been hired as professional staff, the travel is less demanding, I practice my Spanish all day long, and it's refreshing to work for an institution that is respected in the region.

It is not the kind of organization I would recommend to students looking for their first job. Foreign policy specialists need to go to the field, meet the people face-to-face, really learn the language, and try to make things happen in a relatively short period of time. Many more opportunities open up when a job seeker can show a long list of specific achievements and goals realized early in one's career.

Today, I can say I am happy with my career. Each position has been a step up the career ladder; each job has involved me more intensely in Latin American and Third World development and democracy. There has not really been the need for a career shift because each new position has slightly shifted my career for me. I have gone from foreign policy maker to democracy practitioner to development specialist. For the foreseeable future, I hope to stay where I am. The bank is just testing the waters in these new issues of governance. I would like to stay on and help it find its way.

Are there any recipes for finding a rewarding career in a field that motivates and inspires you? Maybe. I believe good careers come to good people. Without sounding too lofty, it is possible to realize your hopes and goals. The easy recipe reads like this: have a passion for your field, exercise patience, practice great perseverance, manipulate the opportune moments, and make use of the right people. Stir gently, let rise, warm, and ENJOY!

3

The M.P.A.:
Careers in the Public Sector

Steven Bosacker

INTRODUCTION

Do you choose a career as the chief of staff to a governor or U.S. member of Congress, or does it choose you? Not to relinquish all matters of self-determination when it comes to working in the public sector, but I don't think attaining jobs here is quite the same as choosing to be an accountant or doctor or electrician. There is, I believe, a big difference because in one sector, timing is everything; in the other, timing is less important, even irrelevant. When I reflect on my jobs in the public and non-profit sectors—congressional aide, campaign manager, executive director to a higher education governing board, management consultant, and chief of staff—timing and demonstrating my preparedness at the time of the job vacancy was everything.

The real choice for me, and I suspect for many public servants, is not necessarily the specific "occupation," but rather the path or career sector. The fork in the road is more frequently represented at various points in life by choosing between the study of social science or business; between pursuing a master's in public administration or a master's in business administration; between getting work in government or a job in a corporation; between toiling in public service or sweating for a profitable bottom-line in the private sector. So far, at every fork in my career path, I've chosen the public sector. Where some people get charged by a great profit–loss statement, I am energized when I have an impact on policy that makes our collective lives better.

I suspect, too, the more nebulous nature of public sector opportunities is why the study of political science over business as an undergraduate student seems risky. College students, including my own nieces and nephew, look at my modest success in the public sector yet question me about the path as they consider their own all-important career choices. They understand more clearly the pre-med and school of dentistry path of my brother or the legal secretarial training of my sister. The courses are clearly prescribed and the result is absolute. If you can hack the challenging studies, you will be rewarded with a profitable and secure career. On the other hand, there is not always a singular professional "job" that awaits you at the end of a social or political science degree. In addition to rigorous study, this path requires a healthy dose of confidence in your own determination and ability to sell yourself at the end—much more demonstration of why *you* are the right fit for a particular job than merely presenting your credentials in the form of a degree.

Public service has been the right choice for me. It is financially profitable enough to live fully and offers every other reward in terms of feeling personally vital in this world. I have never been more professionally exhilarated—and challenged in every which way—than I am right now in my position as chief of staff to Minnesota's governor, Jesse Ventura. As you will learn, it is not a job I had planned for but rather one more example of being ready when the unique opportunity presented itself. Here's my path, and a few lessons along the way, leading to this current adventure (or maybe more aptly termed, "ad*ventura*!").

EARLY PUBLIC SERVICE AND DABBLING IN POLITICS

A bent to public service showed itself early in my life, serving as class president my four years at Waseca High School in southern Minnesota. For that matter, there were probably even earlier hints of a fascination with affecting policy and the thrill of having a voice in our representative democracy as I watched my best friend's mom serve as the first woman on Waseca's city council. She was the one to encourage me and a group of classmates to testify, petition in hand, before the council about constructing a safe bike path around one of our scenic lakes. We never got the path, but something far more profound took root deep inside me.

After high school, I headed to college set on nurturing my musical talent into a lifetime career as either a performer or music teacher. On the side, I always found time to serve on the union board or lead the choir's bass section or work as a resident assistant in my dorm. I also began to seriously dabble in politics. Having been a Republican in my late teens because I didn't know any better, I made the major swing to the center and plunged headlong into John B. Anderson's independent campaign for president in 1980. Little did I know how impactive that centrist experience would be later in my life. About the same time, I switched my major to political science, and went on to get the only "C" I ever received in more than twenty years of schooling. In my very first political science class, I was paralyzed by the question, "Are people basically good or bad?" and never finished the required paper on the topic. Sometimes we're just not ready to tackle something so big. Even now after forty years on this earth, it's a question that would require plenty of deep thought to derive a definitive answer.

The "C" did me in and I dropped out of college. The next three years were spent in the big city of Minneapolis in a variety of private sector jobs—everything from delivering mail at a big banking corporation to managing temps at Kelly Services (yes, "The Kellygirl Company"). These would be my last private sector experiences for nearly the next twenty years. I also went back to school, at night, and finished my bachelor's degree in political science with something resembling a minor in communications. With degree in hand, I quit everything overnight and headed home to southern Minnesota where I hounded our congressman until he brought me aboard his first reelection campaign for a three-week trial period at about one hundred dollars a week (working, as in most serious campaigns, about eighty hours per week). Let's just say he might be the most fiscally conservative Democrat ever to hit Congress! Yes, I said "Democrat." In four short years, I had made the turn from Republican to Democrat, with a worthwhile detour along the way as a John B. Anderson centrist.

BEGINNING THE CAREER: MY RÉSUMÉ'S EARLIEST INDICATORS

I cut my "real political job" teeth on U.S. Representative Tim Penny's campaign as the student coordinator of sixteen college campuses and as assistant to the campaign manager (which included nearly every other organizing function you can imagine). All along, though, I had my eye on the job I really wanted—as a legislative assistant in Washington, D.C. And sure enough, with a 57 percent win, Penny went back to Congress and I along with him. We have growth spurts throughout life, and my first years in Washington produced one of my biggest.

I told someone today, if you're intending to work in policy development or generally in public service, and you have a chance at a stint in Washington, D.C.— take it. If for no other reason than to stand in the middle of the swirl and absorb the good and bad of Washington policy making, it'll be worth the journey. Washington is the nerve center of some of the most complex policy making in the world, and even a low-level exposure to the power of these forces is beneficial to a well-rounded understanding of policy management and administration. Of course actually being "productive" amidst the throes of national governing will pay far greater dividends, and you should take any opportunity that affords you such an experience, be it an internship, a study session, or short-term job.

It was in DC that I decided that public service was the place for me. Two years responding to constituents, drafting legislation, staffing education and labor issues, and generally navigating both the capital "p" politics of DC and the small "p" politics of a congressional office produced a mile-long list of questions that I was sure could only be answered in graduate school. I was also certain that I wanted to be a chief of staff, to be involved in the *management of the whole*—policy, politics, operations, constituent relations, and indeed the elected official himself. So after satisfying a twenties wanderlust with a two-month road trip throughout Europe, followed by a four-month stint working with the Scottish Liberal (i.e., centrist) Party during the 1987 British elections, I enrolled at the University of Massachusetts Amherst and studied public administration.

GRADUATE STUDY FOR THE RIGHT REASONS

Full-time graduate study, after years of working to live and living to work, felt a sinful luxury. Not that it wasn't hard work; I had never been so focused and dedicated to learning. I knew I had, on the outside, two years to be fully exposed to the "theories" supporting success in public service, and along with my mile-long list, I didn't waste a minute. In a class of thirteen, we analyzed and debated the public organizational philosophies of Dwight Waldo, Max Weber, and Norton Long; I read and read and read from Herbert Kaufman, Herbert Simon, and John Rohr; we learned the value of great professors and the importance of challenging them intellectually; and I wrote. Writing had always been a big part of my educational experience, but now I was being asked to construct my own theories of public management and behavior right alongside, and with the assistance of, these historical thinkers. Suddenly the question, "Are people basically good or bad?" seemed a bit more manageable.

My most intensive research activities were devoted to two areas: where one places loyalty when supporting an elected official and how such a decision affects varying levels of "staff control"; and, an analysis of the federal budgeting process and the impact of imposing a two-year cycle on it. Both studies were driven by burning questions from my past experience (heightening the value of taking time between an undergraduate experience and graduate study to live and work in the real world), and by anticipating what might be useful to other future real-life endeavors. Every course I took served as an opportunity to discover what there was never time to understand in a work day, or to immeasurably add to my personal philosophy about public service and management. Take note: graduate work is probably useful regardless of what motivates it, but you'll get the most for your money and more out of your research if it's driven by an honest hunger to sort out some of life's mysteries or simply understand *why*.

Having decided on a path of public service, the master's in public administration was definitely the right track for me. Though the intellectuals surely continue to argue whether public administration is or is not a *true* profession, I chose it and was bound and determined to help make it one. One of the controversies in academic circles is about the level of collaboration with the school's business program. Most public administration programs are introducing more and more from the business school into their required or elective curriculums and vice versa. In my opinion, that's a good thing. The two arenas are getting more blurred in a complex global environment, and an appreciation of both the public and private sectors makes good sense. My best course taken in the business school was one in organizational behavior. In it, class members drew on a personal organizational experience and thoroughly analyzed it using seven metaphors of organization presented in Gareth Morgan's book, *Images of Organization*. Regardless of your path, read the book. To this day I draw on a variety of the metaphors to understand staff behavior, how to solve organizational conflicts, and the importance of my individual actions to a healthy, functional workplace culture.

Ultimately, the most disturbing conclusion I derived from my graduate experience had to do with a broad observation of public administration, not anything that anyone presented in a book. There has been abysmally little attention given by public administration theorists (or our university programs of public administration) to the study and understanding of what I will call our nation's policy-making administration—the support networks and staff who work directly for elected city council members, county commissioners, state legislators, governing boards of all sorts, and members of the U.S. Congress. There are books galore about the origins and peccadilloes of this country's civil service system and executive branch administrations—the folks who work for the city, state, or federal departments of commerce, or agriculture, or housing and urban development. No doubt they still represent the lionshare of professional employment in the public sector. Unfortunately, this disproportion has resulted in a near total disregard for these "other" public employees who are closest to the policy-making activities of our elected officials.

My working hypothesis is that this policy-making administration is ignored, or at least avoided, not because of its smaller size, but because of its "political" nature. Somehow, in this society founded upon the notion that rigorous political debate will produce better policy, we have allowed ourselves to focus on one sector of the public administration as "pure" and to ignore another because it is "tainted" by politics. I have taken loads of great information from my graduate studies and applied it in every job I've held since I left UMass (almost exclusively serving elected policy makers), and any individual student can do the same. Nonetheless, this bias hurts our country and, believe it or not, is partly showing itself today in the breakdown of some of our democratic institutions. The overall poor quality of dialogue, the lack of preparedness of many elected officials, the low level of respect afforded thousands of civil servants by these same democratic institutions and officials could all be improved by greater focus on the enrichment and preparedness of the "policy-making" administration.

USING THE M.P.A. STUDIES AND DEGREE

When I left UMass, I went to work as a management consultant with the Congressional Management Foundation back in Washington, D.C. A small but mighty nonprofit organization devoted to the proposal that well-managed, well-organized congressional offices will produce better policy results for the country, I had found a group that would no doubt allow me to test my grand hypothesis about whether improving and preparing the policy-making administration could produce meaningful results. And test it I did. Once again, my job required that I draw on everything that had gone before—campaigns, my political science and public administration education, and congressional office experience—to be of sound guidance to members of Congress and their staffs seeking assistance. As is so often the case, the congressional offices that sought us out had serious problems, but were generally already enlightened about good management to be bold enough to ask for additional help. We rarely received a call from the offices that needed our help the most. In this job, and when I returned to the Hill a couple years later, it was affirmed to me that congressional staffs who paid attention to good management practices and did productive strategic planning were better able to fully engage the tough policy debates and make a difference. Their "bosses" (as members of Congress are affectionately referred to inside the beltway) were frequently the movers and shakers, the ones who were at the top-of-their-legislative-game in no small part due to a good strategic plan and strong, well-managed support.

I saw firsthand the impact of too much hierarchy or too little organizational trust, the differences in offices motivated by partisan politics versus those dedicated to the best public policy, and the best and worst of how constitutional knowledge or ignorance affected a member's actions. This is to say that in almost every way on any day I was able to apply knowledge gained in college to the management analysis I conducted on behalf of elected officials.

It was also here that I got to contribute to two congressional management manuals, *Setting Course* and *Frontline Management*—books that provide practical advice for establishing and leading good congressional operations in DC and at the district and state levels, respectively. These primers provide a wealth of easy-to-understand information and give any new member of Congress a jumpstart on the business side of their organization.

BACK TO THE HILL AS A CHIEF

I never imagined that Rep. Tim Penny would come calling again, but he did. And after working one more reelection campaign resulting in a 73 percent win, I became his chief of staff in 1992. In graduate school, I had done an in-depth analysis of the "Penny operation" and now I had my chance to put it all to use. Missing were overarching priorities and a common vision that guided all the disparate elements of his congressional operation. The same sense of loyalty from the top down was lacking, as was being delivered upward to the boss. So we forced this soft-spoken Scandinavian official to divulge his hopes and dreams, planned our work, worked our plan, and developed strategies that produced an incredibly loyal staff network around him. Penny retired from Congress in 1984 with the status of a true statesman; certainly due chiefly to his own abilities and hard work, but also enhanced by a small cadre of loyal public servants who served him.

MANAGING AMID THE POLITICS OF THE ACADEMY

When I signed on as the Executive Director and Corporate Secretary for the University of Minnesota Board of Regents, I was completely unaware that we'd soon be at the center of one of the most intense policy debates in the university's history, which focused around how much prerogative the board of regents had to speak to, and actually change, the tenure code at the institution. If Social Security is the "third rail" of federal politics (i.e., touch it—the electrical source for the entire subway system—and you die), tenure is the third rail of university politics. In addition to this intense debate, my public administration skills were thoroughly tested in numerous other ways as the board challenged the closing of General College (a school within the University serving an "underprepared" and largely minority student population); allowed their relationship with the university president to disintegrate, which led to an unconventional search for a new leader; and navigated the sale of the university's hospital and establishment of a seventy million dollar public–private medical partnership—just to name a few.

Serving at the pleasure of the board, and being the only university employee who didn't ultimately report to the president, once again I found myself in that "unpure" place of the policy-making administration. But for those up to the challenge of service with one foot in and one foot outside our public institutions, it's a great place to be. Another piece of traditional political science training that pops up in every public service position I've held is the constitutional notion of the separate branches in public governance. A foundational understanding about the separation of these branches (legislative, executive, judicial), and the check-and-balance authorities of each, is very useful. At the university, it was pertinent to the board's exercise of its oversight duties as well as in drawing a clear distinction between appropriate active governance activities and the inappropriate micromanagement of administrative responsibilities.

WORKING FOR THE "WRESTLER-MAYOR-RADIO-SHOCK-JOCK" TURNED GOVERNOR

I started this chapter with the contention that in public service we don't always have the luxury of picking a job, rather we need to be ready for when a job might pick us. This has happened throughout my career, but never more vividly than with the twelve hours I had to decide about a life-changing career move to serve Minnesota's newly elected governor, Jesse Ventura, in November 1998. At seven-thirty in the morning, two days after the historic election of our first third-party governor, the idea of helping Governor Ventura breezed through my head as I drove to work at the university. I was angered by a cynical radio reporter who suggested that this new governor could not be effective in leading the state. Obviously a plurality of Minnesota citizens believed otherwise in the election booth and in my mind Ventura deserved every fair shake at proving them right. At noon, I mentioned to my former boss and now friend, Tim Penny, that I might offer some volunteer help in my spare time. When out of the blue Penny received a call from the Ventura folks that same afternoon, he suggested they speak with me. By six o'clock that night, I was being interviewed at the dining room table of our new celebrity governor. I would later learn that my very first words to him about working for independent presidential candidate John Anderson nearly twenty years earlier sold him, and as I said good-bye that night, I was pretty certain that the job of heading up his governing organization could be mine. Twelve hours—from the tiniest, innocuous consideration to the likelihood of a lead role. Scary. Despite having so little time to sort out the massiveness of the decision, it has been one of the best decisions of my life.

Nothing has been more satisfying to witness in my public service career than affirming the deeply held belief of our founding fathers that any citizen can serve and be an effective leader. Governor Jesse Ventura—maybe most well-known as a professional wrestler adorned in wildly patterned tights and a feather boa—is one of the best leaders I've encountered. He operates with a set of clearly defined beliefs, is unafraid to challenge the status quo, actually delegates responsibility instead of just talking about it, forgives mistakes, and garners intense loyalty by being loyal himself.

It is in this job that every single element of my personal experience and educational training is intensely used, and some days abused. Throughout this chapter I have alluded to my work in the policy-making administration. Now in service to the head of Minnesota's "executive" branch and its chief executive, I am finally able to fully engage the *pure* public administration—the big bureaucracy and every aspect, good and bad, of a civil service system. As chief of staff, Governor Ventura has charged me with managing the governor's office, Minnesota's twenty-five executive departments and the twenty-five commissioners who head them, and by extension, the 51,000 state employees therein.

The Ventura administration is defined by a set of core "beliefs and budget principles," daily attention to a fresh way of working (disregard for partisanship and staying deadly focused on results), and, most recently, a set of strategic initiatives for the state of Minnesota's long-term prosperity as defined in *The Big Plan*. Here, as in every other post I've held, my admonition to the whole team is to set our sights on truly important goals, plan our work and work the plan. One year in it's "so far, so good"; or as the governor puts it, "The state of the State is great!"

ASSESSING MY FUTURE AT HALFTIME (I.E., 40)

A respected colleague recently shared a concept from the book *Halftime* by Bob Buford that suggests that the first forty years of our lives are about achieving *success*; but it is in the second half of life where we either achieve, or don't achieve, *significance*. I don't know that I subscribe to this theory, but as I look ahead, I do know that every "next experience" is richest when we get to utilize every other experience we've had in getting there. And I suppose that eventually our efforts may indeed add up, or not, to a significant contribution toward our collective well-being.

Even those of us who have spent a lifetime in public service get to that mid-point in life and yearn to do something "more meaningful"; to be more fully aware of the broader benefits to society of our daily efforts. And yet I do recognize, sometimes in the most pedestrian of situations—sipping coffee at Starbucks, snow-shoeing through a state park, watching a minor league baseball game—the impact that my daily work has on the lives of those around me. They don't know and probably don't care, and the contribution may be about as big as one brick in a fifty-story skyscraper, but in the end it's enough for me to know that in some minis-cule way the quality of their lives was improved because I contributed to the making of good public policy. When you add together the millions working daily toward the public good in public service, the miniscule indeed is mighty.

And finally, a few additional tips as you set your own course along a public sector path …

- Be hungry enough but never too hungry for any one job.
- Focus on being prepared and personally ready for the work you want to do. In this competitive world, your true advantage may depend as much on how quickly you can decide to make a move or join a team as on whether you are merely qualified.
- Throw yourself into your work and studies. You've made a decision to be wherever you are and if you're not going to make the most of it, you should move on.
- Bring the theories of your education into the workplace. All those smart people who went before you in public administration professions (deep into the past century), and all those arcane-looking books you read in graduate school, really do hold truths that have been derived by struggles similar to yours and provide meaningful guidance about practices that should be tried or avoided.
- Never underestimate the value of good manners. It doesn't mean you can't also be tough.
- Be proud of your hard work on the public's behalf.

Part II

Advanced Degrees

4

The Academy as Pastoral Policy Shop (or, Campus Activism as Policy Making)

John Brigham

I went to college as an undergraduate from 1963–1967 and I'm still there. This was a notorious period in American political and intellectual life during which college campuses figured prominently in the social unrest characteristic of the period. Not surprisingly, this time taught me about the special place of the college campus in the public sphere. It even filled me with ideas like, "the public sphere," the common good and the general will.

Graduating from a high school on the peninsula south of San Francisco in 1963, I sought a college campus a reasonable distance from home. Three-hundred miles seemed like enough at the time. I also wanted a supportive environment that I thought I could handle. This was, in part, to carry on for my very supportive family, but also so as not to scare them by going off to a wild and crazy place. The euphemism then was "big." You didn't want to go, it seemed, to a place that was too big. Thus, I set off for the University of California, Santa Barbara in the fall of 1963. I have only been away from a college campus for one year in the intervening three and a half decades.

In 1965, the Free Speech movement drew me from the campus at Santa Barbara to the University of California, at Berkeley. There, eight-hundred demonstrators had just been arrested for demanding the right to solicit money on campus that would be used for political causes. This was the Free Speech movement. Not only was it about conflicting views of the campus as a place for political activity, it helped people to see the American campus as a center of political innovation like other college campuses around the world. After two years of college, Berkeley seemed more exciting than threatening.

Berkeley in the sixties would be characterized for many by struggle over the relationship between the university and society. Clark Kerr, the president of the whole UC system, had proposed that the university after World War II had become a "multiversity." He meant that it was a major contributor to the nation's military and industrial enterprise. The modern university was to be supportive of society's needs. It was a good thing, according to Kerr, that the university was part of what former President Dwight Eisenhower had called the military–industrial complex. Students, however, were concerned that much of this contribution was not according to the values they associated with campus life as fostering more critical commentary on society.

The transition to Berkeley was not easy for me. The ferment on campus presented constant challenges. It was common to be stopped on the street or on the way to class to be asked where one stood on the major issues of the day. From a family who avoided talking politics, particularly where there might be differences of opinion, potential differences were the stuff of political discussion and daily life. Often the object was to root them out and take them on. I sought some safe havens while I tried to get used to it all. I worked on the student paper, *The Daily Californian*, where objectivity was expected and I didn't have to make up my mind on the issues. I worked in a boarding house where I had a social life as part of my job and didn't have to create one. But it wasn't too long before I was marching and participating in student government.

The sixties were a time when we chanted "The whole world is watching" to the TV cameras covering demonstrations. Sometimes we returned from classes in the afternoon to scan the TV news for our faces. Of course, we also wanted to find out how our demands were being responded to and whether the campus would be open the next day. The immediacy of the moment and its communal quality made an indelible impression. All the excitement hooked me on the college campus as a source of ferment and political change. College for me was a place were people thought about the human condition and were encouraged to contribute their ideas to issues from how to build bombs to how to stop them from being used.

All this still involved considerable personal growth and sometimes the situations seem odd looking back. I had joined the army's Reserve Officer Training Corps (ROTC) as a freshman at UCSB. By the time I was a junior at Berkeley, training for the military had a whole different meaning. We had military drill at seven in the morning so as not to call attention to this gathering of budding soldiers in the midst of the nation's most radical campus community. One morning I overslept and was called into the commander's office. Ready to be accused of some major offense against military authority I was surprised to find that the commander appeared quite relieved upon learning that not enough sleep was my excuse and that my absence was not intended as a statement about the inherent immorality of training officers on campus.

I graduated from Berkeley in 1967 and went on to graduate school at the University of Wisconsin. Violent struggle broke out on the Madison campus in my first semester over recruitment on campus by the Dow Chemical Company, makers of a jellied gasoline firebomb (napalm) used in the Vietnam War. This was America's heartland and although local politicians blamed "out of state" students like me for the unrest, the truth was that Wisconsin had long been a model for a university that was involved in the life of the community around it. They called it the "Wisconsin Ideal" and it could be traced to the formation of the "land grant college" system under the Morrill Act, which sold western lands to bring in money to build colleges that would educate farmers and teachers.

During my time in Wisconsin, I learned more about the college campus as the key critical and imaginative force in American public policy. Discussions about the war and the structure of American politics in the student union's Rathskeller seemed more important, certainly more intelligent and purer than anything that was going on in the halls of power in Washington. One particularly good friend had already spent time in jail for refusing to serve in the military because he believed conscription to be a form of slavery. On campus we put a premium on integrity in office and honorable policies. Morality seemed like a key, but often missing, element in the making of public policy.

Although college was clearly an important place of social change, it had come to seem too protected or at least I felt too protected on campus. I had trouble justifying my special status with reference to the most pressing issue of the day, the Vietnam War, since I was going to graduate school on a ROTC deferment. In addition, the scholarship that I was required to do for a Ph.D. seemed wrong in substance and it was too far removed from the momentous action that was part of daily campus life to keep my interest. In those days, we didn't want to be professionals looking inward at the knowledge that justified the power of educated men and women. We wanted to think more broadly and to experiment with society itself.

When I left Madison it was to take my involvement in the culture wars into the streets, the workplaces, and the social experiments going on in the world. It seemed important, in terms of the project of constructing a new society, to get into the community. I was going to live in a new way and convey to the people I worked with the need for critical self-evaluation and an awareness of the consequences of American public policy. I moved to the foothills of northern California and at first my wife and I concentrated on clearing land, growing our own food, and chopping wood. Feeling a little isolated and in need of cash we moved into town and I worked in a feed mill, as a carpenter, and as a process server. None of it was particularly political and there was not nearly as much attention to the issues of the day as I had hoped. I did get Conscientious Objector status from the military during this time and I was also offered a job teaching at Chico State, the local branch of the California State college system.

I had only lasted a little over a year away from the campus. I was recruited back to teach because of an unexpected opening. It was a temporary position but it allowed me to think about things and to ask students to join with me. The hardest time for me, maybe ever, was when I was told that my M.A. from Wisconsin was not enough to hold down a position at Chico State. It appeared that I needed to be in a Ph.D. program. I found one back at UCSB. From then on, at one institution or another, from Santa Barbara's magnificent coastal campus to the urban scene of the University of Chicago, from pristine all-women Mt. Holyoke to the large and raucous University of Massachusetts, I have been able to stay on a campus for much of the last three decades.

The American college, particularly the public land grant manifestations with which I was familiar, had come to epitomize, for me, a heady combination of basic research and active contest over how it was to be deployed. I knew the university as a place where those who developed new "polymers" by dividing up petroleum in innovative ways shared their space with young people getting credit for their sculpture or essays on the origins of student unrest on campus. It was a place where the product and the world in which it was to be sold would be examined enthusiastically and money that came in for one would be used by those who ran the place to help support the other.

It went without saying that the college campus, including its contested periphery and its sometimes sensitive, sometimes embracing, surroundings were crucial places of public policy making. Every campus I've been on has some degree of tension with its surroundings. They are part of what sets it off. At the University of Chicago, the back of the Law School on the south side of campus had razor wire to keep the community out when I was there. The north side had streets that went nowhere, to cut down on through-traffic. These were thought to be an innovative form of urban planning. In Amherst, where the university dwarfs the town, students are forced to go off campus to vote and the town police force operates out of a forbidding and very expensive high-tech command post.

The campus has often kept the society out, to one degree or another. But, increasingly, it has seen its destiny linked with its surroundings. Today at public universities we take it for granted that we need to reach beyond public support and interest the private sector in our activities. This is dangerous territory and the development juggernaut threatens to undercut the detachment and critical bent which remains a partial characteristic of the best scholarship. Colleagues of mine warn of the "pull of the policy audience." But, this pull is subtle compared to the push toward interests represented by the large and generous donor.

The traditional campus has idiosyncrasies that keep it a bit detached. For one thing, most college campuses are full of young people for whom this period in their lives would be special. Here, part of each generation is set apart with their special status as student. They are given some room to experiment, to postpone making a living. They are on their own, maybe for the first time. And, remarkably, their program of study is organized around one of the most radical social principles ever devised. This is the idea that it was important to examine and think about life in order that it be worth living.

I did feel strains in my relationship with my campus when, in my thirties, I crossed that divide in years beyond which as students we said we would not trust. I began to seem impossibly older and couldn't pass for one of the students anymore. At that time, in the late 1970s and early 1980s for me, popular media, with shows like "Thirtysomething," began to romanticize the lives of my cohort on the "outside." These were people who had to worry about whether their company would be downsized or eliminated and who seemed to have lots of people near their own age to work with. Even the vagaries of free enterprise, with its intensity around life's changes had a certain appeal for me as I observed them from my protected place in the ivory tower.

These were only minor pangs of envy and longing. Life on campus was just too perfect. In my forties it seemed like bliss. Though my salary was not what it might be on the outside, the security of my position was the sort of thing Supreme Court justices had, and there were only nine of them in the whole country. There were some limits to campus life that seemed to matter then. Often the food was not as good as one could get on the outside. I began to resign myself to the fact that I would not likely have the sort of impact that Karl Marx or even Mario Savio (our leader of the Free Speech movement) had. But, in spite of that I began to get graduate students, young people who would work with me in order to carry on the same activity.

The grad students were closer to my age and also generally possessed the same vision of the special nature of the academy as a place to write and to teach. They had their own interests and in political science those generally bore some relation to the policy sciences. One was interested in the lives of Muslims in America and the discrimination they received. Many were interested in the condition of women and actively participated in feminist scholarship. Some were even drawn to matters of faith as they questioned the relativism of the secular environment that supported the modern academy. In working with such superior students I am not only able to help shape and sustain their thinking but also, because they will soon be teaching in the academy themselves, the ideas of future generations.

In working with these students and in trying to keep my courses from becoming stale, I was able to respond in both my teaching and my research to events of the day. An interest in abortion and the legal politics surrounding it has been constant ever since Irving Schiffman, a colleague at Chico State, expressed surprise in 1973 that the Supreme Court would be so bold as to strike down the anti-abortion laws in most states. His was the surprise of a scholar who cared about an independent and restrained judiciary in a democratic society. This concern would merge, twenty years later, into my critique of an American politics too dependent on high courts and dismissive of politics and public life.

Property remains a passion for me. Beginning with struggles over land use in California and including matters of welfare entitlement, I have studied the phenomenon we call property for years. My passion is fueled when I leave the campus and run into the reach of private prerogatives. Attempting to swim in New England where property ownership extends to the mean low water mark is harder than in California where it extends only to the high tide level. In California, however, the pressure on undeveloped land is intense. Of course no one owns the campus where I work, we just all occupy it for some time or another. Because of this the introduction of private providers of campus services raises questions about the sort of place we want to be and brings my interest in property in line with my commitment to campus life.

My early interest in Free Speech was stimulated by Mario Savio talking about shouting fire in a crowded theater on a very uncrowded bluff on the UCSB campus in Santa Barbara. Currently, I find myself debating the relationship between legal research and the Palestinian cause while sharing pizza and beer at the American Bar Foundation on the Northwestern University campus in Chicago. For thirty-five years, the relationship between law and politics has occupied my scholarly attentions. It is common for Americans to see law as infused with politics and the result is often a degree of cynicism that seems to me to draw power away from the people. Americans have been taught to see courts as superior to legislatures by the last few generations of political science professors. I think this preference for legal processes detracts from our sense that we can govern ourselves.

These questions, and a professional, academic career, have brought me from the relatively isolated campus at Chico to one of the world's capitals where I work in the Law Library of New York University while visiting my wife who teaches there. It is hard to get bored by the academic life when it also involves work as a research and teaching fellow in a fourteenth-century university in the Basque Country whose cloistered campus has been transformed into a modern institute for studying the sociology of law. And, when sabbaticals produce a chance to lecture throughout Australia, as my wife and I did last year, the academic life seems quite stimulating. On that trip we saw as many college campuses as kangaroos traveling from Melbourne in the southeast to Perth in the west and Brisbane in the northeast to talk about America and law. The research and writing that I do on public law and the political process from the academy may not have an immediate impact on the policy debates in Washington, D.C., but it does have a lasting and long-term impact through my students and through my books.

Because of the intensity of all this and the constant change that comes from working in a place where ideas matter so much and the learners are always new, I do sometimes think of even more pastoral scenes and perhaps more "indigenous" political struggle. I think of going back to that place in the foothills of northern California to which I retreated the last time I left the academy almost exactly thirty years ago. Perhaps, in retirement, I would try again at that activism I was so poor at when it had to be combined with making a living. But, on an academic schedule, I am able to go back in the summer and try it out. So far, I have always been inclined to return to campus in the fall to renew the cycle of lectures and writing, students and colleagues, and the ongoing flood of issues that define our time, and always look a little differently from the vantage point of a college campus.

As I write we have just concluded our academic year in Amherst. It is the beginning of that annual time away and I am finishing projects from the year while contemplating what it makes sense to try and do this summer. I face the envy of my peers for what they consider a rather extensive vacation. But here I am, writing about policy and trying to explain the rich engagement that is possible in today's ivory tower. I am still amused by the exuberance of my students a week ago at graduation where, 4,000 strong, they ignored the platform and had their own party on the grounds of our stadium. As they entertained and drenched themselves, it seemed to me that they knew intuitively that on a campus they have considerable freedom to experiment. That what would be rude and disrespectful in some quarters is tolerated as the excess we allow in students and in our youth because we know that these experiments will be the conventional ideas of future generations (and that the Social Security burden of this generation will be considerable). No wonder they are less than attentive when the last generation attempts to instruct them on the proper forms of conduct for a worthwhile life.

5

A State Department Career— and Afterwards

Lowell R. Fleischer

To this day, it remains somewhat of a mystery to me how I became fascinated by foreign affairs and ended up in the Foreign Service for twenty-five years. I was raised in a small town in northeastern Ohio (Salem, Ohio, population then probably around 10,000 or so) in the 1940s and 1950s and never had the opportunity to travel much outside of the state, and certainly not outside of the United States, until college.

I was born in Columbiana, Ohio, an even smaller town best known as the birthplace of Harvey Firestone of Firestone Tire and Rubber fame. We moved to Salem in the early 1940s when my dad gave up his small grocery store/meat market (the details are vague now, but the store probably went under because of the depression) to work at the E.W. Bliss Co, a manufacturer of rolling mills and presses for the steel industry.

The opportunity to write sports for the *Salem News* when I was a junior in high school was the beginning of my interest in the wider world. I had always been a voracious reader, but daily exposure to the Associated Press and United Press International wires sparked a curiosity I did not know I had. I got the opportunity because the sports writer for the paper, a daily with a circulation of about 10,000, had been called up for the Korean War and the editor needed someone immediately. I was writing sports for the weekly high school paper but, truth be known, could hardly type, let alone write coherently—although I assured the editor, Ray Dean, a prototypical old-fashioned small-town newsman, otherwise. For two years, I arrived at the paper at 6 each morning and wrote and edited sports copy (as well as occasional other pieces) until about 9 or 9:30 when I dashed across the street to Salem High School to begin classes. The hardest part of the job was covering high school sports and writing about my friends and teacher–coaches, especially if forced to criticize them. They obviously knew much more than I did about what they were doing. I certainly learned on the job, helped along by the patience and good will of the handful of professional reporters and editors on the staff as well as by the coaches and players themselves. I'm sure this early writing experience with its emphasis on clear expression and quick deadlines helped me in my later career as an analyst for the Department of State.

I am the oldest of four children and the first to go to college. Neither of my parents had the opportunity of higher education, but they saw to it that all four children did. I went to Ohio Wesleyan University mainly because the son of my senior English teacher went there and was editor of the student newspaper, and I wanted to be a newspaperman! As I recall, I applied only to the Ohio Wesleyan, confident that my high school grades and many activities would get me in, and in the fall of 1955, I started there.

I did well enough academically at Ohio Wesleyan but, like many students, spent too much time with extracurricular activities, including student government and the newspaper. I was selected as editor of the paper my junior year and was elected president of the student body the following year. I entered college with the intention of majoring in journalism, which I did. However, thanks to the rigorous liberal arts requirements of the college as well as the insistence of Professor Verne Edwards, who was the one-man journalism department then, I also majored in political science (with enough credits for a second minor in history). Verne wanted all journalism majors to take significant blocks of courses in other departments. It was his philosophy that if you were going to write about some topic, you should have the background and know as much as possible about it. If only all journalists today would heed this still pertinent advice. As I got more involved in political science and government courses, I gradually gave up the idea of a career in journalism, although the image of becoming another James Reston stayed with me for years to come.

The opportunity for frequent contact with university trustees and alumni during these years served further to expand the somewhat circumscribed midwestern world I had known while growing up. Probably influenced by one board member in particular, John Eckler, who was a partner in a Columbus law firm headed by former Ohio Senator John Bricker, sometime in my junior year I decided to go to law school. As I recall, I was accepted at Yale, the University of Michigan, and the University of Chicago. Eventually I decided on Chicago, partly because that is where Eckler had gone, but mostly because they came through with the biggest scholarship. I remember being awed by both the city and the university.

Looking back, I am still not certain exactly why and how I made that decision to go to law school. The idea of going to graduate school had not really entered my mind at that point. I had no burning desire to be a lawyer, but I admired several successful lawyers I knew, and thought that such training would be useful for some kind of public service or politics. About this same time, I became aware of something called the Foreign Service. For some reason, I don't think the Foreign Service exam was given that year; perhaps there were already too many successful candidates on the waiting list. In any case, I did not take the exam then.

Sometime in late winter/early spring of my senior year in college, one of my political science professors (Dr. Robert Lorish, who later taught at Connecticut College), who had become my political science advisor and counselor, raised the question of graduate school with me, implying that I would be "wasting my time" at law school. So began yet more consideration about what I would do when I was graduated. I thought it was too late to even think about graduate school for that fall. Not so, Dr. Lorish advised, giving me a brochure describing the recently enacted National Defense Educational Act, which among other things, provided for three-year fellowships to study international relations at the graduate level. One of the purposes of the act was to encourage universities to upgrade and expand their language and international studies programs. Slots were still available at some institutions because the legislation had been passed so late.

Graduating from Ohio Wesleyan in June of 1959, I decided to pass up law school and accept an NDEA fellowship at the University of Connecticut, which was just beginning a Ph.D. program in what I think was then called the Department of Government and International Relations. As it turned out, I was one of the first, if not the first, to receive a Ph.D. in political science from that institution. So I made the transition from journalism to law to political science. In making this pivotal decision, I still had no idea what I wanted to do professionally, beyond some vague notion of public affairs. The NDEA fellowship did not require any work for the department, but I did eventually teach courses at the university's Stamford branch and became a teaching assistant to Professor Louis Gerson, whose specialty was diplomatic history and U.S. foreign policy. I thoroughly enjoyed this teaching experience, but began to wonder if this was what I wanted to do for the rest of my life.

Somewhere along the way, a couple of my students sought my advice about the foreign service exam. After looking into this for them, I eventually decided to take the test myself. Until the results arrived, I lived in fear that they would pass and I would not. I did pass and after putting the Department of State off for as long as I could (eighteen months), I finally made the decision to enter the Foreign Service. The day I turned in my dissertation I left for Washington to be sworn in. I had already defended my dissertation on "Charles A. Lindbergh and Isolationism, 1939–1941"—with some difficulty, I seem to remember, because at least one of the members of my committee thought it was more a work of diplomatic history than political science.

Many Foreign Service Officers (FSOs) have professional and graduate degrees, an M.A. as well as some significant work experience, which is just about the norm these days. The average age for entering FSOs is now twenty-seven and many have been in the Peace Corps or lived abroad before joining the State Department. I am not aware of the statistics regarding Ph.Ds. In the group of about twenty FSOs, including three women, who entered the service when I did, two of us had finished our Ph.Ds, and at least two others had finished course work, but had not completed their dissertations. In any case, having a Ph.D. does not give one any particular advantage in the Foreign Service. Those with graduate degrees or particular work experience may enter at a little higher level. One may be more likely to be named to a binational Fulbright Commission, as I was in Yugoslavia, or given the opportunity to participate in an academic exchange program, as I did at the University of Massachusetts for a year, but the culture of the Foreign Service does not value a doctoral degree.

Having said that, I have always been grateful that I finished my degree before joining the Foreign Service. With very few exceptions, I think those who entered the service without finishing the degree never got around to it. Because of the somewhat specialized nature of the Foreign Service profession, career options upon leaving are often limited, and with evermore stringent "up or out" promotion provisions in effect, many FSOs are forced to leave earlier than they would prefer. Competition by many able officers for the dwindling number of senior positions is intense. The most recent statistics indicate that the senior ranks are now about 678 compared to 817 in 1993.

Age discrimination at age fifty or so is also a fact of life. Colleges and universities normally are more interested in hiring recent Ph.Ds, perhaps with a published book or articles, rather than someone with years of professional experience, but no recent "academic" work. Having advanced degrees in hand, although no guarantee of future employment, at least provides additional possibilities.

I am glad I decided to enter the Foreign Service and not sorry that I left after twenty-five years, although I do still miss living and working abroad. I suspect that every bright young FSO aspires to reach the highest levels of the Foreign Service and to become an ambassador some day. I know I did. You begin to believe what your boss writes in the yearly so-called efficiency reports. Early on in my career, I was promoted very rapidly, and it was not until several years before I retired (at age fifty), I faced the fact that I would not reach the top.

Looking back, it should have been apparent to me much earlier that I was too independent, too determined to take assignments that appealed to me rather than ones that would have been good for my career. For example, following the year I spent at the UMass (which itself was probably not a very good career move), I chose to become chairman of one of the area studies programs at the Foreign Service Institute, a position that was often a pre-retirement slot and certainly not one that many up-and-coming officers interested in climbing the career ladder would have accepted. I enjoyed the job, however. I also accepted so-called "out-of-cone" assignments, that is, I accepted a consular assignment although I was a political officer. I became the counselor for consular affairs in Belgrade because I wanted to go to Eastern Europe and could not find a political slot at the time. This consular assignment did not help when other political officers on the selection board were considering promotions. In short, other considerations, including family desires, were always more important to me than my career. If I had things to do over again, I would probably try to play the game a little better, and would pay more attention to career moves.

The State Department culture is such that only the well connected thrive. To be well connected you need a patron or mentor and need to focus on charming your supervisor rather than the development of managerial and other skills. One less than outstanding evaluation can kill a career. You also cannot rely on the less-than-transparent assignment process, which almost all FSOs recognize is "wired," which means available only to the select few. Getting good assignments early on ultimately determines later promotions. I had some terrific bosses in the Foreign Service, but with only one exception, none who moved up the ladder and brought me along. One of the frustrations of Foreign Service life today is that many senior officers are trapped in uninteresting assignments from which they cannot be promoted.

I found few frustrations in my early career and many satisfactions. My first assignment was as the U.S. vice-consul in Medellín, Colombia—pre-drug days, of course. In a sense, that random assignment (junior officers in those days had no say in where they were assigned) was to provide the basis for my interest in Latin America and of my career after leaving the Department of State. The Consulate in Medellín was a two-officer post. We had an American secretary, and about six to seven local employees. During my tour there, my boss was called back to Washington to help out on the Dominican Republic desk when the U.S. sent troops to that Caribbean country, so I was left in charge of the post for an extended period of time. Not only did I get involved in textile negotiations with the Colombians (Medellín was the textile center of the country), but I received the difference between my pay and his. This amounted to several thousand dollars and went to finance my first extended trip around South America. Unfortunately, the United States has closed almost all small consulates around the world, and almost the only opportunities available for junior officers are processing visas where they are judged by the number of applications processed. This is one of many practices of the State Department and the Foreign Service that need to be completely rethought. Visas have to be issued, but whether most new FSOs should be sent to visa mills is another question.

After a tour in the Bureau of Intelligence and Research focused on the United Kingdom, another assignment often thought of as out of the mainstream, I went to Santo Domingo in 1968 as a junior political officer where I learned firsthand of the intrusive involvement of the United States in the affairs of this small country. The aid mission was huge and the CIA contingent surprisingly large for such a small country. Even the State Department's political section was staffed with five or six officers. This assignment provided me the opportunity to work with one of the best the Foreign Service has produced, Ambassador John Crimmins. I learned a great deal from him about how to analyze the political and economic situation in a country and, perhaps more importantly, how to deal with politics and the bureaucracy in Washington, lessons that stood me in good stead in later years.

When we left the Dominican Republic, I went to teach for a year at the University of Massachusetts and from there to the Foreign Service Institute. I enjoyed each of these assignments because they put me back into the academic mode. Unfortunately, neither did anything for my promotion possibilities. This may have been the time to consider a change of direction, but I chose to remain in the Foreign Service and entered Serbo-Croatian language training to prepare for an assignment in Belgrade, a tour of duty that provided its own set of satisfactions. This was the mid-1970s when Yugoslavia was still a communist country and still unified under the strong hand of Marshall Tito.

Consular work turns off many FSOs after their first tours of duty on the nonimmigrant visa line in major embassies. When I became chief of the consular section at the Embassy in Belgrade, I had not done consular work since my first tour of duty ten years earlier. The most satisfying moment of my tour in Belgrade was when the United States finally persuaded the government of Marshall Tito to release an American citizen (born in Yugoslavia) who had spent over a year in prison on trumped up industrial espionage charges (taking photographs in a state-run sugar plant). It was also the first and only time my photo ever appeared in the *New York Times*! I had a lot of help in getting the man released, not the least of which was the full support and assistance of Ambassador Larry Silberman. Silberman, a noncareer ambassador of exceptional talent who had been President Ford's Secretary of Labor and now is an appellate judge on the Federal Appeals Court for the District of Colombia, was so incensed over the incident that he persuaded every high-ranking visitor to Belgrade, including Secretary of the Treasury William Simon, not only to raise the issue with high-ranking government officials but to demand the man's release.

In my view, Silberman was a top-notch ambassador and did as well, if not better, than most career officers would have done. However, the consequences of more and more political ambassadors in the better, more important embassies, is that promotion and assignment possibilities for FSOs are reduced. This increased politicization of the Foreign Service, with more and more political appointees as ambassadors, assistant secretaries, deputy assistant secretaries, and even lower ranks, is likely to continue unabated. I personally do not buy into the notion that in order to control foreign policy the president has to have political appointees in these slots.

The one regret I have about my tour in Belgrade was not accepting Ambassador Lawrence Eagleburger's (he replaced Ambassador Silberman) offer to remain in Belgrade and become his political counselor. It would have provided me the opportunity to work more closely with one of the most successful career FSOs who later became Secretary of State under President George Bush. Needless to say it would have been a good career move. In any case, we returned to Washington where I became Deputy Director of the State Department Operations Center and later Deputy Director of the International Relations Division of the Arms Control and Disarmament Agency. After another overseas tour in Venezuela and one in Washington as Alternate U.S. Representative to the Organization of American States, I finished out my career as a State Department Inspector and retired from the department in 1988.

After leaving the Foreign Service I went to work as the Deputy Director of the Washington Office of the Council of the Americas, a business association of U.S. multinationals with interests in Latin America. Again emphasizing that one's contacts are every bit as important as one's skills, I was hired because I had worked for Ambassador George Landau, the council's president, in Venezuela. I later left the council to become a Senior Associate at the Center for Strategic and International Studies, a Washington think tank, and to do more freelance writing and consulting.

All in all, the twenty-five years I spent in the Foreign Service provided an interesting, enjoyable and rewarding career. I traveled to places, met world leaders, and wrestled with important issues that I could never have imagined when growing up in Ohio. Along with most FSOs I know, I complained often about the State Department bureaucracy and the unfathomable assignment and promotion processes. I worried about my wife and children. The State Department still has a long way to go to try to provide meaningful employment opportunities for spouses abroad, for example. As much as my children complained at the time about leaving their friends behind in the United States, today they both look back on living abroad as an experience they not only enjoyed, but one that has helped them in school and in their careers.

It is difficult for me to say now whether I would make the same career choices again if given the opportunity. Even had I gone to law school instead of graduate school, it seems more than likely that I would have ended up somewhere in the policy arena. Although I enjoyed life in the Foreign Service and have no regrets, I am not at all certain I would recommend it for a young person today—certainly not as a career. A tour or two abroad would be useful as well as enjoyable. That would provide insights into the foreign policy process as well as long-remembered personal and professional experiences. Furthermore, it is much easier to find other well-rewarded employment at age 30, or 35, than at 50, or 55. If one stays in the Foreign Service past thirty-five or so, what former FSO David Jones has called the "golden handcuffs" kicks in. Despite dissatisfactions with one's career, the prospect of retirement at age fifty with a good pension has some attractions, so many stay on.

In this day of instant communications when someone from headquarters in Washington can arrive anywhere in the world in a relatively short time, an officer in the field is useful but perhaps not vital. With CNN and other all-news outlets reporting from all over the world with instant, if not profound or thoughtful, analysis, it is logical that the Foreign Service will put less emphasis on reporting and analysis. Foreign Service officers will become high-level customer service representatives whether dealing with foreigners who need visas, traveling Americans in need of various services, or potential investors who need introductions and advice about the local scene. These activities may have their own rewards, but the work is a far cry from the policy analysis and the opportunity to influence that policy that drew most of us to the service in the first place. These days more than ever before, that role belongs not to FSOs but to the lawyers back in Washington who seem to be selected to staff the higher reaches of the State Department and the National Security Council.

6

A Career as an "In 'n' Outer"

Joseph S. Nye, Jr.

INTRODUCTION

"Two roads diverged in a yellow wood / And sorry I could not travel both / And be one traveler, long I stood / And looked down one as far as I could...." I have always loved Robert Frost's poem "The Road Not Taken," but in truth my career is one in which I have traveled two roads, both the academic and the governmental. Some who pursued only one road have gone further in achieving high position or in the length of their list of publications, but I would not trade with them. I have found both halves of my career satisfying, and cannot imagine my life without either. I would like to recommend such a course to others, but I must confess that it is not easy to plan to take two roads, and in my case, serendipity played a large role.

I certainly had no fixed plan to take the roads I took. I grew up on a farm in northwest New Jersey, and that childhood bequeathed me a lifelong love of the outdoors. As a teenager, I wondered about a career as a forester or a farmer. For a spell, I was influenced to think I might want to follow the example of the friendly local minister. My father was in the securities business, and I often felt I would wind up following his footsteps. He loved his work. He used to say that "in my business, you are in everybody's business," and he encouraged me with visits to his office on Wall Street. At the same time, he never tried to control my choice. It was a wise approach that allowed us to remain close without feeling tension or guilt about my decisions. I have followed his example with regard to my three sons, none of whom has chosen an academic path.

When I went to college "down the road" at Princeton, I had no idea what I wanted to major in, much less choose for a career. I found psychology, history, politics, economics, and philosophy all interesting, so I chose an interdisciplinary major in the Woodrow Wilson School of Public and International Affairs. For my senior thesis, I wrote a history of a private firm in Philadelphia as an example of Schumpeter's theory of entrepreneurship. I was gratified to win a prize, but, more importantly, the thesis taught me how fascinating original research and making order out of a chaos of empirical material can be. In retrospect, the most important thing I got from Princeton was a broad basis in liberal arts. I still find myself remembering lessons from my early science and philosophy courses. When students sometimes complain to me that their liberal arts education is not preparing them for anything, I respond that it is preparing them for life. College courses are like building blocks. An undergraduate business degree allows you to pile them into a tall tower quickly. Liberal arts is more like a pyramid with a broad base that does not reach the same early heights. But when the earth shakes, and it likely will more than once during the course of a career in today's world, pyramids are more stable than towers.

CAREER CHOICES AT AGE 21

Senior year arrived, and I had no clear idea of what I wanted to do as a career. At that time, all healthy males faced a period of military service, and I decided to join the Marine Corps. An older friend had just finished officer training for platoon leaders in the marines, and made it sound appealing. Some friends had encouraged me to apply for a Rhodes Scholarship, but I was uncertain about it. By chance, as I entered the library one day to work on my thesis, I bumped into a professor of English whose course I was taking. He asked what I intended to do next year and I replied "Marine Corps Platoon Leaders." He shook his head and said I really should apply for the Rhodes. So I did. I remember at the Rhodes interview being asked what I wanted to do for a career. I had enjoyed writing a column for the student newspaper, so I said that I wanted to try to understand society and write about it. "Oh, a pundit?" they asked. I looked puzzled, but they gave me the scholarship anyway. During the summer after graduation, I worked as a night reporter for a local newspaper. I found that writing as a reporter merely scratched the surface of what interested me. I went to Oxford, cured of any desire to pursue a career in journalism, but with nothing in its place.

Besides postponing my career choice for two years, Oxford had several important effects. One was time to experiment and travel. I thought of becoming a novelist, but after trying some stories, I decided to postpone any such efforts for a later stage in life. Also important was the ethic of public service that went along with the Rhodes. I enjoyed my tutorials in philosophy, politics, and economics, but the most important aspect of Oxford was making foreign friends and expanding my interest in the rest of the world. In particular, I remember long discussions with a friend from Ghana over the future of democracy in Africa. To this day, I believe that making friends who help you see the world through the eyes of foreigners is as educational as any formal course in college. Even if you never want to work overseas, you do not really know what is American until you can compare it with what is not American. And in a world of growing globalization, distant events can have powerful effects on your life and career.

By the end of my two years at Oxford, I was leaning toward a career in government, perhaps in the Foreign Service. At the same time, following the example of another friend, I decided to apply to the Ph.D. program in government at Harvard. I thought that the Ph.D. would give me options if it turned out that I did not like the Foreign Service.

CAREER CHOICES AT AGES 24–28

Some people like graduate school. I found it a period of great anxiety and continual work. There was so much to learn, and everyone seemed to know more than I did. In the first two years, impending oral exams loomed like a sword of Damocles. In addition to endless reading, I worked as a research assistant for a professor and taught sophomore tutorial—and I wanted to finish in four years. Perhaps that is why I do not recommend pursuing a Ph.D. unless you need it. If you want to teach, it is a necessary union card. For most other purposes, it strikes me as a lot of pain for the amount of gain.

The best part of graduate work was writing my thesis. I wanted to get away from Harvard and feel creative again. I also wanted to find out what was happening in the newly independent countries in Africa. The idea for my thesis came from a seminar I took on economic development. Professor Ed Mason had just returned from chairing a World Bank mission to Uganda. He said that economic rationality argued for maintaining the East African Common Market, but it would take a political scientist to answer whether that was possible. That was my challenge. My new wife and I spent fifteen months in Uganda, Kenya, and Tanzania collecting data, interviewing political leaders, and trying to understand how politics and economics interacted in new nations.

Life in Africa was exhilarating, and trying to make sense of what was happening around me proved to be an all-absorbing challenge. I decided to postpone the issue of a job search until I returned to Cambridge to write up my material. One tropical evening in December, standing on the lawn of the East African Institute of Social Research at Makerere University, someone handed me a letter. I opened it and discovered that the Government Department at Harvard was offering me a teaching job. Since I had no other plan, I decided to accept and try it for a while, knowing I could always change if I did not like it. That while turned out to be quite long.

EARLY ACADEMIC CAREER

Having set my foot on the academic ladder, I quickly developed a desire to climb it. I enjoyed teaching, and after a weak start I began to improve my capabilities. But all the signals I received made it clear that progress depended on research and publication. My thesis had won a prize, and I worked hard to turn it into a book. I presented papers based on it at the American Political Science Association and the International Political Science Association. The idea of government service did not vanish, but it receded into the background for consideration at a later date. It was clear that I needed first to succeed as an academic, and that meant I had to pay my dues.

I soon started to plan my second major research project. I had discovered that there was a thriving common market in Central America, even though my thesis had explained why, despite their economic merits, common markets were difficult to maintain in less-developed countries. So I polished up my Spanish (sitting in the same courses as some of the students I was teaching) and applied for a grant to spend six months in Central America. A few years later, I followed my intellectual curiosity to a year in Geneva, teaching and researching regional organizations and the politics of trade more generally. The result was a second book, *Peace in Parts*, which was necessary before the impending decision on tenure.

Tenure is the hurdle that looms in front of all academics at this stage of their careers. One tries to banish it from daily thought, but it is like sharing a bedroom with an elephant. I remember asking Richard Neustadt, a senior member of my department, whether I should try to take a leave from Harvard and pursue a policy job in Washington. His advice: save that for later. Focus on getting tenure first. Other mentors such as Stanley Hoffmann pointed out interesting areas for research and suggested my name for the editorial board of a journal, *International Organization*. That led to further contacts—the famous networking effect—which provided a sense of professional direction. Just as chickens have pecking orders, when academics meet they tend to discuss who is working on what research, and how it ranks in the pecking order. It may seem odd, but it is hard to ignore.

One of the benefits of these early professional activities was making a number of new friends. In particular, Robert Keohane and I found that we shared common interests, common dissatisfaction with the field of international organization as it was then conceived, and enjoyed working together. This led to fruitful collaboration on a number of articles and our book, *Power and Interdependence*. It also produced a lifelong friendship. I think both our ideas were better for our collaboration. Tearing apart each others' drafts and rewriting them both refined and accelerated the work process. The important lesson is not to be afraid of collaboration and not to wear your ego on your sleeve.

Another satisfying aspect of focusing on an academic career at this stage of life is that it has more flexibility in terms of family. In the long run, being able to spend time with my wife and growing children was more important than any aspect of a career. I know that my wife, Molly, thinks that I spent too much time on work, but when I compare the flexibility of my hours during my academic years with the rigidity of my schedule when I was in government, the former has a much better fit with small children.

Molly and I celebrated tenure with a quiet dinner and a fine bottle of wine way above our budget. I would like to be able to say that at age thirty-three, I began to seek a role in government, but there was a complication. I was not a member of the political party in power at that time in Washington. That is the price one pays for waiting until after tenure. You never know when opportunities in government will arise, and if you really want to go in more than anything else, you should probably take advantage when lightning strikes. As it turned out, I was forty when I went to Washington. I spent two years there and returned to Harvard mainly because of the age of my children, but thinking I would like to go back after a few years. Thanks to choices of the American electorate, those few years turned out to be twelve. Planning a career as an in'n'outer is not easy in a democracy!

CAREER CHOICES AT 40

Fortunately, I was excited by the work I was doing on transnational relations and interdependence. Some of the academic writing had policy relevance, and I began to write articles and op-eds in that style. I was invited to join the editorial board of *Foreign Policy* magazine. I attended conferences and meetings on policy issues at places like the Council on Foreign Relations and Ditchley where I developed another type of network. I also participated in a policy study on nuclear energy and trade in nuclear materials organized by the Ford Foundation. It was probably through these writings and contacts that I came to the attention of people involved in Jimmy Carter's 1976 campaign. I submitted a paper or two for the campaign but played no significant role. After Carter won, I was quite surprised to be invited to join his transition team as a consultant on nuclear proliferation. Later, when Cyrus Vance was appointed Secretary of State, he asked me to be a deputy undersecretary in charge of Carter's new initiatives on non-proliferation. It took me no time to say yes.

It took me a lot longer to become good at my job. Two years later, I was presented with the State Department's highest medal, the Distinguished Honor Award, but in my first months I thought I might not survive. At most, my administrative experience was the management of one secretary (and some might say it was the other way around). Here I was in charge of thirty or forty people in the department, and supposedly coordinating a major policy as chair of the interagency committee. Once again, everyone knew more than I did. There was no shortage of experienced bureaucrats who wanted to cut me out of the action, and because Carter's policy was unpopular in some quarters, some figures in the nuclear industry and Congress said they would get me fired. I found myself going to work at seven in the morning and returning near midnight. I sought advice from a wide variety of sources. It was my steepest learning curve since first grade.

In retrospect, I might have adjusted to a major policy job more quickly if I had had an earlier apprenticeship in government. Certainly the second time I went into government, years later, was much easier. It is hard to overstate the difference in the two cultures. One of the big differences is the premium on time. In academic life, time is a secondary value. It is important to get things just right even at the price of being late. In government, an A+ briefing that reaches the president's desk after the foreign minister has arrived in the Oval Office is an F. Timing is everything. And brevity is a close second. I remember academic colleagues sending me seminar-length papers (like I used to write) with solutions to the proliferation problem. They could not envision a world in which I had to read, overnight, intelligence and press clips before the morning staff meeting with the secretary and, after, was caught up in a whirlwind of events until I returned home that evening too exhausted to read anything.

I remember watching some academics who tried to maintain their old habits after they entered government. They either changed or were shunted aside as irrelevant. This does not mean that academic training is irrelevant. On the contrary, it provides the intellectual capital that sometimes allows an academic to set forth a strategy that might escape a career bureaucrat. It is vital to set and maintain priorities and not become a prisoner of one's inbox. But there is little time on the job to develop new intellectual capital.

Partly for those reasons, and mainly for family reasons, I returned to Harvard when my two-year leave expired. I found that there were many intellectual puzzles that arose when I was in government that I had no time to figure out. I was particularly intrigued by the ethical issues involved in foreign policy in general, and nuclear weapons in particular. When I returned to Harvard, I switched part of my teaching to the Kennedy School of Government, where there was more concern for policy issues. There I found that teaching a course on ethics and foreign policy to a bright group of students was a great way to work out my ideas that eventually were published as *Nuclear Ethics*. At the same time, I developed a large course on international conflicts for the core curriculum in the college, and took pride in being able to explain foreign affairs to freshmen and sophomores. Later, the course became the basis for a popular textbook, *Understanding International Conflict*.

CHOICES AT 55

Much as I enjoyed my teaching and writing, I still hoped to spend another period in government. In the late 1980s, I wrote a book, *Bound to Lead: The Changing*

Nature of American Power, which argued that America was not in decline (as was then the academic fashion to predict). I also became very interested in the role of Japan, which some saw as a challenge to the United States. These intellectual puzzles gave me much to chew on, but I missed the chance to affect policy and to use the administrative talents I had belatedly discovered. At this stage in life, there are numerous offers of deanships and college and university presidencies. I had considered, but resisted, such opportunities a number of times. I preferred administration in government, but as such prospects faded after the election of 1988, I began to wonder about succumbing. I tried a period as an associate dean with ambivalent results. Fortunately, I was rescued by the election of 1992.

In 1993, I returned to Washington as Chairman of the National Intelligence Council, the body that coordinates interagency intelligence estimates for the president. Much as I enjoyed working with my friend Jim Woolsey, I was tempted by a policy job that would let me implement some of the issues I had been writing about as an academic. I moved to the Defense Department to become Assistant Secretary for International Security Affairs under William Perry, with whom I had helped to organize the Aspen Strategy Group in the 1980s. If ever I wanted to see the world, this was almost too much of a good thing. In one year, I visited fifty-three countries in fifty-two weeks!

I enjoyed the Pentagon so much that when my two-year leave from Harvard expired in January 1995, I decided to resign my tenure and stay on in government. Finally I cut the umbilical cord! Yet within the year, I was back at Harvard as dean of the Kennedy School, a job for which I had earlier said I did not want to be considered. The major consideration in my change of mind (which took more than a month to decide) was the aftermath of the bombing of the federal building in Oklahoma City. The national debate about government struck me as polarized and confused. I worried about what was happening to public life in our country. I was struck by the irony of the fact that while I was working in government, I was too busy to think about what was happening to government. I decided that the Kennedy School, with it multidisciplinary faculty and its tradition of combining analytic excellence with policy relevance, would provide a base for addressing my concerns. Since returning, I have organized a faculty study group that has addressed issues of declining trust in government (published in 1997 as *Why People Don't Trust Government*) and the effects of the information revolution on government (published in 1999 as *democracy.com*). I do not regret my decision to return to academic life, and I am now wise enough to realize that it is highly unlikely that I would ever return to government.

SUMMING UP

If one is attracted to both analysis and action, a career as an in 'n' outer has a lot to offer. Academic life allows you to follow your intellectual curiosity and to gnaw on interesting bones. Writing provides a sense of creativity. Teaching is fun, and meeting your students in later years is enormously satisfying. In addition, you are able (within limits) to control your own time and agenda. With policy jobs in government you do not control your own time or agenda. There is little opportunity to explore ideas, much less smell the flowers or read poetry. On the other hand, they can be very exciting at times. Not only will you meet the great (and not so great) and be present at fascinating events, but occasionally you can put your own stamp on issues of considerable importance. That is another source of creativity, to feel that you have helped to shape an important policy outcome.

Focusing solely on one or the other may lead to higher achievement in that domain. There are trade-offs, both in time and recognition, from switching back and forth. Some people who choose one road will be jealous and some resentful of intruders and deserters who try to have their cake and eat it too. It all depends on what you want out of life. For me, the in 'n' out approach was worth it, but I enjoyed my academic base in its own right. The biggest problem is the difficulty of planning such a career. Notice what a large role serendipity played in the story I have told above. You can walk in a field with a golf club in a thunderstorm and not be struck by lightning. There is no sense selling short your academic career in hope of being struck by political lightning. If you want both, make sure that you start with the one that will be most satisfying if the other does not happen along. That way you cannot lose.

7

On Being a Woman in Academia and in Research Institutes

Susan Kaufman Purcell

I became a political scientist by accident. During my sophomore year at Barnard College, I was asked to choose a major field. I chose biology and was promptly told that I would have to go to summer school because the science courses that I had taken were not the ones required for a biology major. I could not afford summer school. My father had died and my mother had just begun working as a secretary to support the family. I asked my advisor if there was anything that I could major in without going to summer school. "Spanish," she said. And so I became a Spanish major.

In truth, my professed desire to specialize in biology was never very strong. I enjoyed science, but had no concrete career plans. I entered college in 1959, before the women's movement. I was the first female member of my family to do so. I had been taught to value education, not so much for the thrill of learning but rather because it would give me security and the right kind of husband. My father's death had reinforced the link in my mind between education and security. It was the one thing that no one would ever be able to take away from me.

The next series of choices that influenced my professional career involved summer study abroad. In the aftermath of the Cuban Revolution, private foundations as well as the U.S. government had begun to make large amounts of money available to create a pool of Latin American experts. During my sophomore year in college, a poster on the Spanish Department's bulletin board advertising a scholarship to study during the summer in Guadalajara, Mexico, caught my eye. I successfully applied for it and spent the summer of 1961 living with a family and

studying Mexican history and culture in Guadalajara. The main things I knew about
Mexico were that it was warm and sunny, which appealed to me, and the people
spoke Spanish. It was also foreign, and I was a nineteen year old who had never
traveled abroad.

I often compare what happened to me in Mexico to the imprinting of baby ani-
mals who bond with the first object or animal they see. I became fascinated with
the country and ultimately wrote my Ph.D. thesis on the Mexican political system. During that summer in 1961, however, I had no interest in politics. Mexico's
brightly colored architecture, the songs of its mariachis and its larger-than life rev-
olutionary heroes fascinated me. For the first time I had the sense that the world
was a bigger place than I had imagined and I wanted to experience more of what
it had to offer.

I returned to Barnard determined to spend the next summer in Latin America
as well. I applied for and received another scholarship. This time, I ended up in
Ambato, Ecuador, as a member of an anthropology project. Living alone in four
different Mestizo communities for a week at a time, I interviewed two hundred
families, trying to find out why people were leaving the Andean Highlands and
moving permanently to new jungle towns to the east or working as seasonal migrants
on the tropical coast. Coming face-to-face with such extreme poverty and hardship focused my attention for the first time on the link between politics and poverty.

Upon returning for my final year at Barnard, I was faced with the decision of
what to do next. I knew how to be a good student and had always enjoyed school.
I also did not have a fiancé, so marriage as a solution to my problem was not an
option. I chose, therefore, to continue doing more or less what I had been doing
and get my master's degree in Spanish. I ultimately chose Columbia University
because I received a full scholarship and because the university had a new Latin
American Institute where I could combine my studies in Spanish with courses on
Latin America. During my first year of graduate school, I took three courses on
Latin American politics. I found them fascinating, despite the fact that the field
was so underdeveloped that we were assigned books with titles such as *El Salvador: Land of Lords and Lizards*. At the end of the year, I changed my major to
political science.

Fortunately, my advisor had given his approval, despite the fact that I had not
taken any political science courses as an undergraduate. I was scheduled to spend
that summer of 1964 in Cali, Colombia, as a member of yet another fully funded
summer research group. Knowing nothing about local government and politics anywhere, I decided to use the opportunity in Cali to develop some expertise in these
areas.

Although the research project proved successful, my first full year as a political science graduate student was not. I had spent my college years studying traditionally "female" subjects such as literature, art history, and anthropology. I had
taken a few history courses, but only because I had been required to do so. Polit-

ical science had been optional, so I had avoided it. During my second year of graduate school, therefore, I quickly had to learn not only political science, but history as well. After what I regarded as my trial by fire, I emerged with enough background to consider myself a full-fledged political scientist.

During that year I also decided to become a doctoral candidate in political science, mainly because one of my professors encouraged me to do so and fellowship money was available. In the early 1960s, female graduate students felt more welcome at Columbia than at most other elite universities. Perhaps this was due to its location in a large, politically liberal city. Nevertheless, I never had a female political science professor and often I was the only woman in my Ph.D. seminars.

Following my second year of graduate school, I once again spent the summer in Latin America on a scholarship, this time in Brazil. When I returned to New York, I briefly considered writing my Ph.D. dissertation on Brazil instead of Mexico, but decided that a woman doing political research in an increasingly repressive military regime was not a good idea. I refocused my attention, therefore, on my first love—Mexico.

After fifteen months of conducting research in Mexico City, again with the benefit of a full scholarship, I returned to Columbia to complete my dissertation and seek my first full-time job. I never considered any possibility other than university teaching. The conventional wisdom was that teaching was a good job for a woman, since it would give her the flexibility to combine marriage and family with a career. In the late 1960s, being a professor was still a high-prestige career. On the other hand, I also knew that few universities had or wanted female professors, particularly in traditionally "male" disciplines such as political science. My job search, in fact, provided me with my first experience of discrimination against women.

Despite my excellent record, I was often not invited to compete for jobs at prestigious universities that were interviewing my male colleagues. At one interview, I was asked if I was going to get pregnant and leave. At another school, which was about to become coed and was therefore considering hiring women for the first time, several of the professors made jokes about not being able to take me to the local pub, where they took male candidates, since it did not admit women.

Fortunately, the need for qualified professors of Latin American politics in 1969 outweighed traditional prejudices and I was hired in a tenure-track position at the University of California, Los Angeles (UCLA). I became one of three full-time female professors in a department of about forty-five faculty members. The other two women had been hired six months earlier. Before their appointment, the faculty had always been exclusively male.

Shortly after my arrival at UCLA, the feminist movement arrived on campus. I believed in equality for women, although I never joined any women's organizations or groups. On the other hand, I felt that I wanted to make a contribution and decided to teach a course on women and politics. Unfortunately, I decided to call it "Sexual Politics," the name of a best-selling book of the period. Despite pressure from my department to change the name, I refused to do so. This transformed me into a problematic member of the department. Teaching the course also diverted some of my attention from Latin America and delayed the reworking of my dissertation for publication.

After two years and a warning that I would not get tenure unless my dissertation was accepted for publication, I decided to drop the courses I was offering on women in politics and concentrate instead on the field in which I had been trained. I do not regret the decision, since I regarded Latin American politics as more intellectually interesting than the field of women in politics. In the early 1970s, Latin American specialists were dealing with issues such as the causes of instability and underdevelopment. The field of women and politics, in contrast, was still in the early stages of gathering data about the number and kinds of women in various political positions. I also decided that I could be a better role model for women by becoming a mainstream political scientist.

At about that time, I became pregnant with my daughter and prepared to face the challenge of combining a family with a career. There were no role models in my family. Feminism was not much help, since in 1974 it was not yet oriented toward family issues. When I applied for a maternity leave, I was told that it existed for secretaries, but not for professors. Someone suggested that I write a letter to the chancellor of the university, asking to advance my quarter's sabbatical leave by one quarter so that I could combine research and writing with nursing my daughter. It seemed a humiliating letter to write, but I saw no alternative at the time. The leave was approved and I was able to spend my first four months as a mother at home with my child.

When the leave ended I resumed my teaching duties, but not for long. Within nine months my husband, who was a political science professor at a different university, and I were living in Mexico on a fellowship, collaborating on a research project dealing with business–government relations. This proved to be the beginning of the transition to the next phase of my career.

I was thirty-three years old and had recently been granted tenure. I also had become increasingly ambivalent about teaching. On the one hand, I enjoyed working with young people and helping them learn how to formulate and think about ideas and issues. On the other hand, I was tired of interacting professionally mainly with other academics and longed to be more a part of the "real" world. I also disliked what would later be called the "political correctness" that had begun to permeate the university in the mid-1970s.

After fifteen months in Mexico, I moved with my family to Washington, D.C., where my husband and I became joint fellows at the Woodrow Wilson Center for Scholars. I had never lived in Washington before. Nor did I have much experience in dealing with foreign policy issues. My field was comparative politics, with a focus on Latin America. My approach had been very cerebral. I looked upon foreign political systems as a jigsaw puzzle, and I wanted to understand how the pieces fit together. What I studied had always seemed quite peripheral to my life. In Washington, in contrast, the focus was on the interests and security of the United States, my own country. Finally, I could engage both my intellect and my emotions. When I resumed my teaching at UCLA in September 1977, it was with a determination to find a way to return quickly to Washington.

By September 1979, I was back. I had received an International Affairs Fellowship from the Council on Foreign Relations. The purpose of the fellowship was to give ivory-tower intellectuals a dose of reality by enabling them to spend a year in government. It also worked in reverse, allowing people in government to spend a year at a university or think tank gathering their thoughts. This fellowship changed my life. It brought me into contact with the so-called foreign policy establishment of the United States and allowed me to place my Latin American expertise in a global context.

I originally had begun working on the State Department's Policy Planning Staff as an assistant to the person in charge of Latin America. When he suddenly left that position, I asked my boss if I could replace him. My courage was the result of a feminist book I had recently read called *Games Your Mother Never Taught You*. It said that women, no matter how talented and hardworking, would go nowhere unless they asked for what they wanted. So I asked if I could replace the departing staff member. My boss said that I lacked sufficient foreign policy expertise. I asked him to try me out for a few months. Fortunately for me, he said yes.

I served on the State Department's Policy Planning Staff from January 1980 through June 1981. My tenure began during the last year of the Carter administration, following the Soviet invasion of Afghanistan, and ended after the first six months of Ronald Reagan's first term of office. During those eighteen months the United States had three secretaries of state—Cyrus Vance, Edmund Muskie, and Alexander Haig. The Sandinistas had recently taken control of Nicaragua and Marxist guerrillas were gaining strength in El Salvador. Cuba was actively engaged in helping both.

I learned more in my eighteen months in government than I had in a comparable period of time in academia. The work was challenging and exhilarating. Almost everything I did involved the Central American conflict. My job included writing talking points for the secretary of state, participating in interdepartmental planning meetings, and writing briefing papers for my boss. For the first time, I was forced to combine knowledge and ideas with recommendations for action. Here, finally, was the reality I had been looking for.

My experience in government also helped me define my own political views. I had managed to reach the age of thirty-seven without having done so, or so I thought. As it turned out, I did have fairly clear political ideas, but had never really had to articulate them. In the course of writing talking points, without much guidance, for three secretaries of state, I discovered that I was either a conservative

Democrat or a moderate Republican. Carter's foreign policy seemed too liberal for a period of the Cold War characterized by active Soviet attempts at expansion into the so-called third world. Reagan's early policies, on the other hand, appeared too willing to give military regimes in Latin America and elsewhere the benefit of the doubt.

I also learned that permanent full-time government employment was not for me. I missed seeing my name on the documents that I wrote. I found it unsatisfying to write papers by committee. I also missed being able to offer my own opinions on the issues to public audiences. On the other hand, I learned so much in government and found the ability to help shape U.S policy so satisfying that I hoped one day to be able to return.

In the meantime, I was faced with an important professional decision. UCLA had informed me that I had to resume teaching or forfeit tenure. I had taken four years of leave over the preceding six years. My colleagues had begun to question my commitment to the university. I had my doubts as well. My husband recently had resigned from his university and begun a new career as a political risk analyst with a New York bank. Although he offered to return to California with me if I wished to stay at UCLA, I knew that he really liked his new job. I also did not want my husband and I to live in different cities, which would deprive our seven-year-old daughter of one of her parents. I finally decided to return to New York, the city where I was born and educated, and look for a job there.

Within several weeks, I received a job offer from the Council on Foreign Relations in New York. The council had decided to hire a full-time Latin American expert for the first time. The job offer was conditional. I had one year to develop a two-year project proposal and raise $200,000 to fund it. If I was successful, I could remain at the council during these two additional years to run the project.

I raised the money and stayed at the council for eight years. It was like being a kid in a candy store. I attended as many of the meetings dealing with U.S. foreign policy as possible. For the first time, I was able to spend my days learning and thinking about areas other than Latin America. At the same time, as Director of the Latin American Project, I was able to focus the study groups I organized on contentious issues of U.S. foreign policy toward the region. This was a long way from the highly intellectual approach I had taken toward Latin America when I was a professor.

While at the Council on Foreign Relations, I had an opportunity to dramatically change the direction of my career. I was offered either a full-or part-time position as a political risk analyst, focusing on Latin America, by a New York bank. I declined the offer for personal reasons. My marriage had ended three years earlier and I shared joint custody of my daughter with my former husband. My daughter was ten years old and still struggling emotionally as a result of the divorce. Her father's private sector job required him to work long hours and travel a lot. I did not see how I could be a good mother to my daughter while working at a less flexible and more time-consuming job in the private sector. The part-time job was not a solution either, since for financial reasons I would have had to complement it with another part-time job.

Although I did not move to the private sector, by the late 1980s I was ready to change jobs. I could not expand my program at the council. Nor were there any opportunities for me to move up to another position. The president of the Americas Society, a nonprofit educational institution focusing on Latin America and Canada, happened to ask me if I knew of anyone to fill a position there as a program director. I did not, but implied that I might be interested in moving to the Americas Society if a higher-level position were available. He called the next day and asked me what I wanted. I asked for a vice presidency and the opportunity to create and run a public policy program. He responded favorably and I immediately accepted his offer.

The Americas Society is an affiliate of the Council of the Americas, a nonprofit business organization of mainly Fortune 500 companies with investments in Latin America. Shortly after taking my new position, the Soviet Union collapsed and the Cold War ended. President Bush announced a new Enterprise for the Americas Initiative, which encouraged and helped consolidate a series of market-oriented reforms in Latin America. The expansion of trade and investment replaced security issues on the U.S. policy agenda for the Western Hemisphere. I did not know it then, but it soon became clear that I had landed in the right place at the right time.

Specifically, I began to "retool" myself intellectually, reading heavily about free trade, privatization, the benefits of foreign investment, and the ways in which political and economic liberalization were related. I also began organizing public programs and study groups around these topics. Essentially, I successfully applied the programming expertise I had learned and used at the Council on Foreign Relations to a new set of issues at the Americas Society and Council of the Americas.

I should mention that shortly after agreeing to move to the Americas Society, I was offered the Latin American staff position on the National Security Council in the new Bush administration. Once again, I declined the offer. Accepting it would have either meant moving my daughter to Washington and thereby separating her from her father, or leaving my daughter in New York with her father and missing out on my daughter's high school years. I did not tell this to the Bush Administration, out of fear that I would not be considered a "serious professional woman." Instead, I said that I had just accepted a job in New York and did not want to break my word to my new employers.

I do not regret my decision. I have enjoyed the past decade at the Americas Society and Council of the Americas and have learned a great deal about how the private sector operates and the issues that concern it. During these same years, I was also invited to join the board of directors of Valero Energy Corporation, a Fortune 500 company, and several mutual fund boards managed by Scudder Kemper Investments.

I have served, and continue to serve, on a number of nonprofit boards such as the National Endowment for Democracy, Freedom House, and the Women's Foreign Policy Group. And in addition to continuing to speak and write on issues concerning Latin America and U.S. policy toward the region, I do occasional consulting for private companies, nonprofit groups, and the U.S. government.

I do not know if there is another job change in my future. I enjoy my current position, which is not surprising since I essentially designed it. As vice president of the Americas Society and Council of the Americas, I have the freedom to think, write, and speak about the ever-changing political and economic landscape of Latin America. My job also allows me to interact on a daily basis with the people who influence developments in the region. On the other hand, if an opportunity to do something new and even more exciting and satisfying were to present itself, I certainly would explore it and might be tempted to take it.

As I look back on the various stages of professional life, three conclusions seem obvious. The first involves the extremely important role that scholarships and fellowships have played in my professional development. They enabled me to attend Columbia University over a ten-year period cost free. They also made it possible for me to spend four summers studying or conducting research in Latin America before taking my first job. Finally, fellowships allowed me to spend three years in Washington, D.C., first as a guest scholar and then as a member of the State Department's policy planning staff.

I have no doubt that I would have attended college even if I had not received scholarships. It is much less likely, however, that I would have gone to graduate school and become a specialist in Latin America without the opportunity to spend some time abroad. This may be less true now. When I was young, foreign travel was much less common than it is today, at least for middle-class girls. The fact that I received scholarships and fellowships to study and conduct research abroad developed new interests that might have remained undiscovered had I spent my early years only in the United States.

The second conclusion involves my gender. As a woman, I have almost always chosen jobs that have given me the flexibility to combine work with marriage and children. The one exception was my eighteen months in the State Department. It was the exception that proved the rule. Once I realized how difficult it was to spend time with my child while working in government, I declined the opportunity to reenter government several years later. If I had to do it all over again, I would make the same decision.

I believe that despite the achievements of the feminist movement, which are many, young women today still confront the traditional problem of balancing a career with motherhood. In recent years, many young men have also begun to value a more balanced life. A career in academia or in a so-called think tank remains a good option, provided that one is willing to forgo great wealth.

The third conclusion concerns the importance of being proactive in pursuing what you want. I feel that this is especially important for women, many of whom have been socialized into believing that taking the initiative is unfeminine or unnecessary. Throughout my career, I have rarely been offered jobs without asking for them and persuading those doing the hiring that I was a qualified candidate. In several cases I had to redefine the position into a more interesting one or create something where nothing existed before.

I used to envy people who knew exactly what they wanted to be when they "grew up," since it is obviously easier to get what you want if you know what you want. This may be true. My own experience has taught me, however, that in the absence of certainty, things can turn out well if we are able to recognize potential job opportunities, think creatively about them, and then aggressively pursue them.

8

Law and Public Policy

William D. Rogers

The notional template of career passages, which this volume addresses, is close to my actual experience. But not all passages are equal. I sense that I controlled the early ones—those through school and into a profession. It was otherwise with the later passages—those that led me eventually to a senior foreign policy position in the State Department. I chose my education and my profession. The rest was accident.

The early choices seem almost inevitable now. For as long as I can remember, I was interested in public policy. My grandfather had been a political figure in New Jersey, a judge on the highest court, twice candidate for governor and a New Dealer. An uncle was a lawyer. He and several of his brothers were Princetonians. So I gravitated to Princeton, and to the School of Public International Affairs there. My father was a chemist. I had little interest in the sciences. So when I had the good fortune to get a D in chemistry, my father was finally persuaded to abandon his secret hopes for me in his chosen field.

In the same way, Yale Law School seemed the natural next step. An offer of a history fellowship at Wisconsin was not very tempting; teaching about the past was too remote from the great issues of the time. I graduated from Princeton in 1948, and came to adulthood as the nation emerged from World War II. The consolidation of Soviet power in Eastern Europe posed large challenges. The United States was busy with the postwar architecture of new international financial and political structures. Law school seemed, as I turned twenty-one, to present the broadest range of opportunities to be a part of this new world.

I did passing well in law school. The next major juncture in my career came in the form of an offer of clerkship to the former dean of the Law School, Judge Charles E. Clark, on the then-great Second Circuit Court in New York. Accident, which came to play so great a role in my later passages, made its first appearance. The clerkship offer came to hand only because Yale Law Professor Fred Rodell admired my wife. On that account he mentioned me to Judge Clark.

And Judge Clark, at the end of our year together, recommended me to Justice Stanley Reed of the Supreme Court. I became his law clerk in 1952. Thus, with fortune's hand once again at play, my wife and I found ourselves in Washington, and I, working at the peak of the nation's judicial system.

The next major choice, in my case at age twenty-six, was where to practice when the one-year Supreme Court clerkship ended. I had offers from New York. But somehow the glamour of drafting trust indentures escaped me. The then-microscopic Washington law firm of Arnold, Fortas & Porter was in the market. Its principals were gutsy lawyers. Each had had a stint of public service—Thurman Arnold as Roosevelt's antitrust enforcer, Abe Fortas as Under Secretary of the Interior, Paul Porter as Ambassador to Greece and OPA Administrator. And they were much in the press, representing Owen Lattimore and other targets of Senator McCarthy. The national witch hunt was at its peak in the early 1950s and Arnold, Fortas & Porter was in the middle of it.

Thus the choice: a comfortable, well-remunerated life of commercial law in New York, or a new and financially shaky Washington firm, brash and reckless enough to take on America's leading demagogue in the civil liberties struggle of the century. The choice was easy—for me. I thank heaven for a wife who was also ready for a bumpy ride.

And so it came to be that I began my legal practice by a total immersion in the loyalty cases. This proved totally absorbing. The firm was in the courts and congressional committees for years, and in the papers almost every day, battling for the victims of the national madness and for freedom of speech

It was everything a young lawyer with a taste for public policy could hope for. Owen Lattimore's searing experience at the hands of his Senate persecutors was for me a splendid fight and a heady delight. Thurman Arnold made the point well. He regularly reminded us, "If someone has to go to jail, be sure it's the client."

As it happened, Abe Fortas had had responsibilities for Puerto Pico, then an American colony, when he was at Interior. While I was clerking with Judge Clark, he and I had drafted the new judicial code for Puerto Rico, one of the legal instruments by which it achieved self-governing commonwealth status in 1952. So it was natural enough that Fortas should ask me to work on the firm's Puerto Rican matters with him. The nation's witch-hunting madness began to burn out in the mid-1950s. Our loyalty case load declined. As a result, not by design but by chance, I became immersed in Puerto Rico's gallant economic development programs—

its Operation Bootstrap. And with its leader, Teodoro Moscoso. He became my client.

Throughout the 1950s, I was more than happy with a life in the law. It had an ample component of policy. I gave little thought to public service. That changed drastically with the election of Jack Kennedy. His inspiration was the stuff of legend; his call, that we ask what we could do for our country, hit home.

Opportunity met desire, when President Kennedy called Moscoso to Washington in late 1961 to head up the Alliance for Progress. At the swearing-in ceremony in the White House—a rare event, and testimony to the importance the new president gave to Latin America—to my astonishment, just before raising his right hand, Moscoso whispered to me that he wanted me to join him as counsel to the Alliance. The program was then located in the AID Agency within the State Department. I suggested he come to dinner. When we got home, my wife lowered the boom on him; she made it clear she was holding Moscoso responsible for derailing a promising career. Arnold, Fortas & Porter had no tradition of younger lawyers decamping for public service—or tolerance of it. There could be no assurance that I could return to private practice there.

Still, it was no contest. I had not planned for a career shift at the ripe age of thirty-four. The invitation was unforeseen. But the prospects were too intriguing to pass up—engagement in the economic, social, and political regeneration of the hemisphere, amply funded, backed by an inspiring and dedicated president. The switch was more happenstance than design, but a happy happenstance indeed. I accepted.

Paul Porter likened public office at the time to the Jesuit priesthood, with the same vows of poverty, chastity, and silence. I can only think of the change as positive. Bracing as the Arnold, Fortar & Porter work had proven, saturated as it was with public policy issues, to enter the service of one's country after a decade of private law practice was a moving experience.

Within days, I was in the Dominican Republic bringing the first tranche of U.S. aid to the post-Trujillo regime. My wife and I were in Mexico, one of the targets of the Russian missiles in Cuba according to President Kennedy's address, at the height of the Cuban Missile Crisis. I was the legal officer responsible for clearing hundreds of millions of dollars of high-impact, high-visibility school, road, hospital, and technical assistance projects for Latin America.

From this I extract the principle that career change in one's thirties is likely to be healthy but hard to plan. After half a dozen years at one desk, a new one is almost always a bracing and invigorating affair. A shift to public service after one's first third of a century is close to ideal, if it involves new responsibilities for affairs of public consequence. But the odds of such an offer are low, or at least they were in my case.

My wife adds a further insight about such passages. In my career, I have switched from private law practice to public service and back three times. On each occasion of my entering government she has pointedly reminded me that I was woefully lacking in the experience appropriate to my new public responsibilities. And each time I left public service, she has pointed out, I had finally learned the job and my resignation was a net loss of national expertise. This may be another way of expressing the value of career shifts. They do indeed compel one to pick up new responsibilities and undertake new challenges.

In my case, however, and I suspect in most, there is a point where the curve of satisfaction at policy levels in the national government begins to turn down—perhaps when the work becomes too familiar and the effort more routine than new. The frustrations of pushing options against the tide of bureaucratic inertia and fiefdom-preservation can outrun the satisfaction of making a dent on policy. Government is different from the private sector, particularly the great national government. Businesses and law firms are hierarchical. The public power of the United States is allocated in mysterious and changing ways between three branches of government. Congress is contentious in defense of its prerogatives, increasingly so in the foreign affairs field. It delights in imposing its will on the executive branch, perhaps particularly so in the case of the State Department. The executive branch is balkanized amongst a multitude of operating agencies. And within State, the conflict of views between the regional and the functional bureaus, and between the desks and the far-flung ambassadorial outposts they supposedly serve, as well as vertically between all levels from the Secretary to the lowliest FSO, is constant and unremitting. Edwin Corwin was right. He wrote that the Constitution's foreign relations arrangements are "an invitation to struggle." There comes a time when even the most hardy and the most dedicated can find this a bit wearing.

Or at least so it was in my case. I began to think of returning to private practice. Kennedy's assassination in 1963 was a blow to the Latin Americanists in the administration. Johnson promised the Alliance for Progress continued support. But with the new president there was enough change in the tone of our relations with Latin America to inspire reflections about another career switch.

My reservations reached a critical point with the U.S. incursion into the 1965 Dominican Republic. I resigned in June, not with a full-throated public blast but with strongly expressed private reservations about the use of force in our hemisphere. Somewhat to my surprise, Arnold, Fortas & Porter welcomed me back.

The return to private practice was seamless. One Friday I was sitting at my desk in the State Department, signing loan authorizations; the following Monday I was in the law firm library researching some issue of legal interest as if I had never left. Indeed, this proved to be the case each of the other times I returned from government to private law practice. Not long after I returned, the firm became Arnold & Porter. Fortas was drafted to the Supreme Court by Johnson. Not long thereafter Fortas called me to have lunch with him at the Court. Over coffee he said that the president wished to know if I would like to be Ambassador to Brazil— and how close I was to Bobby Kennedy. As it happened, I had come under Bobby's spell. We had spent no little time discussing Latin America. He had acquired his late brother's passion for the region. The Dominican intervention had appalled him as it had me. So without much thought, I said to Fortas that the answers were "No" and "Very." Fortas' probe about Kennedy was an expression of Johnson's passion for loyalty. What I would have said to his first question if he had not asked me for proof of that loyalty I cannot say. Perhaps piqued though I was, I was also being true to my career plans; it was not the first, or the last, offer of an overseas chief of mission assignment that I received and rejected over the years. On the other occasions I contented myself with the observation that I would do anything for my country but leave it.

In all events, the astonishing Fortas offer and my rejection were decisive. Unplanned encounters have outsized consequences. Is it a consolation to reflect that the person who did get the ambassadorial nod in Brazil in my place was kidnapped by terrorists shortly after his arrival?

But this was not the end of the accidental events. Late in 1965, George Ball, then Under Secretary of State, called to say that he had proposed to the president the nomination of a certain prominent American to head up an interagency task force to determine the U.S. response to the unilateral declaration of independence by the Ian Smith regime in Rhodesia. The suggestion had leaked to the press. Johnson killed the nomination. Would I take it? With much less consideration than the decision deserved, I said yes. Fortune plays a role; so does spontaneous opportunism.

Thus began another stint in the State Department. Confirming my wife's observation, I knew nothing about Rhodesia. This was a different continent and new—largely military—considerations. To return to government after a brief tour back at the law firm was the farthest thing from my thoughts. But if unplanned, it was welcome. I learned something about the use and misuse of power in far off places. I reported, with Ball, our recommendation to the president that the United States not support a British reinvasion of Rhodesia—and had the satisfaction of seeing the recommendation accepted. This was certainly just as well. Johnson was getting us deeper and deeper in Vietnam. I was scarcely the only one who thought that one remote war was more than enough for the United States in the late 1960s.

The British prime minister came to Washington. Johnson delivered his decision. I returned to my law firm.

One of my colleagues in the Alliance for Progress had been Dr. Edgar Berman, an expert on family planning and demography. He had arranged for us both to discuss the demographic aspects of Latin American development with the pope in Rome. Berman happened also to be Vice President Hubert Humphrey's friend, physician, and intellectual bodyguard. We stayed close through the late 1960s, after we both had returned to private life. When Humphrey got the nomination of the Democratic Party in 1968, Berman delivered a message that Humphrey wanted me to be his assistant secretary of state for Latin America if he won. Again a matter of the purest chance.

But Humphrey did not win, Nixon did. Not once did I contemplate returning to government in a Nixon Administration.

Until 1974 I practiced fairly typical Washington law—civil trials, administrative agency proceedings, antitrust. And all quite happily; I never seriously considered the options that some of my colleagues exercised, departing private practice for either teaching or a corporate officership. For the first, the money was not attractive; for the other, the intellectual horizons working for a single firm seemed too constricting.

Throughout, however, I maintained an involvement in public affairs. The opportunities were legion: President of the New York Center for Inter-American Relations, the American Society of International Law of which I became president for several years, the Georgetown Foreign Service School on whose board I served. The Vietnam War was at fall tilt then. I published my share of articles critical of U.S. policy and the U.S. international legal justification for the war.

So it came as something of a surprise again when in early 1974 the legal adviser to the Department of State told me that Henry Kissinger wished to know if I was interested in that position—which I declined—and, shortly after, whether I would head the Latin American Bureau of State. I declined this as well. But again, it was fortune intruding. So far as I can reconstruct the matter, Kissinger probably had had a word about me from David Rockefeller through Nelson Rockefeller for whom Kissinger had worked and who had become vice president when Agnew self-destructed. I was not contemplating a career switch at that point. I was forty-three years old. More importantly, I did not want to be associated with the Nixon Administration in its dying days.

Then occurred one of the more astonishing events in my life. In August of 1974, on the day Nixon resigned and while he was winging his way back to California, Kissinger called me. Would I reconsider the Latin American offer? The country needed to pull together. He needed a team. I went to see him at State. Kissinger can be persuasive. I gave him copies of my anti-Vietnam War papers. I aggressively added that I would resign if the CIA engaged in destabilization efforts in Latin America on my watch and asked him to call me the next Monday. He did. Kissinger said I had not changed his mind. I accepted.

And so began a relationship that has survived the years. It was a tie I could not have planned. It has led me, in a strange and mysterious way, into paths that I could never have anticipated.

I remained in the department, first as assistant secretary for Latin America, then as Under Secretary for International Economic Affairs, until the end of the Ford Administration. Kissinger handed me a capacious mandate: to oversee Latin American relations; to represent the United States in the North-South Dialogue in Paris; to speak for him in the financial crises which struck the Pound, the Peseta, and the Lira in

1976; to negotiate normalization of relations secretly with the Castro government; and to work with him in the effort to bring an end to apartheid in Southern African.

Indeed, in 1976 Kissinger asked that I become his deputy secretary, the second-officer in the department. The offer reminded me of nothing so much as Groucho Marx' quip that he did not want to belong to any club that would have him. In the event, the idea was vetoed by the Ford White House, then locked in a death grip contest with Reagan for the Republican nomination. One wonders what would have happened if Ford had beaten Carter in 1976. Kissinger would have remained the towering commander of our foreign policy. I would probably have continued at State. Fortune again.

Ford lost. I returned for a third time to the practice of the law. Again, the transition was painless. Indeed, I observed at the time that a return to private life, at least a Washington law practice, had its rewards. One could sleep an hour later, watch government and politics up close, work in the same international arena as one had done during public service—and avoid the buffeting which seems to come with public territory.

My firm, which had been overwhelmingly domestic in the early days, had begun to build an international practice. It blossomed in the 1980s. We took on a number of Latin American countries in the great Latin American debt crisis. We became counsel to the international financial institutions in their U.S. court litigation.

In this period, in my fifties, I entertained no great longing for another career switch. My professional life was varied enough. I undertook several out-of-office chores in the international arena. Howard Baker, then majority leader of the Senate, asked me to act as his personal adviser on the Panama Canal Treaties. Later I provided good offices to the two countries in the final ratification controversies. At the behest of the government of Panama, I went to Nicaragua the day the dictator Somoza left and the Sandinistas took over. My orders were to provide legal advice to the new government. In 1983, I joined Kissinger as senior counselor to the National Bipartisan Commission on Central America. This absorbed the better part of a year in preparing the evidence and the report for President Reagan with respect to the bloody insurgencies in that troubled land. I went on a year's sabbatical to England to join the law faculty of Cambridge University. And in 1996, for a change of scene, my wife and I went to London where I headed up the expansion of Arnold & Porter's European presence.

Perhaps the most energizing aspect of my professional life for the past two decades has been my continued involvement with Henry Kissinger. I helped him in editing the several volumes of his memoirs. I have advised him on a variety of legal matters. And I have served as a member of his small but dazzlingly successful consulting firm.

In short, I suppose, the highly diverse efforts that I have put my hand to, even as I maintained my law partnership, have suppressed any thoughts of a formal career shift for the last twenty years. Perhaps the crazy quilt of activities outside the law office has been quite enough change.

Nor have I contemplated retirement; the firm asked me to stay when I passed my seventieth birthday, the magic moment of departure stipulated in the partnership agreement.

Does my varied career experience suggest some lessons for others? I am not sure. I have followed an erratic course, strewn with accidents and diversions. The best I can suggest are a few tentative generalities:

- For someone aspiring to international relations, and particularly public service, a foreign language helps. I have Spanish and middling French. Foreign languages continue to open doors, even as the world is increasingly English-fluent.

- Chance is pervasive—being at the right place at the right time, having a friend who has the ear of an appointing authority. One can put one's self in the way of chance. It is possible to improve the odds, by diligent pursuit of public policy matters and being known as one who does so. But precision and perfect foresight in plotting a path to senior public policy appointment is impossible. Career shifts into high office are dependent variables. The independent variables are one's reputation and ability, throwing oneself into such political and policy activities as come to hand, the good fortune of occurring to someone as a likely candidate when an opening appears, and the foibles of the electoral process.

- Withal, to land in a senior Washington position, it helps to be in Washington. A position on the Hill or at a think tank in the Capital enhances one's chances.

- I have a sense that a graduate degree also helps, and perhaps that a law degree helps most. They may not be necessary. They are certainly not sufficient. One can shift the probabilities in one's favor. What is both necessary and sufficient at the end of the day is luck.

- I think there is a greater chance of moving up to a policy position in government—whether in the legislative or the executive branch—if one starts at the entry level. The odds are not in favor of policy aspirants who spend ten years outside government and away from Washington, whether teaching or practicing law, and expect to be offered a significant policy job. Many aspire to appointments. Few receive them. The numbers of those in mid-career who think about public service vastly outnumber those who serve.

- One reason is that ten years out of school one's income is often higher than one can expect in government. Sacrifice is not to everyone's taste. In addition, the transaction costs of entering public service these days—filling out endless forms, disclosing one's intimate secrets, enduring the agony of long FBI delays, suffering through the Senate committee hearing process in the case of presidential appointments—these have a depressing effect on the mid-career people who contemplate a transition.

- Yet, improbable as it may be, and unattractive, though the nomination process is, to serve one's country is exhilarating. I would not have traded a minute of it.

Part III

Life as a Policy Wonk

9

Close to Home:
Working in State Government

Steve D. Boilard

John F. Kennedy famously remarked that "mothers all want their sons to grow up to become president, but they don't want them to become politicians in the process." It's difficult to help develop policy without becoming enmeshed in politics. But this is the objective of my current work.

I am on the staff of the California Legislative Analyst's Office (LAO), which provides nonpartisan budget and policy advice to the state legislature. It's an intellectually satisfying place to work, although the office's reputation for excruciating accuracy and pathological objectivity can be hard to live up to.

I was born thirty-nine years ago at the southern side of the San Francisco Bay area—a region known today as the Silicon Valley. Twelve years ago I married my wife, Christine, and seven years ago I became a father to young Ian Christopher.

I always enjoyed school. I collected a few college degrees somewhat haphazardly, alternately working for a living. I figure I'll go back for another degree before I'm done, but where and, more to the point, what, I haven't yet decided.

EARLY CAREER CHOICES

Like most people, I wasn't born with a desire to influence policy. Rather, I grew up with the expectation that I'd follow in my father's footsteps and become an engineer. Two years of college course work toward an engineering major cured me of this. Liberated from my delusions by a series of mediocre grade reports, I jumped to the social sciences. Not only did the social sciences better fit my interest in human activity (versus the activity of electrons and their kin), but political science in particular fed my desire to understand world events and my nascent fixation with the governance of societies. I couldn't be accused of over-researching my new choice of major: it was enough that my good friend was majoring in political science and recommended it, and I'd had an interesting class in civics in high school.

Suddenly, college was relatively easy. It's amazing what a difference one's choice of major has on one's grades. Despite my wandering for two years in what was known as the "dark side" of campus (the science buildings), I somehow managed to attain a bachelor's degree four years after taking my high school diploma.

So there I was, twenty-two years old with a B.A. in political science from an obscure campus of the University of California. Like many recent graduates, I wasn't sure what I had just been trained to do. But I did know the next step. Since I had taken my degree with a "public service" emphasis, I was expected to serve a three-month internship. I'd lined up an internship with one of the party caucuses of the California Senate—the same as my friend who'd recommended the major a couple of years earlier.

Internships, as any career counselor will tell you, are invaluable for developing hands-on experience, learning how an organization works, and making professional contacts. They are not, however, a good way to earn money. Mine, like many others, paid nothing. The trick is to try to parlay the internship into either permanent, paid work at the same organization, or to use it on your resume to land a "real" job elsewhere. In my case, at the end of three months, I was enticed away from the state internship by a paid internship (eight hundred dollars per month) in Washington, D.C., working for a U.S. congressman. This, too, was a three-month stint, and at the end I returned to Sacramento to do more unpaid work for the state Legislature—hoping that something permanent would turn up.

After a couple of months I managed to obtain a job as "campaign coordinator" for a state senate campaign. This had real potential, for if the candidate won, I would be virtually assured a job on his staff in the Capitol. However, the voters in the district did not see it this way, and voted to cut off this career option to me.

POST-GRADUATION OPTIONS

It was June 1984—I was twenty-three years old with a bachelor's degree, brief experience at the State and U.S. Capitols, and a failed campaign under my belt. I had no money and no immediate job prospects.

At the time this seemed bleak indeed. But in retrospect, my quiver was far from empty. I had a flavor—though little more than this—of the state and national legislative processes. I had seen glimpses of the political side and the policy side of government. I had walked precincts and tacked up campaign signs. I'd had some heady, politically charged experiences—for instance, meeting larger-than-life politicians such as U.S. House Speaker Tip O'Neill and California Assembly Speaker

Willie Brown. Don't infer from this any level of "expertise" or status. But these scattered and tenuous experiences provided some texture to the two-dimensional processes and institutions I had studied in textbooks.

The point is that legislatures—like other institutions—have their own cultures. To succeed, or even to simply survive, one has to understand the mores. One has to be able to comport comfortably, to adopt the attitudes. And as trite as it sounds, this is learned only through experience.

Rather than use my small experiences with legislatures and legislators as a springboard to a legislative career, however, I accepted a "graduate student assistant" position with an executive agency in the state bureaucracy. To a young college graduate, the distinction between working for the legislature and working for the governor may be of small importance. It's all the "government," isn't it? But the cultures are entirely distinct, and there are reasons that a legislative employee would never answer to the appellative "state worker." (More on this shortly.)

In any event, the press secretary I'd worked for in the legislature now was a division chief in a midsized department. She knew of my plight and offered me a job. The "catch" was I needed to be a graduate student. So I immediately enrolled in a Master's program in the local state university's government department. By day I worked in the policy development section of the state housing department, and by night I either attended classes or did homework. The schedule was more tedious than onerous. But it provided me with money, experience, and graduate training.

Soon I became a permanent employee—a bona fide civil servant. I learned the ins and outs of the classic bureaucracy. It's not pretty. Mostly the sloth of the culture impressed me. The egalitarian but anti-meritocratic rules of civil service can create a stultifying atmosphere. Initiative is discouraged and morale is low. Employees and managers are obsessed with the time clock. There is bitterness about "having" to work. But it was my first "real" job, and I was happy to be supporting myself.

In fairness, I should note that bureaucracies are designed to implement programs that, in theory and often in practice, benefit society. The department I worked for administered programs to help develop affordable housing in the state. My role was to monitor legislation that affected our programs, and to evaluate local implementation of relevant state laws and regulations. I and my coworkers had almost no influence on the development of state policy. However, we did have some (small) control over how these laws were administered.

Mostly, though, I looked forward to the night classes. They involved heady discussions of politics and government unconstrained by bureaucratic indifference or petty political spats. It was refreshing to be part of a group that shared ambition and an interest in politics. The part-time program took five years. At the end, I knew I had to get out of the bureaucracy. I desired more of the brainstorming, critiquing, and solution-seeking that characterize (the ideal of) the policy process. Eventually I set my sights on a new career that would provide adequate mental challenges:

I would become a college professor. For that, I needed a Ph.D. So it was back to graduate school.

AN ACADEMIC INTERREGNUM

The doctoral program took four years. This is quick, but unlike many of my fellow students I was married. This imposed a discipline on my activities (no endless hours at watering holes and coffee houses) and provided financial wherewithal (no need to wait tables at night). Finding a tenure-track college job is something else again. In the area of political science, and I presume most social sciences, a would-be assistant professor needs to be willing to relocate to just about anywhere in the country. This is a case where academic pedigree matters, and mine was second tier. (Foolishly, I put little thought in selecting a graduate school, and simply returned to the UC campus where I'd received my bachelor's.)

After taking my doctorate, I ended up at a Midwestern university with about fifteen thousand students. It was a nice enough campus and town. For five years I taught undergraduate classes in the government department. But I increasingly experienced disillusionment as the reality of classroom instruction clashed with my idealized vision of academe. Most students are not motivated by a love of learning, many are poorly equipped for college study, and few are willing to take an active role in their learning. I'm sure my expectations were unrealistic, and that many of the traits for which I damned the students were traits I'd exhibited as an undergraduate. But this disillusionment about academia conspired with other factors—such as an inability to shed my sense of being an outsider in that part of the country—to direct my career focus elsewhere. The idea of influencing policy (rather than teaching about it) seemed attractive. Weighing the options, I resolved to return to the west and take a policy-related position *not* within the civil service. (My earlier experience in state government still left a bitter taste.)

This meant either an "exempt" (i.e., exempt from civil service) position under the governor or a staff position with the legislature. Once again contacts I'd made at the state housing department came in useful. A former coworker (and still good friend) pointed me to the office of the legislature's nonpartisan fiscal and policy analyst. It was an ideal setup. Like most offices connected with the legislature, the LAO is not part of the civil service and, thus, more meritocratic. Unlike most legislative offices, the LAO serves the entire legislature (Republicans and Democrats alike), and thus is largely free of political and ideological constraints. Moreover, it affords an opportunity to have a direct influence on policy.

ADVISING THE LEGISLATURE

The California Legislature created the LAO in 1941 in an effort to arm itself with independent fiscal expertise to scrutinize the governor's annual budget proposal.

Up to this point, legislators felt poorly equipped to evaluate the governor's revenue projections, workload estimates, and other fiscal assumptions. As a result, they found it difficult to ensure that their policy priorities were reflected in the budget that was ultimately adopted. Over the past six decades the LAO has expanded its scope beyond the budget and today advises the legislature on a broad range of fiscal and policy matters, analyzes selected legislation, suggests changes to state programs and laws, and prepares an objective analysis of ballot measures for the state's voters.

A joint budget committee, comprising members of both the Senate and assembly and both Republicans and Democrats, appoints the legislative analyst. Beyond that, the committee largely allows the legislative analyst structure the office, select staff, pursue issues, and develop recommendations independently.

LAO's nonpartisan, independent nature makes it somewhat rare among government entities. After all, virtually all federal and state departments are ultimately headed by a chief executive (president or governor), who is typically elected on a partisan ballot. While constitutions, civil service laws, and various equal protection statutes limit the politicization of these departments, they are strongly influenced by the political and ideological biases of the chief executive.

Legislatures, obviously, are even more directly and unabashedly governed by partisanship. The professional identity of virtually all legislative staff is in some measure defined by party, and most committees march to the tune of the party leaders. Nevertheless, many state legislatures now have an independent fiscal office similar to LAO. At the federal level, the congressional budget office plays a similar role.

Working as an analyst at LAO is something of a cross between academics and espionage. The academic thread of the job is partly evident in the requirement that all analysts hold advanced degrees. In our academic mode, analysts research issues which have relevance for state policy makers. As researchers we use an expertise developed through constant study and programmatic monitoring. We read trade journals and attend conferences in our assigned subject areas. We go "into the field" and observe the operation of state programs—anything from parks to prisons. In this way, we're able to build practical and theoretical knowledge of state governmental operations.

While we're not exactly spies, we do serve as the legislature's "eyes and ears" in monitoring how the various state departments implement programs, which, after all, are created by the legislature. We measure programmatic performance (driver licensing, water quality improvements over time, etc.) and programmatic efficiency (number of hospital beds provided per million dollars, length of time and amount of money required to build a mile of highway). We look for questionable expenditures buried in departmental budgets, and attempt to expose wasteful purchases (such as overpriced computers or unnecessarily large fleets of vehicles).

While our budget work has policy implications, we also make policy recommendations more directly. LAO places important issues on the legislature's agenda by issuing reports on policy-related matters. These reports, which are typically picked up by the press, outline issues that we believe deserve the legislature's attention. The reports typically frame questions for legislative consideration, and offer one or more recommended solutions. For example, we recently released a report on the usage of car pool lanes, and suggested some ways the legislature could make these more efficient.

As an advisory body, the LAO has no regulatory or legislative powers. We simply provide the legislature with well-researched information and nonpartisan advice. It is up to the legislature to consider this information in its political context, including such matters as constituents' interests, party ideology, and strategic voting considerations. Frequently these contextual concerns win out, and our recommendations are not adopted. But this does not cause undue grief in our office, for at least two reasons.

First, some of our greatest influence on policy comes in the longer term. While the legislature may not act immediately or in the way we recommend, our influence may be seen in the framing of the issue. Groups outside the legislature, such as the press and interest groups, as well as legislators who voted in the minority, may continue to pursue the issue. In addition, as a Sacramento-based columnist wrote recently, while LAO may not be able to stop bad ideas from becoming law, it does remove the legislature's ability to plead ignorance when predictably bad policies go awry.

The second reason we can be philosophical about our advisory role is that policy making (versus policy analysis and recommendation) can be a messy, contentious process. The charms of this work—brokering deals, massaging egos, dancing with lobbyists—are not for everyone. For the most part, the legislative analyst's staff are happy leaving these tasks to the elected representatives, and content themselves with their advisory role. It's a comfortable balance of influencing policy without having to make it.

LIFESTYLE CONSEQUENCES

Few get into the policy business with the intention of getting rich. An entry-level professional in state government can expect a salary in the thirty-thousand dollar range. Without taking on management duties, this would top out in the seventies or so. Benefits for civil service employees and legislative staff compare favorably with many private sector jobs—decent health, dental, and medical insurance, a day or two vacation each month, sick leave, deferred compensation plans, and so forth. Paid holidays for state employees tend to be more plentiful than those available in the private sector. In addition to the usual holidays such as Christmas and Thanksgiving, California's government acknowledges a number of commemorative days, such as Columbus Day and Martin Luther King, Jr. Day. This brings the number of paid holidays to about fourteen.

The legislative process tends to be seasonal, and so does our work. Our office puts considerable effort each year into our seven-hundred page review of the governor's budget proposal. The proposal is released January 10, and our analysis of it comes out in mid-February. For that six-week period, we work many evenings and weekends. Analysts typically put in about 100 to 150 hours of overtime during this period. These hours are available as "compensatory time off," or CTO, later in the year.

In the springtime we work with the legislature's budget committees to amend and pass the state budget. Our role is essentially to make our recommendations in budget hearings. This is when we have most of our direct contact with legislators, which is valuable not just for influencing policy, but also serves to keep us in the Capitol loop and exposed to the particular interests and concerns of our "bosses." Once the two houses pass their versions of the budget, we play the role of honest broker in conference committee, recommending compromises so that a single budget bill can be passed and placed on the governor's desk.

Once the budget is passed by the legislature and signed by the governor (by June 30, according to the state Constitution), the work of an LAO analyst shifts back to a more leisurely, academic mode. Much of the CTO earned in the winter is used at this time. When CTO is coupled with vacation time and state holidays, analysts can spend a lot of time away from the office during the summer.

Much of the fall is spent doing general background research on the departments and programs we are assigned. This can involve site visits, departmental briefings, conferences, or simply catching up on reading. Again, the pace is quite relaxed, and the mood in the office is congenial and collegial. It's a restorative time that helps prepare the office for taking on the next budget in January.

On the whole, the lifestyle consequences of this type of career can be described as "balanced." The remuneration is not high, but it is enough to support a reasonable middle-class lifestyle. The work is not stressful—except perhaps for six weeks in the winter. Analysts perform a variety of roles in the legislative process throughout the seasons of the year, though overall a somewhat academic culture is maintained. Professional satisfaction is derived from knowing that one's work is recognized as authoritative, even if it isn't always acted on.

CONCLUSIONS

Among the many careers available to students of political science, state government affords both advantages and shortcomings. Weighing the good and bad depends on one's own biases, of course. In general, state government is best for those whose interests focus a bit closer to home than the national or international level, while desiring to avoid the more parochial and pedestrian concerns of local governance. State politics can be petty and provincial, to be sure, but also can encompass profound and weighty issues. Working at the state level affords a balance between being a small cog in an enormous federal process, and a large player in a picayune local process.

The person considering such a career would be wise to study the state's history, demographics, and culture, as well as the formal legislative, electoral, and budgeting processes. Time spent—even as an intern—in both the legislative and executive branches would provide a more complete view of the different governmental cultures, and this would provide a valuable professional edge, whichever the branch one chose to make his or her professional home. Finally, one should consider carefully the level of politics one is comfortable with. There are those who thrive on it, and there are those who prefer to be insulated from it. LAO is something of an anomaly in this regard, for in general one will encounter a tradeoff: more involvement in policy requires more involvement in politics, and avoiding politics reduces one's influence on policy. As JFK noted, our mothers will have to accept this.

10

The World of the Washington Think Tanks

Howard J. Wiarda

The Washington think tanks are among the most influential actors in the nation's Capital. Usually when we study political science, we concentrate on interest groups, political parties, and government institutions; but now we recognize the need to study public opinion, PACs (Political Action Committees), and the media as well. To this list of key policy-influencing institutions we must add the think tanks.

As the name implies, think tanks do a lot of the government's thinking for it. It may seem inconceivable that, with a work force of about four-and-a-half million persons (including the military), the federal government cannot think for itself. Obviously one should not overstate the case, but the fact is that most federal agencies are so overwhelmed by day-to-day decisions, routine procedures, and paperwork that they seldom have the opportunity to engage in background research, long-range planning, or the careful weighing of policy options. That is where the think tanks enter in: they engage in research, try to think and plan for the long term, and recommend policy options. As Norman Ornstein suggests elsewhere in this volume, think tanks also serve as transmission belts for ideas and research between the world of the universities and that of Washington policy making, between the media and the government, between the political parties, and between interest groups and public officials. They are also very interesting places to work.

EARLY DECISIONS

When I decided to concentrate on political science, I knew that I wanted not only to study politics but to influence the policy process. Early in my undergraduate career at the University of Michigan, I had majored in engineering but soon discovered I had little talent or interest in advanced calculus even while I did well in history and English. After switching out of engineering I still stumbled from major to major (English, philosophy, journalism) until finally settling on history and political science, meanwhile writing for *The Michigan Daily* and throwing myself into the intellectual and political life at the university.

Graduation loomed; I had several interviews for bank and private sector management training programs, but I still had no idea what I wanted to *be* or *do* in life. So I went to see my favorite teacher, told him I was very interested in Latin America (the Cuban Revolution was a red-hot issue then), and asked about graduate schools. He told me the University of Florida had the best Latin America program in the country; that was, perhaps naively, the only school to which I applied and that's where I went—a decision that I have never regretted. I received superb training at Florida in political science, Latin American studies, and international relations; did well in the program there (lots of writing, no more calculus!); matured, and really found myself personally and career-wise.

When I finished my master's degree, like many students, I was tired of school, as I'd been in it for seventeen straight years. So I flirted with taking a policy job. I took the State Department and CIA entrance exams, never heard again from the former, but passed the latter, and was invited to Washington for an interview. It was a "spooky" experience, literally: I was told to meet someone in a raincoat on a street corner; we took an unmarked bus to the Langley headquarters; I had to be accompanied at all times even to the bathroom; there were no pictures on the walls for fear of "bugs"; and the psychological examiner asked me (1) if I thought of the agency as a draft-dodging opportunity, and (2) if I loved my mother more than my father—or the other way around! I decided the CIA was not for me, went back to grad school with a three-year National Defense Education Act (NDEA) Fulbright-Hays Fellowship, and earned a Ph.D.

I took a job teaching Latin American and comparative politics at the University of Massachusetts, Amherst. Fortunately I liked to write and do research, and published a lot. Tenure and promotion came early and I was a full prof. at the age of thirty-seven. I became active politically in the election campaigns of 1976 (Jerry Ford was from my hometown in Michigan) and 1980 (again voting for a loser, Jimmy Carter), did two years of post-doc work at Harvard and MIT, and retooled as a specialist in international relations and foreign policy. During this period my writing focused more on foreign policy issues (human rights and transitions to democracy) and I consulted frequently with the Department of State and other Washington agencies, in the process becoming better known at the policy level. I'm sure it was partly on the basis of using Harvard stationery that I was invited to go to Washington on a permanent basis.

It's a funny story. After the 1980 election, Jeane Kirkpatrick, just named as ambassador to the UN, called to invite me to join her staff in New York with the rank of ambassador. I didn't know Jeane well or agree with all her policies, but the position sounded attractive. A couple of weeks later, after we'd already gotten all excited about moving to New York, Jeane called again: she had offered more ambassadorships than she had available, was terribly sorry, but would I be interested instead in a foreign policy position at the American Enterprise Institute for Public Policy Research (AEI), one of Washington's leading think tanks? The AEI position thus came to me as a consolation prize.

I was forty-years old when I went to Washington more or less permanently, and I have often debated with myself, since I'm interested in policy, about whether I had waited too long to make the move. There are arguments on both sides. On the one hand, if I'd gone to Washington earlier, I might have had an interesting foreign policy (or CIA) career, worked my way up the bureaucracy, and perhaps eventually gotten to an interesting policy position. On the other, by spending fifteen years in academia, I had established a scholarly reputation, had published widely, and was already known for some of my policy research and positions. I have many times been introduced to someone in Washington who responded, "Oh, Prof. Wiarda, I'm so happy to meet you and I've read your stuff back in college." Such responses are not only nice for the ego but they give you immediate access in the agency involved; they also mean that when I write something and mail it off to policy influentials, it is now actually read and taken seriously, rather than simply being weighed on some dean's tenure–promotion scale. So on the question of going into policy making directly out of college or grad school, or waiting until you have your own independent reputation as an academic or in some other pursuit, there are good arguments on both sides. But if you decide on the academic option, you should still start early in writing policy-oriented papers and becoming acquainted with both political and career policy-making leaders.

INTO THE THINK TANK WORLD

During my early years in Washington, five major think tanks vied for political influence. Moving from left to right, on the radical side was the Institute for Policy Studies (IPS), an extremely liberal, often Marxist, anti-establishment think tank that emerged out of the student revolts of the 1960s and 1970s and that was generally opposed to all U.S. foreign and defense policy. Slightly left of center was the Brookings Institution, close to the Democratic Party and best known for its liberal economic analyses. The broad middle is occupied by the Center for Strategic and International Studies (CSIS), the only think tank to focus exclusively on foreign and defense policy studies and whose ranks included former National Security Advisors

Henry Kissinger (moderate Republican) and Zbigniew Brzezinski (moderate Democrat). The American Enterprise Institute for Public Policy Research (AEI) was the counterpart of Brookings: slightly right of center, emphasizing market economics versus the Keynesian-managed economy orientation of Brookings, and split between the moderate Ford–Bush wing of the Republican Party and the neoconservative, or Reagan, wing. The far right was occupied by the Heritage Foundation, whose research product was often sloppy, but was enormously successful both at fundraising and exercising policy influence.

The world of the think tanks also includes some influential organizations outside of Washington: the RAND Corporation and Hoover Institution in California, the Mershon Center at Ohio State University, and the Foreign Policy Research Institute (FPRI) in Philadelphia. Meanwhile in Washington itself some other think tanks have increased their staffs and therefore their influence over the years: the Carnegie Endowment (liberal), the Council on Foreign Relations (establishment), the Cato Institute (libertarian), Trans-Africa (Afro-American issues), and the Urban Institute (governance). At the same time, the success of the big think tanks has spawned a host of smaller imitators: more specialized groups that usually focus on one or two issues and that have small staffs and budgets but often lots of (unpaid) interns.

AEI was a real eye-opener for me, a superb introduction to the Washington social whirl and the world of policy making as viewed from a think tank perspective. It may have been the high point of my career. I wrote more and learned more about Washington policy making than at any comparable time in my life. In those days, in the early years of the Reagan Revolution, it was often assumed that AEI, along with its ideas and personnel, was running the U.S. government. Naturally, since it enhanced our own reputations, we did nothing to disabuse people of that notion. And sometimes it was actually true! With my experience at AEI, all my earlier policy writing, done from an academic perspective, seems romantic and naive.

My first few years at AEI, 1981–86, were idyllic; but not all think tank experiences—or even AEI after the glory years of the early 1980s—are so glamorous. To begin with, the pay was considerably higher than in my university position, and it could be supplemented handsomely by private writing and speaking engagements. Second, at AEI the senior scholars all had their own personal secretaries and research assistants; in addition, the support staff (for meetings, conferences, television appearances, an so forth) was superb. Third, virtually unlimited financial support was available for travel and research—welcome after the sparse resources of my university. Fourth, AEI had its own editorial staff and publishing outlets, which all but guaranteed that anything the scholars wrote got published (my dean once complained, "Wiarda, every time you *sneeze*, it gets published"). Fifth, AEI had a marvelous, gourmet, and very elegant dining room where we could entertain our friends royally as long as it was for "business purposes," which in Washington, D.C., covers a broad territory. So we had all the major foreign policy players over regularly for lunch, dinner, even breakfast: Secretary of State Al Haig, CIA Director Bill

Casey, Lt. Col. Oliver North, senators, congressmen, journalists, staff aides. As one of my new colleagues remarked, "AEI is like a university except that it has no students, no grading, no committee meetings, no administrators, and wonderful perks; what could be better than that?"

Other issues were a little more complicated. When I asked about tenure, AEI trotted out Gottfried Haberler, a famous old economist who attended the Paris peace talks in 1918, as proof that you could stay there until age 110 and not have to worry about tenure. But later, when AEI got into financial and managerial trouble, I was very happy that I had only gone on leave rather than resigning my tenured position at UMass. When I asked about academic freedom, AEI assured me that it genuinely believed in the competition of ideas and that no one would ever tell me what research agenda to pursue, let alone what conclusions to reach—this proved to be surprisingly true, even though as a moderate and centrist I sometimes felt uncomfortable among the conservative "true believers" at AEI. My fears about academic freedom were also assuaged by the quality of the research scholars and associated fellows at AEI who may have then constituted the best political science "department" in the country and who could not be stuffed into any simple ideological straightjacket: Austin Ranney, Warren Miller, Evron Kirkpatrick, Samuel P. Huntington, Michael Novak, Ben Wattenberg, James Q. Wilson, Richard Neustadt, Howard Penniman, Giovanni Sartori, Nelson Polsby, Richard Fenno, Anthony King, Richard Rose, Thomas Mann, Norman Ornstein, Michael Malbin, Robert Pranger, Harold Saunders, Robert Goldwin, Walter Berns, Jeane Kirkpatrick, and Judith Kipper. I was pleased and excited to join this distinguished group.

WHAT THINK TANKS DO

The main reason to opt for a think tank career is, of course, to have the opportunity to influence policy rather than (as in a university) just study it. The bigger think tanks are well known in Washington and to policy makers, so the statements, writings, and television appearances of their major scholars are often paid close attention. When you're at one of the major Washington think tanks, you're assumed by policy makers (rightly or wrongly) to be at the top of your field; or else just by being associated with one of the major think tanks, what you say or write has importance because it's assumed the position you take is representative of a larger constituency. In other words, in Washington you're important, not so much as an individual (unless you're a celebrity like Kissinger) but because of your specific think tank association; this also means that, when you leave your think tank position, your influence also drops off considerably.

Think tanks operate in different kinds of ways. AEI and Brookings are best-known for their long, serious studies that often influence legislation. But CSIS, while not eschewing scholarship, is more action oriented, putting together high-level commissions or congressional study groups to directly impact the policy process. IPS is mainly a naysayer and is so outside the centrist mainstream as to have little effect on policy. The Heritage Foundation was famous for providing instant (overnight) analyses for congressmen and policy makers; but as the country became more conservative and business oriented, its budget grew exponentially and its research product improved as well.

At AEI we used a variety of means to try to influence the policy process. First, AEI (like Brookings) had an unusually large number of serious academic scholars and we sought to influence policy through our research and writing. The difference from academic life was, however, that at AEI, our writings were actually read and had influence—augmented by AEI's skillful press and public relations office who taught us how to get our writings into the policy process, to the right people, at the right time. Second, there was television: again the AEI public relations and press people were clever at getting us on, as guests or "talking heads," the major TV news and discussion programs; AEI was also unique in producing its own TV programs and having its conferences covered by CNN or C-SPAN. Third, we were often invited as expert witnesses to testify before Congress— although I became so disgusted by the intensely partisan and even "circus-like" atmosphere of some of these hearings, for example, on Central America, that for a time I refused to testify.

There are many other avenues of influence that over time I, now beginning to operate as a Washington "insider," learned to maneuver in and manipulate. First is the "revolving door" syndrome between government and the think tanks: in the early 1980s about thirty people each from AEI and the Heritage Foundation, plus about fifteen from CSIS, went into the Reagan Administration at high levels. I went into the State Department for a time and did work for the CIA, Department of Defense, and U.S. Information Agency, thus becoming something of an "in'n'outer" like Joseph Nye in this volume; but I now regret not having spent longer time in government service, not only because of the contribution I thought I could make but also because it would have given my writing a more practical bent. Second, after working in the Washington think tank world for a couple of years, I got to know an awful lot of people in Congress, the media, labor, business, lobbying, and the executive branch; these contacts were invaluable when I needed information for my research or wished to channel advice or position papers to the right people in "the system." Third, in part because of my writings, but mainly because of my position at AEI, which was thought to be a powerful influence on administration policy, I was often sought out by lobbyists, congressmen and their staffs, U.S. ambassadors headed for Europe or Latin America, Latin American presidential candidates, members of the National Security Council (NSC), and so forth, who wanted to get my views—and, no doubt, thought that because of AEI's prominence, I would call the White House right after our meeting and convey my blessing on their political ambitions or policy preferences. It was a heady experience for a former academic to be consulted and exercise influence at such high levels—and I confess to succumbing, for a time, to a familiar Washington malady: a sense of exaggerated self-importance.

For the Washington think tanks at senior levels, there's no such thing as a boring day. Often, in Washington, it's said that if 80 percent of your work is routine and boring and 20 percent creative and interesting, that makes it all worthwhile. At the major think tanks the proportions are often the reverse: 80 percent interesting and only 20 percent routine. No other job or occupation that one can think of can match those numbers.

I'm an early bird and a self-starter, enthused about my work, so I was usually at my office by six. Those early morning hours before the secretaries and staff got in were quiet and peaceful, and I did most of my policy writing—for me, not a chore but something I love to do—during that time. From about ten o'clock until noon I usually worked on AEI programs, arranging conferences, going over guest lists, making phone calls, and setting up seminars. These administrative tasks are relatively easy when you've got your own staff, as well as the AEI's to do the legwork. Lunchtime was from noon until two o'clock, either at the AEI dining room or by invitation at one of the other think tanks, at Congress, the executive branch, or private restaurants—always with interesting companions.

During the mid-afternoon I'd be back at AEI, reading, doing research in the institute's fine private library, or writing policy memos. But by four o'clock it was usually time for a seminar hosted by us or another institution, or a presentation (usually for a fee) to some private group. By six o'clock Washington's social swirl kicks in and I'd often have two or three receptions to go to followed by dinner at the Carnegie Institution, the Council on Foreign Relations, or one of the foreign embassies. What a life!—although I must confess all the fancy food and drinks were hard on the waistline, liver, and blood pressure. During that first year in Washington, my family had stayed in Amherst so our daughter could finish high school with her class; so all this intense socializing had a double purpose: I quickly learned the Washington players and all the ins and outs, *and I* didn't have to cook! The next year when my family joined me, I cut down on the social life and consumption somewhat, even while staying very active in policy.

It was fun and stimulating being "in" on policy making during this period. The Falkland Islands war between Britain and Argentina, the Central American conflicts (Nicaragua, Guatemala, El Salvador), Mexico, the Third World debt crisis, human rights, transitions to democracy in Latin America and elsewhere were all hot issues. I must have been at the White House and State Department at least once a week during this period and at the Defense Department, Congress, and CIA once a month. In 1983, I was asked to serve as the chief staff person on the National (Kissinger) Commission on Central America; in 1985, President Reagan invited me to become a member of another presidential commission on social and economic modernization in the Third World. As a centrist, my purpose in these activities, as well as my writings, was to return policy to the middle and to carve out a careful, multifaceted policy that would be acceptable to the feuding political factions and offer hope of long-term change. We worked on elections in Central America, human rights and democracy issues, and the peace process in El Salvador and Nicaragua. It was exciting to move in high policy circles and to actually exercise influence.

But then in the late 1980s, AEI went into a financial and administrative crisis from which it is only now beginning to recover. The crisis had to do with weak management at the institute, changed tax laws that made it less attractive for big donors to fund AEI, personnel and political changes at the big foundations that had supported AEI in the past, changing political priorities and personnel as we transitioned from Reagan to Bush, and a sense among donors that, since "our guys" (Republicans) were in power anyway, there was no need to fund AEI. In terms of career choices, however, the crisis at AEI also taught me some valuable lessons: (1) how fickle Washington policy making is (and the think tanks that focus on policy), gravitating from one crisis or issue to the next with little sense of continuity or long-range policy thinking; (2) how nice it was, when the going got rough, to have a solid academic reputation and a tenured professorship to fall back on; (3) how quickly you can be forgotten once your think tank hits the skids or another party comes into office. If you take any of these negatives personally, you can easily get depressed in Washington when the inevitable denouement comes; but if you recognize to begin with that it's not you that counts so much but your institutional position (AEI), then when the phone stops ringing so often you don't feel so badly. As they say, if you want a true friend in Washington, get a pet rock!

When AEI imploded in the late 1980s, a large number of my colleagues there found themselves not only out of a job but also almost literally out in the streets; they had nowhere else to go and quite a number still have not landed on their feet. I was fortunate to land a visiting professorship at George Washington University, a major research grant from the Twentieth Century Fund to write a book about democratization in Latin America, and another think tank position at the Foreign Policy Research Institute (FPRI). These positions were interspersed with stints back at UMass, so I could hold onto my permanent position there. Then, in the early 1990s, even though I had no prior military experience, I held a professorship at the National War College ("The Harvard of the military schools," according to Colin Powell) for five years, where I learned a lot about how the "military mind" and the Defense Department work. I also negotiated a senior research position at the Center for Strategic and International Studies (CSIS), the centrist think tank. Having both a War College and a think tank position in Washington was an attractive combination, but UMass made a very attractive counter offer and also offered me an endowed chair that included research and travel funds, secretarial assistance, a research assistant, and a large salary increase. Plus my family loves Amherst. So I accepted and now I have the best of all possible worlds. I have a full professorship, an endowed chair, and wonderful students in the marvelously congenial

Department of Political Science at the University of Massachusetts; I teach there three days a week and cram all my courses into those days. The other two days I spend in Washington at CSIS, a combination which enables me to enjoy the benefits of teaching, research, and writing in Amherst and at the same time to stay plugged into the Washington policy and think tank world.

I've had a particularly exciting and challenging academic policy career over a thirty-year period but not everyone can be as lucky as I've been. Such a dual career track is not for everyone and many of us who go this route have mixed feelings about it. It's perhaps instructive that my academic colleagues are sometimes green with envy over the policy influence and opportunities I've had, while my Washington colleagues can't conceive why anyone would give up a tenured, bucolic career in academia for the sake of all the nastiness, back stabbing, and mindless bureaucracy that are part of influencing policy in Washington. For while a career in Washington is exciting, attractive, and seductive, and offers the opportunity for power, influence, and wealth (as Washington says, "You can do well while doing good"), it can also be terribly disruptive or even destructive to family life, personality, and character. When Clinton aide Vince Foster wrote in his suicide note, "Here [in Washington] they make a sport of destroying reputations," many of us knew exactly what he meant.

It is not my intention to end on a sour note; quite the contrary. For me, going to Washington was the high point of my career; I would not trade that experience for anything. I wrote more, published more, learned more, and had more impact on policy—my main career goals—than at any other time in my life. On the other hand, I can also appreciate why one would want, or even need, to leave Washington from time to time, or maybe permanently. In that case, it sure is nice to have other options, an alternative career, to fall back on.

11

Influencing Policy on an International Level: Life and Work in a United Nations Agency

Elizabeth D. Gibbons

INTRODUCTION

Since I received my undergraduate degree twenty-five years ago, I have been work-ing in the field of international economic and social development. In some small way, I was prepared for this career by a cold war childhood of mixed cultural influ-ences—my American father met my European mother when he was deployed in France as part of the first NATO troops, and they brought their children up out-side Boston, Zurich, and London. I was also influenced by the puritan tradition of New England by which those of us privileged enough to have an education are obliged to contribute to the betterment of society. Changing countries at an early age, I was exposed to new languages and surprising values, as well as poverty and discrimination in a way that would not have been possible had I remained in the Boston suburbs.

I was fortunate that my parents ensured that I got the best possible education. I went first to Hampshire College, then Smith College, where I graduated from in 1976. I began my career in New York City, working for Lutheran World Relief (LWR), a faith-based non-governmental organization (NGO) funding projects throughout what was then known as the "Third World." In 1983, I obtained my master's degree from Columbia University, then was hired by the United Nations

Children's Fund (UNICEF), where I remain employed. During my career, I have lived in six countries, visited well over fifty, and held twelve different positions. It is only now that I realize that the career shaped by these immensely varied experiences falls into three distinct passages, each of which, to my surprise, was launched from an academic institution. My first passage began when I was completing my undergraduate degree, and ended following my first experience living and working in a developing country (Togo 1979–1981). My second passage began in graduate school and came to an end with my first experience leading a UNICEF office and program (Haiti 1992–1996). I have now entered my third passage, which began in 1997 when I took a sabbatical to write about the impact of sanctions in Haiti; at this point, I do not know when or how the third passage will end. As will be evident from the paragraphs that follow, rather than by a well thought out plan, the passages of my serendipitous career have been governed by chance, circumstance, and my own reaction to opportunities presented to me.

THE FIRST PASSAGE: CAREER CHOICES AT AGES 19–21

By the time I was twenty, I was clear that I wanted to work in international economic and social development. I do not remember ever debating about any other choice of career. While still an undergraduate, I knew that I did not want to go straight to graduate school; the reasons seemed obvious: without the experience of a few years of working, how would I know what extra knowledge and competencies I needed?

Despite being clear on my direction, I was very haphazard in my academic preparation, majoring in European history, dabbling in political science and only taking one course in Latin American Studies with a semester of Spanish. My rationale was that analysis of history, particularly the history of political transitions, allowed one to understand the present sociopolitical dynamics.

I had decided that I wanted to work for a non-governmental international development organization, since, as a member of the Vietnam War generation, I abhorred anything related to the U.S. government. This automatically precluded me from joining the Peace Corps, which would have been, and still is, the most obvious route to obtaining experience in international development. Doggedly, I sent letters and cajoled interviews with all of the NGOs and foundations who were doing development work overseas. Everywhere, I was told the same thing: come back when you have experience abroad. Meanwhile, I supported myself working fourteen-hour shifts at an outdoor restaurant in midtown Manhattan, carrying trays of food from the cellar up two flights of stairs to the baking pavement. After a particularly hectic day, my boss said, "Liz, d'you think it's easy? It ain't easy." I have gone back to those words many, many times in the years since.

I was lucky though, at Lutheran World Relief where the man who interviewed me was an elderly pastor, close to retirement and willing to take a chance on me.

Thus, initially as a volunteer, I began the first job of my career. Since the person for whom I was working was in charge of programs in Africa, the direction I had planned, with studies in Spanish and Latin American affairs, was suddenly changed; this happenstance, and the fact that I spoke French, sent me to the Afro-Francophone world for the next twenty years. My job as program assistant for LWR in New York was a perfect first job; I learned a lot about many things, but especially about professional behavior. The disadvantage was that without any experiential frame of reference in Africa, my project analysis did not have the depth I knew I really needed. After a couple years, I revived my objective of working overseas, and started applying to other international organizations, when I was appointed to an LWR post that had opened up in Togo, West Africa.

THE FIRST PASSAGE: CAREER CHOICES AT AGES 24–28

I arrived in Lomé, Togo in January 1979. I was twenty-five and enthused about the adventure that awaited me; from the moment of my arrival, on the trip from the airport to my room in the compound of a Togolese family, my senses were swamped with incredibly powerful impressions—the hot moist air, the flickering oil lamps of the market women's stalls lining the road, the welcome meal that awaited me, so spiced with red pepper that it made me blow my nose, and the chickens squawking in the yard.

My work was divided between the capital, Lomé, where I spent one week every month helping SOTOPRODER, the Togolese NGO managing the project I'd been assigned to, in administration and fund-raising, and three weeks in the northern provincial town of Kanté where, it was said, government officials who had fallen out of favor were sent as punishment. My job there was to manage what was then known as an "integrated rural development project," which meant that it aspired to respond to the basic needs of the population it served. The project's main component was the introduction of oxen plowing to farmers who, until then, had only used a short-handled hoe to produce their subsistence crops. The project also helped farmers organize themselves into cooperatives and grow a new, higher-yielding variety of crops. Key to these advances was the year-round availability of water, addressed by digging a rainwater catchment dam in each participating village, and by planting gardens on the dam's downstream side.

One may well ask what technical capacity did I conceivably have to manage such a project, and the answer is, of course, I had none. However, the Togolese in the project and local government services had ample technical capacity. What they did not have was planning and management capacity, and this was what I brought to the project, in the most elementary fashion.

Since I had never managed other people before, in addition to the cultural adaptation, I had to learn how to build a team, and a team that consisted only of men, men coming from a culture where women occupy a distinctly secondary position, in a society where polygamy was common. To my surprise, this did not seem to seriously affect my authority, less because of my personality than my essential exoticness, by which I was viewed less as a woman and more as someone from outerspace. In most countries where I subsequently served, this remained true: the role I played was so far outside the realm of the possible for women from the country, that I was rarely seen as a woman. Instead, I was just a foreigner, in some ways a more difficult role to play since one is often seen less as a person, and more as a resource.

Never again would I have the opportunity to work at the community level; those two years in northern Togo served as my future basis for understanding the hidden dynamics of solidarity, social conflict, and social change in traditional societies. Among the many things I observed was what little control rural people in poor countries actually have over their lives. Not only were they victims of the weather, but of governmental policies that distorted the profit they could obtain from their back-breaking work, and left them without basic social services. Working for a non-governmental organization, I realized I would never be able to affect governmental policy; only governmental bodies with substantial resources could do that and so ensure that the small changes in quality of life that development projects introduced were sustainable. It was largely for this reason that I decided to go to graduate school in economics and planning, as these were the skills multilateral institutions, such as the World Bank and the United Nations, most needed for influencing government policy. I was accepted to Columbia University's School of International and Public Affairs. My work experience was considered to add such a lot to the student body that I was awarded a full-tuition scholarship, which further vindicated my decision to delay going to graduate school.

THE SECOND PASSAGE: EARLY CAREER

I had a stimulating, but uneventful two years in graduate school, and greatly enjoyed being back in New York. As I was keen to work for an organization with both the mandate and the resources for influencing policy on a national or even international scale, I had set my heart on the World Bank's Young Professional Program. However, to my dismay, I was not accepted to this competitive program (I did not yet know that I would work at the World Bank years later, and find it was really not my type of place at all). Crestfallen, I pursued other options in a desultory fashion. I had ruled out applying to the United Nations or any of its agencies on the mistaken assumption that my U.S. nationality was an insurmountable handicap. Graduation was a few days away when I got a call from a friend who had been in charge of the UNICEF program in Togo; then posted in Madagascar she told me that she'd given my name to her boss in Nairobi who was urgently looking for an assistant. The interview was set up for the day after graduation, and the lingering gaiety of the night before made me feel quite cavalier about the appointment, which I considered more as an obligation to my friend than the opportunity to set my career on a whole new direction. Perhaps because of this casual attitude, the interview was a big success. Within three months I was off to Nairobi, a staff member of the United Nations Children's Fund, UNICEF.[1]

My first job with UNICEF was as Assistant Program Officer in the Francophone Section of the East Africa Regional Office in Nairobi, Kenya; I was responsible for providing administrative back-up to the UNICEF offices in Burundi, Rwanda, Madagascar, Comoros, and Djibouti as well as for helping my colleagues conduct needs assessments, negotiate and plan programs with the partner governments, and prepare project proposals and budgets. It was very different work than I'd had in Togo, most obviously since I was totally cut off from community-level contacts, but also because instead of contributing directly to development change, I contributed indirectly through my colleagues managing the other offices. Nonetheless, I did learn about how national policies are planned and contributed, in a limited way, to children's health, education, and community programs managed by the governments in the francophone countries.

I enjoyed my first job at UNICEF, but I especially enjoyed living in Nairobi, a large, cosmopolitan city with many diversions, and in Kenya, whose safari parks and pristine beaches enticed many friends to visit. I had developed a wide range of contacts and a strong attachment to my life there. So when an organizational restructuring resulted in my job in the francophone section being abolished, I was not at all prepared to move to a new country and leave behind all that I had come to love about Nairobi. However, I had no alternative, it was either resign from UNICEF, or accept a posting in Zimbabwe. This was the first occasion when I was forced to confront the tremendous personal costs of the international career I had chosen; the move out of Kenya would destroy a social support network upon which I depended. Torn about what to do, I finally decided to go to Zimbabwe, but only for one year, after which I would resign from UNICEF and give priority to my personal life. In Zimbabwe, I had a perfectly agreeable time and a very interesting job as Program Officer for Education. But I was still determined to leave UNICEF; at the end of the year, I returned to New York once again.

By leaving UNICEF and a promising career at the age of thirty-four to give priority to a more rooted, less vulnerable personal life, I made my first attempt to live without the incredible stimulation and professional satisfaction of international development work. I was delighted be back in New York especially since I earned my living from consultancies and was free from the fear of suddenly having to uproot myself and head off to another country. I enjoyed the consultancies, which allowed me to avoid management responsibilities, concentrate on one assignment instead of being atomized into many, and occasionally produce creative and original work some of which, years later, became organizational policy. At first I was happy with all the travel involved in an international consultant's life, as I was still curious about new countries, provided I could return to my New York base. But after a while I became disenchanted, as the travel was very disruptive to constructing a satisfying personal life. In addition, as a consultant, it was impossible to judge the value of my work; once the final report was handed over, I could not follow-up to see how my recommendations were applied and with what result. Eventually, this lack of professional satisfaction led me to accept a staff position at UNICEF's New York headquarters.

By 1990, I had been working in international economic development for fifteen years, years during which I enjoyed the satisfaction of seeing my energy and creativity have a positive impact, at least some of the time, on the lives of hundreds of people in Togo, and thousands in East Africa. The project in Kanté proved to be sustainable and would still be going strong almost twenty years after my departure; my work with SOTOPRODER had allowed this local NGO to grow and manage a project portfolio ten times what it had the year I arrived. I had learned that the longer one is in a country, the less one understands, and that it is only by getting to this point that humility gives you hope of ever understanding anything. Without any real plan on my part, my career had advanced in both complexity and in rank, and I continued to find much of the public servant's work highly stimulating. Nonetheless, I had not managed to settle down in my personal life, in part because of the frequent moves. Living in physical as well as cultural isolation forces one to develop a protective shell, a shell that becomes hard for others to penetrate. One's frame of reference logically becomes the world, rather than the community, and others may find this either awesome or off-putting.

By 1992, the year I turned thirty-nine, I had been working at the UNICEF headquarters as Chief of the Program Information and Management Unit for two years. In this position, I enjoyed the satisfaction of developing and writing program planning policies that influenced the whole organization in every one of its 160-odd country offices. However, there were other aspects of the job that really did not suit me at all. So I began to get restless to return to the field, the heart of UNICEF's work.

I had returned to New York in 1987 because I wanted to reconstruct a personal and a family life that had been denied me in the years I moved around Africa. I partially achieved this goal; although marriage still eluded me, I had reactivated a network of old friends, managed to spend more time with my parents and siblings and bought an apartment that grounded me in Manhattan and ended my nomad status. These were personal gains that I was loathe to surrender by moving thousands of miles away, and so I decided that I only would accept a posting in the Western Hemisphere. At the same time, I wanted the challenge of a hardship country where interesting social and political change was taking place; the obvious choice was Haiti, a poor country under an economic and diplomatic embargo. The very day I had decided to announce to management my interest in being considered as UNICEF representative to Haiti, the deputy executive director approached me: "We can't find anyone willing to go to Haiti; would you be interested?" Despite a rather unflattering implication that I was somehow the choice of last resort, the offer, coinciding with my own selection of Haiti, confirmed my destiny with this troubled Caribbean country that was only a three-hour flight from New York.

THE SECOND PASSAGE: AFTER 40

In September 1992, I arrived in Haiti with almost ten years of UNICEF experience, very little of which, I was surprised to discover, could be applied in unique circumstances of the time.[2] Diplomatic and economic sanctions imposed on Haiti following the September 1991 coup d'état against the democratically elected President, Jean-Bertrand Aristide, meant that the UN could not manage any programs through the usual government structures. Instead of supporting development programs that, by definition, seek to improve the conditions in the country, we were limited to providing only life-saving humanitarian assistance. Since all of UNICEF's program planning and implementation policies are oriented to work with government, we were left to develop our own alternative strategies, alternatives that had to accommodate various political agendas at both the national and international level. I was totally unprepared for the acutely political nature of the work, by which the actions of the UNICEF-Haiti office could have implications as far away as the UN Security Council, the General Assembly of the Organization of American States, and the White House, all of which were keen that humanitarian assistance not distort political objectives for restoring democratic rule. Work under sanctions was totally new to UNICEF, and headquarters could only advise me "to use my best judgement" when navigating the politically mined waters that the office had to cross to implement its mandate.

With the experience of sanctions, my faith in the noble ideals of the United Nations was severely tested, forcing me to confront moral dilemmas and other hardships. UN-mandated sanctions produced consequences—poverty, malnutrition, and a breakdown in health services—that violated the human rights of the poor and led, indisputably, to increased disease and death among Haiti's children. Of course UNICEF, as a UN agency, supported the sanctions policy, but still had to try to carry out its mandate for children as best it could. To help in this effort, UNICEF, together with the United Nations Fund for Population Activities, commissioned the Harvard University School of Public Health to carry out a study to identify those sectors of society that had suffered the worst humanitarian decline under the embargo, so that we might mobilize resources to reverse that decline. When the study was released, indicating that sanctions were among a complex set of factors contributing to a rise in child mortality, the news hit the front page of *The New York Times*, and caused an uproar, since the information could be used to undermine the international policy for punishing the de facto government and reinstating the elected president, then in exile. The following day, the White House press secretary stated that the government had concerns about "questionable" methodology used. However, although officially discredited, the study did ultimately lead to a reassessment of U.S. humanitarian policy and an increase in assistance to Haiti.

Situations that challenge your basic values arise frequently when working for the United Nations. Actions taken to maintain peace and security are not always going to protect fundamental human rights, or civilian access to basic services.[3] Faced with these challenges, it is tempting to discard one's internal moral compass, and take the easy route, as we could have, for example, by not publishing the Harvard study, or by succumbing to political pressure to withhold measles vaccines during a lethal epidemic (the democratic forces believed that saving children's lives would bring credit to the de facto government). I knew that I would have to live with the life or death consequences of these decisions for the rest of my life; they were decisions that tested my faith in myself, my judgement, and my basic morality in ways that are inconceivable in ninety-five percent of other jobs.

Apart from the spiritual crisis that coping with such moral dilemmas provoked, living conditions under an economic embargo were quite aggravating, and added further stress to a stressful situation. Fuel could only be obtained on the black market at a very high price, electricity use was reduced to three to six hours per day, and at one point we went six weeks without a single spark of power. The lack of electricity is a lot more irritating than one might imagine, for it reduces you to a prisoner of small decisions—scheduling your reading or your shower to coincide with the time when the power comes on, rather than when you choose, or deciding how many times you can open the refrigerator door before all the cold escapes.

Fortunately, in Haiti, as in most countries, respect for child rights and protection for children is a rallying point around which rival groups can come to consensus. Faced with the country's long history of political, economic, and social divisions, accentuated by the coup d'état and sanctions, UNICEF served as a catalyst for bringing together political and social actors who viewed each other with suspicion. Throughout my four years in the country, two under economic sanctions and two working with the reinstated democratic government, using the child rights convention as a means to mobilize, we helped create a neutral space to enable many diverse groups to work together: networks of NGOs and community groups to deliver humanitarian services; the state and NGOs to improve the standard of health and education services; the private sector to establish a child rights foundation using Haitian capital; rival political parties to come to consensus and ratify The International Convention on the Rights of the Child in parliament, and to commit, at election time, to a joint child rights platform in the national interest. All of these alliances, catalyzed by UNICEF, but whose success was due to the commitment and vision of local leaders, contributed to national policy development and implementation. Ultimately, these policies had an impact on the lives of several million Haitians.

Managing a multicultural office is one of the UNICEF representative's most important tasks, especially when the local staff is politically polarized as was the case when I arrived in Haiti. One can have no influence on national policy without building a coherently focused UNICEF team able to "keep its eyes on the prize" of serving children. The team is composed of international staff (about ten percent of the total) who come and go every three to four years, and local staff who observe frequent, de-motivating changes in top management ("Oh no! Here comes another one!") that often leave them hunkered down in safe positions, passively resisting the lead of a new head of office who they know will be transferred in a few years. In addition to gaining the confidence of the local staff and overcoming their resistance to change by motivating them with a compelling vision, the UNICEF representative has to build coherence among the international staff; in Haiti, I had colleagues from Africa, Latin America, North America, and Europe working with me, each with his or her own cultural and linguistic perspective. Consequently, as head of the office I had to be perceived as understanding, tolerant, fair, and having no biases (individual or cultural).

THE THIRD PASSAGE: SABBATICAL

The experience of four years in Haiti challenged me, both professionally and personally, more profoundly than any other experience before or since. The complex situation demanded the utmost of my existing abilities, and forced me to develop new talents that I would otherwise have never known I possessed, talents for political analysis, for persuading and mobilizing diverse forces around a galvanizing idea, for dealing with the media, and for leading a large, multicultural but politically polarized office. Together, we had developed new programming methods that reached more children than ever before. The International Convention on the Rights of the Child had been ratified and child rights were being promoted and protected by networks of organizations throughout society. So, by the end of 1996, much as I loved being in Haiti, I felt I had contributed as much as I could and that it was time for a new team to take over. Despite the professional satisfactions, the moral dilemmas imposed by sanctions had taken an immense personal toll; being forced to support sanctions while knowing that the consequences were killing children and driving thousands of families deep into degrading poverty was profoundly traumatic for me. Even though two years had passed since sanctions had been lifted, I still felt that I was not ready to go to another country, and that the best way to recover would be to take a sabbatical and gain the personal perspective that I knew writing about sanctions would provide. UNICEF graciously agreed to my request and I was accepted as a visiting scholar in the UN Studies Program of my former graduate school.

I left Haiti in December 1996, and began my The Visiting Scholar Program at Columbia University in January, the dead of winter. While I audited a few courses during the first months of my sabbatical, I found to my surprise that after four-teen years working overseas, four in the high-octane environment of Haiti, I had absorbed by osmosis much of what I thought I needed in additional academic train-ing. Halfway through the semester I abandoned my courses and headed for the library. Meanwhile, I could not help noticing the huge gulf that separates acade-mia from the hands-on work at the front lines of political change, where I had been. I was very surprised that not one of the professors approached me, even informally, to find out more about the Haiti experience that had been front-page news only two years before. I felt very shy about approaching them, feeling some-how inadequate in expressing personal drama in geopolitical terms. Of course this gulf between the two world of academia and policy impedes policy development. On the one hand, those academicians who develop international policy are cut off from its source and its consequences in the field. On the other, those of us, such as UNICEF representatives living through political transitions, have few means of channeling our experience into the policy debate, as we are more likely to be doers than thinker–writers. By the same token, academics do not often seek out knowledge of on-the-ground experience, which may threaten existing paradigms.

However, once I had entered the academic realm, and written a draft of my book, I was astonished at the openness and collegiality with which I, a complete unknown, was received by famous scholars who were doing recognized research on sanc-tions and human rights. Many graciously agreed to read my draft and even pro-vided detailed comments. I had written a book on Haiti sanctions as therapy for myself with no expectation that anyone would even read it, let alone that it would eventually be considered worthy of publication. I thus remain as surprised as I am grateful that, through the intervention of a Haitian friend, the draft fell into the hands of Georges Fauriol at the Center for Strategic and International Studies, where it was eventually published under the title *Sanctions in Haiti: Human Rights and Democracy under Assault*. Through this experience, I learned the power of the writ-ten word, and that those of us working at the front line of sociopolitical change can be heard if we put pen to paper.

Despite the perspective that my sabbatical gave me, as 1997 progressed, I con-tinued to feel that I was not ready for a new field assignment, so I was fortunate when a position as senior policy officer opened in UNICEF's New York Headquarters Office of Emergency Programmes (EMOPS). EMOPS also represents UNICEF with the UN Secretariat's Office of the Coordinator of Humanitarian Affairs (OCHA), which supports the humanitarian response of the UN agencies operat-ing in crisis countries. At the time, the UN Security Council had requested OCHA, also responsible for coordinating the UN system's humanitarian policy, to provide it with information on the humanitarian impact of sanctions as well as on possi-ble mechanisms for reducing that impact. Thus my experience in Haiti, as well as the research I completed during my sabbatical, were fed through OCHA directly into sanctions policy development at the highest levels of the United Nations, where it had the potential to influence decisions on a global scale.

However, for a variety of reasons, I was unsuited to the EMOPS assignment as it ultimately evolved. Senior management recognized this and offered me a number of other positions that included a promotion, but I did not feel I could accept them, either because I doubted that I would enjoy the job or because I would have had to live far away from the Western Hemisphere. After my return from Haiti, I had become more attached than ever to my Manhattan apartment and my life in New York. Finally I proposed to top management that I be posted to Guatemala, a lateral move that had the benefit of offering me the possibility to learn a new language, work in an unfamiliar culture, in the stimulating post-conflict context of a newly democratizing country. However, the personal cost of moving to yet another new country where I knew no one was higher than ever before.

As I write, I have been in Guatemala just a year, the first six months of which I felt as if I had a head cold with the mighty struggle to master the language muffling my understanding, as well as my verbal capacity. This was a difficulty that I had totally underestimated, and greatly reduced my effectiveness in the key roles of a UNICEF representative—advocacy and alliance-building. Despite this initial handicap, I find the country's sociopolitical context fascinating, and the work challenging, which offsets the familiarity of tasks that I as representative carry out, tasks that are essentially the same as those in Haiti.

THE THIRD PASSAGE: EXPLORING OTHER OPTIONS?

As I deepen my understanding of Guatemala, I ask myself how long one should stick with a career of missionary proportions, a career that demands such intense personal commitment, such perception, and such sacrifice? At forty-six, I have yet to come up with my answers, but as I consider whether I should explore other options beyond UNICEF, the questions I ask myself are:

- Do I still have the empathy to become passionate about changing the situation of poverty in which far too many people still live, or, in an attempt at self-preservation, have I hardened my heart too much to care?
- Can I live without the incredible stimulation and constant challenge to one's understanding of the world that a UNICEF career provides?
- Am I becoming too blasé, considering that "I've seen it all," or am I still open to learning?
- Do I have the energy and emotional stamina to pack up and move to yet another country?
- Will I be happy being a bystander to sociopolitical change instead of working at the front lines of political transitions? Would I be able to feel I am making the contribution to society towards which my superior education obliges me?

SUMMING UP

Although I am left with a raft of questions after a public service career of twenty-five years, a few of which have allowed me to influence policy on an international level, I do have some answers. The first is that it is a career that has required me to be open to learning; this has proved much more important than any specific academic training, with the possible exception of language training. My education provided me with a highly developed capacity for analysis, an ability to think, to present ideas in an orderly way, and to write and speak clearly and articulately in at least two languages. These are skills that have proved invaluable throughout my career, in ways that I never could have imagined—for they allow me to analyze my environment and present my conclusions in a convincing manner. Obtaining developing country experience early on solidly grounded my career, and ensured that I knew what I wanted before going for a master's degree.

By choosing a career in public service, I have always been in a position to initiate change, and, by convincing local actors, have a small influence on the quality of life for hundreds, then thousands, and ultimately millions of people. For me, in the end, this has been very satisfying. A career in a United Nations agency, where no day is like the next, where one learns to live with uncertainty, political turmoil, instability, and constant moral dilemmas, is also a career in which one can truly make a positive difference in people's lives.

Nonetheless, all these benefits come at an extremely high personal cost, a cost that needs to be carefully considered. Life and work a UN agency, and moving countries every few years, can be and often is both lonely and stressful, especially for women. Family life is often impossible to construct or maintain, not only for women but also men, and the rates of separation and divorce are quite high. Moreover, the risk of becoming a person who never feels at home anywhere is significant, only partially offset by the benefits of being able to fit in just about everywhere.

At the same time, as "change agents" in an international organization, you need to be able to live with constant doubt. Are the socioeconomic changes set off by our good intentions truly beneficial, or simply disruptive, disorienting, or destructive to the participating communities and countries? We are forever being confronted with evidence that our interventions may not be in the best interest of the people we innocently aim to serve; we have to learn to live with this ambiguity every day, and come to terms with it.

However, if the aim is to be of service, and at times, to influence international policy, there are an infinite number of ways that a career in a UN agency allows you to do so, both within the organization itself, and within the countries where you serve. Moreover, a career in international economic and social development also allows for considerable personal growth; I am constantly learning, about people, cultures, and politics, and picking up a huge amount of general knowledge on the way. If I weren't so before, I have had to become an open, observant, curious, flexible, and tolerant person, with an indispensable sense of humor. I have learned to deal with despair and exhilaration, with the startling contrasts of visiting people in the poorest slums, and meeting with the President of the Republic, all in the same day. My patience and diplomatic skills are constantly put to test, and this has increased my self-discipline. All of this personal growth is rewarding, and fundamentally worthwhile.

In conclusion, as my first boss said years ago, "D'you think its easy? It ain't easy." Yet life and work in a United Nations agency is immensely rewarding, and personally fulfilling. Thus I recommend this public service career wholeheartedly to anyone who can live with its demands, dilemmas, and ambiguities, and who aspires to influence policy on an international level.

NOTES

1. UNICEF is an independently funded agency of the United Nations, mandated to support programs and projects that protect children, help to meet their basic needs for health, education, nutrition, and clean water, and that contribute to developing self-reliant communities, nations and governments that place a high priority on children. In 1990, following the entry into force of the Convention on the Rights of the Child, the UN General Assembly gave UNICEF the mandate to advocate for the protection of child rights, which included political, civil, economic, social, and cultural rights without discrimination due to race, sex, religion, location, or economic status.

2. The political and humanitarian dimensions of my work in Haiti during the embargo years are fully discussed in my book, *Sanctions in Haiti: Human Rights and Democracy Under Assault* (Washington, D.C.: Center for Strategic and International Studies and Praeger Press, 1999).

3. For numerous examples of this see Jonathan Moore (ed.), *Hard Choices: Moral Dilemmas in Humanitarian Intervention* (Lanham, MD: Rowman and Littlefield, 199b), and William Shawcross, *Deliver Us From Evil: Peacekeepers, Warlords and a World of Endless Conflict* (New York: Simon and Schuster, 2000).

12

The Satisfactions of Nonpartisan Policy Analysis on Capitol Hill

K. Larry Storrs

Nearing another major turning point in my life, I look back with satisfaction on more than forty years of involvement with Latin America and more than thirty fascinating years of dealing with U.S.-Latin American policy issues[1]. For the last twenty-five years of my life, I have been attempting to provide objective and nonpartisan analysis on Latin American policy issues to Congress as an analyst with the Congressional Research Service of the Library of Congress. These policy issues have ranged from the Panama Canal treaties in the 1970s, and the provision of military aid to El Salvador in the 1980s, to financial assistance to Brazil and trade and drug trafficking issues with Mexico in the 1990s.

This chapter attempts to tell the reader what route I followed to gain this position, what I do on a daily basis in my job, and what I learned along the way that would be useful to future policy wonks. A sketch of my life fits nicely into three periods: training, college teaching, and policy analysis on Capitol Hill.

TRAINING

Public policy analysis in a major metropolitan area is a far cry from the farm in a small town in Utah where I was raised. I believe it was my involvement in debate (where you spoke on both sides of an issue), as well as student government and service clubs in high school and college, that established my interest in politics and public policy. In my early years of college at the University of Utah, I thought of becoming a lawyer or a high school teacher, possibly the coach of the debate team.

My interest in Latin America came in my early twenties, at the midpoint of my undergraduate studies, when I served for two and a half years as a missionary in Brazil for my church. This experience gave me immediate and firsthand contact with the poverty and difficulties affecting people in less developed countries, and it made a lasting impression. I learned to love the Brazilian people, to be fascinated with Brazilian culture, and to see the country's great potential, while honing my skills in speaking Portuguese. These were the years when Brazilian confidence was demonstrated by the inauguration of a new and modern capital in Brasilia, but Fidel Castro's rise in Cuba was creating a host of issues in Latin American countries and in U.S.-Latin American relations. I was anxious for the United States to take positions that would advance development in these countries and promote greater understanding among the countries. My missionary experience required a break in my undergraduate schooling, but it taught me things that could not be found in textbooks. It set my life on another course and gave greater focus to my future studies.

After my return from Brazil, I completed my undergraduate studies at Brigham Young University, with a major in political science and a minor in history. In keeping with my new interest in Latin America, and with the Cuban Revolution in the daily press, I took courses on Latin American history and politics, advanced Portuguese, and international relations, along with other courses on American government and comparative government. Although I enjoyed my courses on constitutional law, and considered the possibility of going to law school, I finally decided to focus on Latin American affairs, and to go to graduate school in political science with the career goal of teaching political science at the university level. I admired the sense of community and the free exchange of ideas at the universities that I had attended and the many universities I had visited on debate tournaments. I cherished the thought of dealing with ideas and students through teaching, and I imagined that I would advance understanding of Latin America and influence U.S. policy toward Latin America through my teaching and writing.

Applying at a time when the U.S. government was encouraging the study of Third World countries, I was lucky enough to receive a fellowship funded by the National Defense Education Act (NDEA). This fellowship supported graduate studies in government (political science) and Latin American Studies at Cornell University, in a program leading directly to the Ph.D. I never considered taking a break after my undergraduate studies or in the middle of my graduate studies for non-educational experiences because of my previous break in schooling. Although the prospect of a program leading to the Ph.D., with no master's degree in between, was risky and a bit daunting, I reasoned that it was a necessity to become a college professor.

My graduate training and completion of my doctoral dissertation stretched on for many years and intersected with my early teaching career. My first three years of course work at Cornell were invigorating and broadening, with courses in international relations, international law, and Latin American studies as well as American government and political theory. I was advised and required to take a broad array of courses because I would be teaching in a political science department where expertise in more than one area was expected. In the classroom, I learned about U.S.-Soviet relations, the Sino-Soviet conflict, U.S. executive-legislative relations, and the Mexican and Cuban Revolutions, with the Cuban Missile Crisis of 1962 giving these studies a sense of great immediacy. Outside the classroom, the Cornell community was embroiled in the domestic struggles for civil rights and greater equity in society, and, with mounting intensity over the years, in the debate over U.S. policy toward Vietnam, given Cornell's special emphasis on Southeast Asia.

After completing my comprehensive doctoral examinations (known as comps), I received an NDEA-related Fulbright-Hays Fellowship, and, newly married, I returned to Brazil in the mid-1960s for a year and a half of research on my doctoral dissertation. Brazil was in the early period of two decades of military control following the 1964 military coup that ousted a civilian government perceived as being too sympathetic to Cuba and the Soviet Union, and too inclined to adopt radical domestic policies. In the United States and in Brazil there was an active academic and policy debate about the role of the United States in support of the coup and the subsequent military regimes and the extent of repression and human rights abuse.

My dissertation on Brazil's "independent foreign policy" from 1961 to 1964, when it was less aligned with the United States, was a bit controversial since it focused on Brazil's changing policies toward the United States, Cuba, and the Third World, and contrasted the independent policy with the policies in earlier and subsequent periods. My training and my dissertation research hooked me forever on the quest to understand the linkage between domestic and foreign policy and the intricacies of U.S.-Latin American relations. I returned to Cornell for a short time to continue writing my dissertation but was forced to work on it for more than a few years in the first years of my teaching career while I was developing course lectures and in the early years of raising a family. I was satisfied and relieved when my dissertation was completed because in my case I would have had only a B.A. without it.

Among the lessons from my graduate school experience that I would pass on to future policy analysts are the following: it would have been wiser to have entered a program with a master's degree to allow more flexibility and security; to have taken more courses in economics to better understand the numerous political economy policy issues that have emerged; and to have completed the dissertation before being immersed in teaching without trying to make it a definitive work in the discipline.

COLLEGE TEACHING

My first career passage, in my early thirties, was to eight years of teaching political science in college, in keeping with my planning and academic preparation. Academic positions were more available in those days, and I never really considered any other option. I looked forward to the prospect of teaching about U.S. policy and Latin America, and to engaging in discussions with students. One nice feature of teaching that I appreciated was that the less structured but demanding schedule of teaching allowed me to spend considerable time at home when my sons were young.

My first year of teaching was at Vassar College in Poughkeepsie, New York, at the time a small, undergraduate, liberal arts college for women where I taught American government, comparative politics, and Latin American politics. I enjoyed working with very bright undergraduate students at Vassar, and especially advising students on their senior honors theses. The campus community was in ferment that year as it considered whether to remain a women's college or become coeducational.

The rest of my teaching career was at George Washington University in Washington, D.C., a major university where I taught undergraduate and graduate courses on Latin American politics, U.S.-Latin American relations, and international relations. I enjoyed the urban campus at GWU, with the mix of graduate and undergraduate, full-time and part-time, younger and older students, in disciplinary and interdisciplinary programs. It was stimulating and demanding to have students who were from Latin America and other foreign countries, or who were working at the nearby State and Defense Departments or other policy organizations. I had a chance to work closely with many students writing theses and dissertations on major policy issues as the culmination of their graduate school training.

In my Latin American courses, the major topics of discussion included the growing militarization throughout the hemisphere, the disillusionment with President Kennedy's Alliance for Progress, and the implications of the U.S. policies of isolating Cuba, intervening in the Dominican Republic, constraining Allende in Chile, and supporting military regimes, such as those in Argentina, Brazil and Chile. In my international relations courses and in the campus community, the major focus of attention was U.S. involvement in Vietnam, with several demonstrations on campus against university institutes or programs with contracts with the Department of Defense. Since GWU is the closest campus to the White House, it was often the base of operations for many of the big anti-war student demonstrations during those years.

Looking back at my years of teaching I remember it as a stimulating and enjoyable time, with many satisfactions, that helped prepare me for a more policy-relevant opportunity, although the demands of teaching and advising students often left too little time for research and publication. I enjoyed college teaching so much, in fact, that I have been a part-time instructor on four separate occasions at various area institutions, teaching courses on Brazil, Central America, U.S.-Latin American relations, and South America.

POLICY ANALYSIS ON CAPITOL HILL

My second career passage came in my late thirties when I became an analyst, later specialist, in Latin American affairs in the Foreign Affairs Division of the Congressional Research Service of the Library of Congress in Washington, D.C. The Congressional Research Service (CRS) is the part of the Library of Congress that works directly with members, staff and committees of the Congress, with a mandate to provide objective, nonpartisan, and timely analysis. CRS serves many purposes: it is a "reference library" where congressional staffers may obtain all sorts of information; it is a "think tank" where members and staff may try out ideas and gain perspective; and it is a "treasury of synthesis" where staffers may obtain concise and up-to-date summaries and analyses of policy issues and legislative action.

Acting in the very partisan environment of Capitol Hill, CRS analysts take pride in providing objective and nonpartisan information, and in being an institutional memory for the Congress. Our pride is enhanced by the fact that CRS products bear the names of the authors, a privilege that is somewhat unique in the federal government. We produce balanced reports, even when our clients would prefer a more definite policy slant, with the knowledge that we influence policy by providing much needed analysis and evaluation, but unlike staff or policymakers in the executive and legislative branches, we do not make recommendations or policy decisions. After twenty-five years at CRS, I am very comfortable with the nonpartisan role, and feel that my experience in debate and teaching, where I tried to understand both sides of an issue, prepared me for this niche in the policy process.

Over the years this position has given me an opportunity to associate and interact with wonderfully cooperative and helpful colleagues in CRS, with hard-working members and congressional staff, with dedicated staffers in the executive branch, with very knowledgeable fellow Latin Americanists outside the government, and with devoted staff members with human rights and advocacy groups. It has given me opportunities to travel on occasion to Central America, Mexico, and Brazil; to observe elections in El Salvador and Mexico; to conduct seminars and to make presentations on a host of subjects, including the Caribbean, El Salvador, Mexico, and Brazil; and to spend an academic year at the National War College with civilian and military colleagues. It has even given me an opportunity to explore my earlier interest in law through the study of legislation and issues with legal ramifications, and through extensive involvement with the union that represents CRS employees. Most of all, the position has given me a great appreciation for the extensive role of the Congress in the formulation of U.S. foreign policy toward Latin America and the world.

In a daily routine that involves responding to congressional inquiries with strict deadlines, writing reports and memoranda on the most current policy issues before Congress, and reviewing other colleagues reports, I have been privileged to work on many of the major Latin American issues over the years, with the choice of topics being dictated primarily by congressional requests and the congressional agenda rather than personal choice.

In the mid-to-late 1970s, I worked on issues relating to U.S. relations with Chile and Panama, providing background material and analysis on both countries, and traveling with a congressional delegation to Panama. With regard to Chile, concern about the role of the United States in the 1973 military coup that ousted President Salvador Allende led to hearings on the role of the CIA in foreign policy by the select committee chaired by Senator Frank Church, and concern with the human rights conditions under the dictatorship of General Augusto Pinochet led to a termination of U.S. assistance to Chile. With regard to Panama, the very heated and public debate on the merits of the Panama Canal treaties, with eventual transfer of the canal to Panama, culminated in the razor-thin approval of both treaties by the Senate with a one vote margin, and in the approval by both houses of legislation creating the Panama Canal Commission that operated the canal until the end of 1999.

In the 1980s and into the 1990s I wrote primarily on the hotly contested issues relating to Central America and the Caribbean, tracking the congressional conditions on military aid to El Salvador and Guatemala, the congressional prohibitions on covert assistance to the "contras" in Nicaragua, the recommendations for the region of the bipartisan Kissinger Commission, and the enactment of the Caribbean Basin Initiative with trade preferences and economic assistance. Eventually, with Congress playing a supportive role, the conflictive parties reached peace agreements in El Salvador, Nicaragua, and Guatemala, and elections became the norm. U.S. assistance to the region helped to support the peace processes at various times, and also provided relief following Hurricane Mitch in 1998. I also dealt with issues relating to the congressional tightening of sanctions against Cuba with the Cuban Democracy Act of 1992, and to congressional conditions on U.S. assistance to Haiti in the mid-1990s under Presidents Aristide and Preval.

Beginning earlier but with greater attention in the 1990s, my research focused on Mexico and Brazil, within the context of the Bush and Clinton Administrations' initiatives to promote subregional and regional free-trade regimes in the hemisphere.

With regard to Mexico, I have dealt with issues relating to Congress' approval of the controversial North American Free Trade Agreement (NAFTA) in 1993, congressional concerns with guerrillas in Chiapas and political assassinations in 1994, and congressional resistance to the large financial assistance package for Mexico in 1995 following the devaluation crisis. I have also analyzed issues related to congressional measures to control illegal immigration and to strengthen the border patrol in 1996, and congressional initiatives to strengthen regional and bilateral drug control programs, including unsuccessful efforts to decertify Mexico as a fully cooperative country in recent years, and passage of the Foreign Narcotics Kingpin Designation Act in 1999.

With regard to Brazil, I have written on trade, environmental, and assistance issues, ranging from Brazil's designation as an unfair trading partner in 1990 under the congressionally mandated Super 301 provisions, to Brazil's leadership of the Southern Common Market (Mercosur) and its reluctant stance toward the Free Trade Agreement of the Americas (FTAA), to the IMF's package of financial assistance for Brazil in 1999 following devaluation. I have also analyzed the Summits of the Americas in 1994 (Miami) and 1998 (Santiago) that reflect the growing cooperation within the region.

During my career I have seen Latin America change from statist to free enterprise, from militaristic to democratic, and I have observed relations with the United States change from tense to cooperative. I have observed in detail how relations with Mexico changed from difficult and somewhat remote to friendly and incredibly interactive, and I have been able to see Nicaragua, El Salvador and Guatemala move from a state of conflict and insurgency to peace. I have had the opportunity to observe the Mexico with a single dominant party become the Mexico where many governors, the mayor of the Federal District, and the majority in the Chamber of Deputies are from opposition parties. I have seen inflation-riddled Brazil bring inflation under control under President Cardoso's Real Plan and survive economic hardship following devaluation in early 1999.

Looking back, I feel satisfied and pleased with my career as a policy analyst. Among my major accomplishments, I have completed over two hundred CRS reports[2] and memoranda for members of Congress and congressional committees; and I have prepared congressional committee documents on Panama,[3] inter-American relations,[4] the Panama Canal Treaties debate,[5] and Administration statements and Truth Commission findings on El Salvador.[6] I also made numerous contributions to the *CRS Review*[7] (the Service's digest of policy research) and to the annual volumes on Congress and Foreign Policy[8] printed by the House Foreign Affairs Committee. I jointly authored a chapter in a book on public opinion and aid to the Contras[9]; and wrote draft reports for congressional delegations to Panama[10] and to the Mexico-U.S. Interparliamentary Conferences.

During my career, I have been involved in some of the most exciting and controversial policy issues in the last quarter of a century. At the same time, I have enjoyed the stability and consistency of living in the Washington, D.C. area for more than thirty years, and of working almost exclusively in two institutions, with friends and colleagues that I admire and respect. Despite the demands of my career path, my employment has permitted me adequate time for my family and my other interests, including service with my church and periods of time as a soccer coach and as a scoutmaster.

Based on my experience, I would certainly encourage would-be policy wonks to enter the world of policy analysis, whether as a teacher, a reporter, an advocate for a certain group, a policymaker in the executive or legislative branch, or, as in my case, as a nonpartisan analyst. For those who are interested in a career involving policy analysis, I would advise you to seize opportunities to learn to speak and write clearly and concisely, to get good disciplinary or interdisciplinary training, and to acquire as much practical experience as you can through internships and employment opportunities. For those interested in a career relating to Latin American issues, I would advise you to learn the relevant languages, and to have some practical experience living in the region.

At this point in my life I have passed up opportunities for early retirement, mostly because I continue to enjoy what I am doing, and as I approach the traditional age of retirement, I am still trying to decide when I will leave CRS and what I will do in the future. So far the satisfactions of working on Latin American policy issues at the Congressional Research Service have outweighed any other options, although the appeal of spending more time with my wife and grandchildren is gaining weight.

NOTES

1. I would like to thank my wife and sons, a number of CRS colleagues—Nina Serafino, Mark Sullivan, Maureen Taft-Morales, and Joan Davenport—and Howard Wiarda for helpful and constructive comments.

2. On El Salvador, for example: *El Salvador Aid: Congressional Action, 1981–1986, on President Reagan's Requests for Economic and Military Assistance for El Salvador,* CRS Report 87–230F, 1987; *El Salvador Highlights, 1960–1990: A Summary of Major Turning Points in Salvadoran History and U.S. Policy,* CRS Report 90–177F, 1990; and *El Salvador Under Cristiani: U.S. Foreign Assistance Decisions* and *El Salvador Under Calderon Sol: U.S. Foreign Assistance Decisions,* CRS Issue Briefs 92034 (1989–1994) and 94048 (1994–1999). On Mexico, for example, *Mexico-U.S. Relations: Issues for Congress,* CRS Issue Briefs IB10047 (1999–2000) and IB97028 (1997–1998); *Mexico's Counter-Narcotics Efforts Under Zedillo, December 1994 to March 1999, CRS Report RL30098 (1999);* and *Mexican Drug Certification Issues: U.S. Congressional Action, 1986–1999,* CRS Report 98–174 (1998–1999). On Brazil, for example, *Brazil Under Cardoso: Politics, Economics, and Relations with the United States,* CRS Report RL30121, April 1999.

3. Senate Foreign Relations Committee, *Background Documents Relating to the Panama Canal [1825–1977],* Committee Print, 95th Congress, 1st Session, November 1977, 1688 pp.

4. Senate Foreign Relations Committee and House Foreign Affairs Committee, *Inter-American Relations: A Collection of Documents, Legislation, Descriptions of Inter-American Organizations, and Other Material Pertaining to Inter-American Affairs,* Joint Committee Print, 100th Congress, 2nd Session, December 1988, 999 pp.

5. Senate Foreign Relations Committee, *Senate Debate on the Panama Canal Treaties: A Compendium of Major Statements, Documents, Record Votes and Relevant Events*, Committee Print, 96th Congress, 1st Session, February 1979, 560 pp.

6. House Foreign Affairs Committee, *Comparison of U.S. Administration Testimony and Reports with 1993 U.N. Truth Commission Report on El Salvador,* Committee Print, 103rd Congress, 1st Session, July 1993, 57 pp.

7. For example, "El Salvador—New Challenges for U.S. Policy," and "Central America's Economic Development—Options for U.S. Assistance, *CRS Review*, February 1989; "Brazil's Position on GATT Trade Talks," *CRS Review*, May–June 1990; and "Cuba in a Changing World: Options for U.S. Policy," *CRS Review*, January–February 1991.

8. For example, "Congress and El Salvador," in House Foreign Affairs Committee, *Congress and Foreign Policy—1981*, Committee Print, 1982; and "Congress, Central America and the Caribbean," in House Foreign Affairs Committee, *Congress and Foreign Policy—1983*, Committee Print, 1984.

9. "The Reagan Administration's Efforts to Gain Support for Contra Aid," in Richard Sobel, ed., *Public Opinion in U.S. Foreign Policy: The Controversy over Contra Aid* (Princeton: Princeton University Press, 1993).

10. House Committee on International Relations, Subcommittee on Inter-American Affairs, *The Panama Canal and United States-Panama Relations—Report of a Study Mission to Panama, March 17 to 20, 1977*, Committee Print, 1977.

13

Up and Down Pennsylvania Avenue: Congress and the Executive Branch

Victor C. Johnson

Great careers aren't for everyone. There are other kinds—secure careers, remunerative careers—and they're all valid. If you want a great career, my advice is: Stop trying to plan it. In my experience, great careers aren't planned. They're serendipitous journeys, full of accidents, chance encounters, risks taken, opportunities seized, mistakes that turn into opportunities, plain luck . . . and some sleepless nights wondering if it will all work out. Of course, ability counts. The better you are at what you do when taking this journey, the greater the chance that you will navigate the journey successfully.

I've had a great career—one that I could have neither planned nor predicted when I was in school. And at age fifty-eight, it's not over yet! I still haven't learned to plan successfully where I'll be five years from now. But at least I think I know how I got where I am now.

My father was a Ph.D. chemist, and my mother was a Ph.D. pharmacist (albeit, in keeping with the times, a housewife who never practiced her profession). But the conversation around our dinner table was often about politics and world affairs. The only thing I've ever known about my career was that I wanted it to be in some sense international. I did eventually get a Ph.D., but not because I planned it that way or because I felt that I had to equal my parents.

In college (University of California Riverside and Whitworth College, 1959–63) I first majored in history, then changed to political science. At some point I asked my advisor what a person who was interested in international relations should do for a career. His immediate answer: Get a master's and join the Foreign Service. And for a time, that's what I thought I would probably do.

Fortunately, however—being eternally undecided about what I wanted to do— I first joined the Peace Corps. It was one of the smartest things I ever did, not because it enhanced my career in any concrete way, but because it changed me as a person and taught me things about the world and about life that I could not have learned in any other way. The experience of being a Peace Corps volunteer in Liberia almost forty years ago still influences my thinking about international issues.

While in the Peace Corps I began to think seriously about pursuing the advice I had received as an undergraduate and joining the Foreign Service. I applied to master's programs with that in mind, and I began the Foreign Service examination process. However, by the time I returned to the United States at the end of 1965, I was rethinking my career objectives. The Vietnam War had become a major issue in U.S. politics. I knew I couldn't support the war, or indeed much else about foreign policy, and I knew my job in the Foreign Service would require me to do precisely that. I decided instead that I wanted to build on my Peace Corps experience by pursuing a career in international development. In 1967 (at age twenty-six), with my master's thesis from San Francisco State almost done, I took a two-year job as a training associate with the Ford Foundation's international development program in Bogota, Colombia. Through the accident of being offered that job versus another, I learned Spanish and my career turned in the direction of Latin America.

During my two years in Bogota, I rethought my career yet again and decided that what I really wanted to be was a professor of international relations—to influence policy through analysis rather than administration. In 1969, I enrolled in the University of Wisconsin-Madison to pursue a Ph.D. in political science. But while I was there, the bottom fell out of the academic job market. As I was completing my dissertation, I was having zero success at finding a teaching job. Finally, I packed my car and moved to Washington, D.C., figuring that if I couldn't teach foreign policy, I would try to practice it. It was 1975; I was thirty-three.

I landed my job with what was then called the House Foreign Affairs Committee through both persistence and sheer luck. It was a classic case of being in the right place at the right time. I began my House career with the Subcommittee on International Economic Policy and Trade. I had no in-depth experience with the subject matter dealt with by that subcommittee, but that's not uncommon in Congress, where your ability to gain the trust of a member of Congress and to work the congressional system is often more important than your knowledge of the subject matter. You learn the subject on the job, and you learn how to tap the experts when you need to.

I could never have known it until I experienced it, but I was born to do that job. I discovered a latent talent for (and a joy in) using congressional hearings and contacts with experts to formulate coherent policy, and in using the congressional process to further the adoption of the policy. I was able to experience the thrill of playing a key role in the formulation and adoption of important foreign affairs legislation that remains on the books to this day—legislation that probably either would not have passed or would not have been as good were it not for the skills that I found within myself and developed through the process. As I grew professionally, though, I began to experience the frustration that went with not being the top staff person on the subcommittee. I wanted to be a subcommittee staff director—one of the best jobs in the world, given the right chairman and the right Congress.

It happened serendipitously, and in a way that brought together my Latin American and my congressional experience. No career advisor could have told me how to do this; it had to just happen. One day in 1979, when I was taking a few days off to move, my boss called to tell me that a freshman congressman from Maryland named Mike Barnes was planning a trip to Mexico and needed a Foreign Affairs Committee staff person to accompany him. No one wanted to go until finally they got down to me, the only one too junior to say no. Because I spoke Spanish and had been to Mexico several times, I was elected. So I left my wife with a house full of boxes (not something I would recommend) and began to plan the trip. I spent several days in Mexico with Congressman Barnes.

The next year, Ronald Reagan was elected president. As a Democrat, I won't characterize Mr. Reagan's presidency, but it was probably the best thing that ever happened to my career—a career that came to be defined in many ways through my role in opposing the Reagan Administration's policies in Latin America. It was clear that under President Reagan, Latin America was going to be a key area of contention between Democrats and Republicans. House Democrats were concerned because the chairman of the Subcommittee on Western Hemisphere Affairs at that time was seen as too conservative and too inactive to be able to serve as the Democrats' point person on Latin America policy, and they began to cast about for an alternative. In January 1981 (I was forty), I returned from a trip to Africa to discover a revolution brewing in the committee. The same Mike Barnes whom I had taken to Mexico, then a second-term member, was being promoted to unseat the sitting chairman of the subcommittee. He succeeded, he knew me, and in February I was appointed staff director of the Subcommittee on Western Hemisphere Affairs. It was unusual for a chairman to be unseated, and unheard of for a second-term member to do it. It made my career.

I served as staff director of that subcommittee for twelve years, under three chairmen, which is also unusual, because staff does not often survive one transition in the chairmanship, let alone two. During the 1980s, I was a key player in all of the contentious debates over—and legislation concerning—U.S. policy toward Latin America. And I discovered another talent I had: leading a staff. Congressional staffs are extremely small (mine was three to four people), and we were up against the enormous bureaucracies that served the administration. But we held our own. It was extremely gratifying when George Bush became president in 1989 and proceeded to adopt many of the policies toward the region for which we had been working for eight years. And it was good to be able to work with the administration rather than against it for a change.

There could have been no better job. There is no bureaucracy in Congress. You report directly to your principal. His or hers is the only approval you need to act. Many people, I suspect, go through entire careers in an executive branch bureaucracy without having anything like the impact on policy that you can have as a subcommittee staff director in the House. And if you work for a member whose values and policy orientations you share, as you should, you can gain enormous satisfaction from pursuing and sometimes achieving policy objectives that really matter to you. The work is extremely hard and can be very stressful; policy consequences of some magnitude, not to mention political reputations, are riding on how well you do your job. But I have a very low boredom threshold; I don't believe I ever experienced a boring day in twelve years as a House subcommittee staff director. And to think I wanted to be a professor. Thank God no one wanted to hire me for *that* job!

In my congressional positions, I interacted with many Foreign Service Officers, and I realized that this career was never what I really wanted. Being a little person in a big organization, following orders, was not the right thing for me. The more freewheeling, more political, less bureaucratic environment of the Congress, with its vastly greater scope for individual responsibility, was more suited to my strong policy orientation and my independent spirit.

A subcommittee staff director's job is really two jobs. On the one hand, you administer a subcommittee, which holds hearings and publishes hearing records, produces legislation, receives foreign visitors, conducts study missions abroad, interacts with other congressional offices and with executive branch agencies, and so forth. You propose an agenda for the subcommittee and, once the agenda is approved by the chairman, you carry it out. You meet with members of the public and speak before groups that have an interest in issues before the subcommittee, respond to correspondence to the chairman pertaining to subcommittee business, and answer constant phone calls. All these activities have to be planned and staffed, and it is the responsibility of the staff director to ensure that the subcommittee staff has everything covered and is operating at maximum effectiveness.

On the other hand, you are the chief adviser to the chairman on policy issues within the subcommittee's jurisdiction. This requires both strong policy analysis skills and an understanding of the political interests of the chairman. You advise the chairman on positions he or she should take, write speeches and statements, meet with constituents, and serve as a policy resource for the chairman's political party. And where the two jobs intersect—where judgments need to be made regarding how the subcommittee can best serve the political interests of the chairman and the party—your judgment is crucial.

I was often asked what a typical day was like. One of the things I loved about the job was that I could never answer that question. There was no typical day. Every day presented a new series of challenges as we worked on a variety of issues, each of which was at a different stage of the policy process, from issue conceptualization through final legislation. Each had its own political ramifications, and each called for a different strategy. The only thing you could be sure of was that, whatever you were working on, it was about to be interrupted by something else.

But there's one drawback. As a subcommittee staff director, your quality of life is almost entirely dependent on the chairman to whom you report. If she or he is good, you have a good job. If not, you don't. And there are so few jobs of a comparable level in Congress that it's very difficult to switch to another one if, through congressional turnover, you happen to acquire a boss you don't want to work for. Eventually, this happened to me, and I had a couple of rough years, including achieving the passage of legislation with which I did not agree.

But in 1993, for the first time in twelve years, a Democrat became president, and that opened up possibilities for high level jobs in the executive branch. I applied to the Clinton administration for several such positions, but there was only one I really wanted: Regional Director for Inter-American [Latin American and Caribbean] Operations at the Peace Corps. And sure enough, one day the phone awoke me at eight in the morning while my wife and I were vacationing on the West Coast. The White House personnel office had tracked me down and was offering me that job. Thus was I enabled to fulfill the dream of many Peace Corps Volunteers: to return to the Peace Corps in a senior staff position (I was fifty-two). And, serendipitously again, I was gone when the Republicans took over the Congress in 1995, at which time many Democrats lost their jobs overnight.

The Peace Corps is one of the noblest expressions of the American character, and I will always be grateful to President Clinton and Peace Corps Director Carol Bellamy for the appointment. It was an enormous privilege to serve with that organization and to watch young volunteers (and not so young—the oldest I saw was in her eighties!) do incredible things in Latin America and the Caribbean. Many in my generation worry about what will happen to the country when the supposedly self-absorbed and materialistic younger generation takes over. I don't worry about that, because I saw our future leaders serving with enormous dedication and effectiveness as Peace Corps Volunteers in small towns and urban *barrios* throughout the hemisphere. When they take over, the country will be in good hands.

Nevertheless, in terms of professional job satisfaction, the bureaucracy was in many ways a disappointment. I was dedicated to fulfilling the Peace Corps' mission in Latin America and the Caribbean; to me, that's what the job was about. I spent precious little time on that. Amazing amounts of my days were devoted to doing stereotypical bureaucratic things that I had not experienced before because I had not worked in a bureaucracy: sitting in endless meetings that decided nothing, fighting bureaucratic turf battles with those outside the office who sought control over our operations, coping with the effects of decisions that increased demands and took away resources. I learned firsthand the truth of a Peace Corps' saying: The miracle of the Peace Corps lies in its continuing ability to thrive despite repeated attempts by the staff to screw it up. I was fortunate to have a wonderful staff that was able to help our region be a leader in the agency, and I took a certain vicarious satisfaction from that. But my own contribution consisted mostly of fighting to preserve their independence to do their jobs. The job paled after awhile.

But I'm glad I had the experience, and I still think it was the best job in the executive branch. As I observed my colleagues with other agencies—particularly the State Department and AID—I understood that there weren't many executive branch jobs I would have wanted. Many people seemed to me to be in the jobs because they wanted the title. A presidential appointment is, after all, prestigious. But once in the position, many seemed to see their mission less in policy terms than in bureaucratic terms. As one who had spent much of my career dealing with real issues, it seemed unsatisfying to me. My executive branch experience helped me realize how fortunate I had been to "luck into" a series of good congressional jobs, relatively unencumbered by bureaucracy and fights over titles.

The kind of career I've had is full of excitement and fulfillment—and also full of risk. I never had a tenured or secure job with the federal government. In every job I've had, I could have been fired immediately, without notice and without recourse. I worked for four subcommittee chairmen in my seventeen years on the Hill, and each one could have been my last. I was never on a career track, where one progresses naturally from one level to the next. Despite the help of serendipity, I've worked hard to find every job I've held. For me, that was the price of interesting work, and I paid it willingly. But you never know how long you will be able to play out the string, to parlay one job into the next.

My string lasted slightly more than twenty years. It ended on January 20, 1997, the day of President Clinton's second inauguration. The Peace Corps had a new director, he wanted a new team, and that was the date he chose for the transition in my job. There was nowhere to go from there, no other government job I wanted. At age fifty-five, my government career ended in the same unplanned and unprogrammed way it had begun, and I had once again to face the perennial question: *Now* what do I want to be when I grow up?

As always, the answer was not what I thought it was. I first tried to move back in the academic direction that I had thought I wanted to follow thirty years before. That didn't work out for a variety of reasons. As I write this at the turn of the millennium (at age fifty-eight), I'm settling into what I hope will be my last full-time job as advocacy director for a nonprofit association that promotes international education. It's a job that enables me to continue my international career, to use my knowledge of the policy process, to learn a new field (educational exchange), and to learn the sociology and politics of the nonprofit world. It presents significant satisfactions and challenges, and I'm looking forward to the next few years. And then—who knows? The only thing I know is this: Whatever I might think the future will be, that isn't what it will be.

What lessons would I have you draw from my experience, other than the fundamental one provided in the first paragraph? Perhaps these. First, there's no "right" pattern of educational preparation, except to get a good education. I interrupted my education between my bachelor's and master's and again between my master's and my Ph.D. That was right for me. It was an integral part of my experimentation with different things while I was trying to figure out what I wanted to do. If I had it to do over again, I would not get a Ph.D., because it had no real value for the career I eventually pursued—at least, not yet! But of course, I didn't know what career I would pursue. I would say, get a good undergraduate education (your major is unimportant), get a little experience, and then get a good master's degree. Then get out there and try things.

Second, if you follow my career pattern, you will experience failure. When you have a nontenured job, you're always applying for jobs. Remember this from someone who has probably been rejected for more jobs than has anyone else in the United States: The job you desperately wanted, but didn't get, probably wasn't really the job for you.

Finally, in the words of the great bard of my youth, Bob Dylan, the times they are a-changin'. There are still great careers in public policy—indeed, more than ever. But you can't pursue *my* career, because the Congress that I worked in doesn't exist anymore. I was privileged to work in the House during a period from the '70s to the '90s when the institution was led by serious, policy-oriented people who sought to achieve a serious impact on foreign policy. That is no longer the case. Congress is not into serious legislation anymore, least of all in foreign policy, and the committee for which I worked with pride—now renamed the International Relations Committee—has fallen off the face of the earth. This may, surely will, change again. But from the perspective of today, if I were to start over, I could not have the career I had in the House. Like all generations, you will have to forge your own roads. Enjoy the journey!

14

Dealing with the Media

Norman Ornstein

For the past fifteen years, I have been a resident scholar at the American Enterprise Institute for Public Policy Research, one of the most significant think tanks in Washington. I am surrounded by about fifty other scholars and fellows[1] in areas like foreign policy and defense, economics, social policy, demography, politics and public opinion. AEI has its own magazine, *The American Enterprise*, and its own publisher, AEI Press. Several of my colleagues write syndicated columns. One, Ben Wattenberg, has his own TV show on PBS, called, appropriately, *Think Tank*. I and my colleagues write books, hold seminars, write articles in magazines and newspapers, testify in front of Congress, meet with public officials, diplomats and foreign dignitaries, talk to reporters, speak to conferences, conventions, boards of directors, and other groups.

Probably the question I field most frequently is, "What does a think tank do?" Here is at least one answer to the question. A good think tank acts as an intermediary between the world of ideas and the worlds of politics, policy making and journalism. Scholars and fellows at think tanks have one foot solidly in the academic camp, keeping up with scholarly research in their fields and the scholars doing the work, and the other in the policy/political world. They are able to converse readily with actors in both worlds, using (or at least understanding) academic jargon, and translating it into common parlance for a non-academic audience. Their own research is usually geared to real world public policy problems, and they use their knowledge of history and the scholarly literature, their analytical abilities and their insights into the policy process to aid policy makers, journalists and the public in their understanding of policy options and consequences.

My field is American politics. These are some of the things I do from my perch here at AEI. I write about Congress, the presidency, elections, campaign finance, public opinion and the press, and the connections of all these areas to policy, including foreign policy, health policy, budget policy, and others. I do so in a variety of formats in a variety of places. I write a column for the Capitol Hill newspaper *Roll Call* called "Congress Inside Out," and write as a member of the Board of Contributors for *USA Today*. I write from time to time in the *Washington Post*, the *New York Times*, the *Wall Street Journal* and other newspapers.

I write and edit books such as *Vital Statistics on Congress* (published every two years since 1980, and done in collaboration with Thomas E. Mann and Michael J. Malbin), *The Permanent Campaign and Its Future* (edited with Tom Mann), and *Campaign Finance: An Illustrated Guide*. Every two years, three of my colleagues (Ben Wattenberg, Karlyn Bowman, and Bill Schneider) and I conduct a monthly series of seminars called "Election Watch." A group of fifty to one-hundred people, including journalists, embassy representatives from many countries, Washington representatives for corporations and trade associations and academics, come to these sessions to hear us analyze the election trends and engage in dialogue with us.

Since 1982, I have been an election analyst with CBS News, spending most of each biennial election week in New York preparing for the election eve coverage, and sitting in the studio on election eve, working with Bob Schieffer and his producers to cover House and Senate races. I do year-round television analysis and commentary in many other places, like CNN, *Nightline*, *NewsHour with Jim Lehrer*, and *The Charlie Rose Show*. (I have also done some television comedy, most notably with Al Franken on Comedy Central for both the 1992 and 1996 presidential campaigns.) I do some radio analysis, on National Public Radio and on the *Diane Rehm Show*, among others.

I am active in a lot of other ways. Over the past few years, I pulled together a small group of scholars and others[2] to come up with a pragmatic approach to campaign finance reform; our product, called "Five Ideas for Campaign Finance Reform," was endorsed by the League of Women Voters, supported in an ad campaign including in a television commercial featuring Walter Cronkite. Several of our ideas were incorporated into various reform plans, including the later versions of the so-called McCain/Feingold and Shays/Meehan bills, as well as the proposals made by congressional freshmen in 1998.

We also created a new approach on so-called issue advocacy, which became translated into the Snowe/Jeffords Amendment, accepted by the Senate that year. In this instance, I worked with the best scholars in the field, including Dan Ortiz, Tom Mann, and Josh Rosenkranz. We analyzed the problem, and debated various approaches. University of Virginia Law Professor Dan Ortiz drafted practical language to fit the law, and we worked it over through several iterations. When Senator Olympia Snowe of Maine called to discuss new approaches to reform, I had an alternative to suggest to her; she convened several of her colleagues, and ultimately she, Senator Jim Jeffords of Maine, Senator Carl Levin of Michigan and several other senators and their staffs took our draft and channeled it, with members of our group as sounding boards, into appropriate legislative language. Our group worked hard to bring the fruits of academic research on elections and campaign money to our proposals, and to make the research relevant for journalists and policy makers alike.

Tom Mann of Brookings is my regular collaborator in many areas (including the campaign reform one). In the early and mid-1990s, we directed "The Renewing Congress Project," which focused on wide-ranging proposals to reform Congress, many of which were incorporated into recommendations made by a joint committee of Congress on reform, and into reforms implemented in the 103rd and 104th Congresses. In 1999, we directed a project, co-chaired by former senators Bob Dole and George Mitchell, to reconsider the Independent Counsel statute.

Currently, we co-direct the "Transition to Governing Project." This project is designed to focus on a phenomenon often called "the permanent campaign"—the tendency in recent years for campaigning to be a continuous, year-round activity, which is intruding regularly on what should be a distinct process of governing. We want to find ways to create more of a focus during the campaign on governing itself, by the candidates, the press, scholars, and voters. We also want to understand better what happens in the period after the election and before elected leaders take office, including the formal transition that begins the day after the election and ends with the swearing-in of Congress and the presidential inauguration, and to improve on procedures during that time. And we hope, in the process, to gain a reconsideration of the rules and norms we have put in place surrounding the nomination and confirmation of officials to policy positions in a new administration. We hope to expedite the process by which presidents get their people in place and make it easier for nominees to serve, all without sacrificing the legitimate need to assure their ethics and preserve checks and balances.

To do all of this (or at least to try to do these things) we are moving on a variety of fronts. We have pulled prominent scholars together to do a book on the nature and origins of the permanent campaign. We are talking regularly to journalists to encourage them to make governing a significant focus of their coverage of the 2000 campaign, and hope to have comparable impact on the debate commission that arranges the presidential candidate debates.

We are working with prominent members of Congress like Senators Fred Thompson (R-TN) and Joseph Lieberman (D-CT) and with other important organizations like the Council for Excellence in Government to focus attention on what will be needed to govern after the campaign is over. In the heat of the campaign, it is hard but necessary to look ahead to things like nominations and appointments. We are working with the Council on Foreign Relations to improve the campaign dialogue on governing in the foreign policy area. We are encouraging the presidential candidates and their advisors to think about the transition and the governing process before the election, not just to wait until afterward to devise a governing strategy. With other partners, we are preparing software to make it easier for new appointees to fill out the myriad of disclosure forms required of every nominee.

On another front: in 1997, I was named by President Clinton to co-chair (with Leslie Moonves, president of CBS Television), a presidential advisory committee on the public interest obligations of digital television broadcasters. Directed to report recommendations to the vice president, we became known as the Gore Commission. This commission, with twenty-two members drawn from broadcasting, the public interest community, academia and other fields, met numerous times to consider the coming transition from analog to digital broadcasting. Congress, in 1996, had granted at no cost a valuable share of the public airwaves to broadcasters to create digital stations. The question was what public interest obligations would go along with this grant of space on the communications spectrum (including the sensitive issue of free time for political campaigns). We issued a report with a series of recommendations in December of 1998. Many of them, including those in the area of political discourse, are being debated vigorously now, and may be considered by the Federal Communications Commission in 2000 and 2001.

I also spend a lot of time on the phone talking to reporters, something I began. to do in the early 1970s when I was a junior assistant professor. I dutifully returned phone calls, and therefore got a lot of calls. I found it valuable to talk to reporters, both to improve their stories by giving them some historical or analytical perspective, and to learn something from savvy people who were spending their time on the ground covering policy fights, political maneuvering, or election campaigns. I also found that quotes increased my name recognition and broader legitimacy in Washington and elsewhere.

As one consequence, I got (and get) quoted a lot in newspapers and magazines enough that in 1986, *Washington Monthly* magazine did a cover story on me as the "king of quotes." The article was more about the Washington press corps and its tendency to use the same sources, but it created a focus on me as a "quote machine" that continues intermittently today. A similar focus has come from television appearances; NBC a few years back dubbed me the "king of sound bites." Each year, some reporter runs a column counting my quotes, and those of other analysts (like Tom Mann), and proclaims one of us the "winner."

We laugh at this. Neither of us aspires to be a "king" in this area, and we have found in recent years that conversations with reporters less frequently involves give-and-take and a mutual learning experience, and more often a desire by a reporter to get a predetermined point of view in a story. At the same time, stories on evening news shows have gone from an average of two minutes to less than one, and "sound bites" that were once twenty seconds or more now tend to be three or five seconds. Fortunately, there are still a number of reporters of the old school who are diligent, deep, interested, knowledgeable and fair, with whom I talk regularly and share information, theories, and observations. So I still spend time talking to reporters, but less than I used to, and for less mutual benefit.

The career I have now evolved over many years. I did not start out knowing what would happen. There were not many models for the kinds of things I do now. It evolved, and to some degree I improvised, moving from a traditional academic base to a role more channeled to public education and public discourse.

When I started at college I had no real idea what I wanted to be. The University of Minnesota was a huge place and I was a very young commuter student—living at home in a suburb of Minneapolis, taking the bus to school every day. Although I was a Minnesota native, I had not gone to high school there, and I did not start out with a core of close friends. It was traumatic at the beginning. But I found U of M to have an ethos comfortable to undergraduates; faculty tended to be open and friendly and a small effort on my part got attention on theirs.

I managed to develop close relationships with a number of faculty members in several departments. I did not have a traditional major. I figured out a way in the system to "graze" across several interesting areas and avoid some of the boring departmental requirements by crafting an interdepartmental major with concentrations in four areas (political science, sociology, mathematics, and economics). I found mentors especially in political science and sociology. By my junior year, I was helping in several research projects. The faculty members I knew—including Walter Gerson in sociology, and David RePass, Bill Flanigan, Tom Scott, Gene Eidenberg, and Frank Sorauf in political science—appealed to me as role models, and seemed to lead nice, comfortable, and interesting lives.

By the middle of my junior year, I had decided two things. One, I wanted to be a Congressional Fellow—Gene Eidenberg, who taught both legislative and presidential politics, had spent a year under the auspices of the American Political Science Association working on Capitol Hill, and his stories and anecdotes from that time animated all his classes. Second, I wanted to follow my mentors and become a professor. By my senior year, my twin objectives drew me to apply to graduate schools in political science.

Another of my mentors, David RePass, had come through the University of Michigan's Survey Research Center, and his enthusiasm about his experience there, along with my awe at the theoretical elegance of *The American Voter*, convinced me to go there for graduate school. Michigan was actually a larger and more impersonal environment for me as a graduate student than Minnesota had been as an undergraduate. But I did find good mentors there, including Jack Walker, Donald Stokes, and John Kingdon, gained enormously from a hugely talented collection of fellow graduate students, and learned a great deal from involvement in Michigan's fabled Survey Research Center and its national election surveys.

After two years of course work, I took my comprehensive exams and applied for a Congressional Fellowship. To my surprise and relief, I won one (as did my fellow U of M graduate student Tom Mann), and in 1969 we both headed for

Capitol Hill. There, I spent one of the most fulfilling years of my life, working in both the House and the Senate. In the House, I worked for Rep. Don Fraser of Minneapolis, who was chairman of a reformist caucus known as the Democratic Study Group (DSG), and was vice chair and later chair of the McGovern/Fraser Commission that rewrote the rules for selection of delegates to Democratic Party nominating conventions. I worked particularly on congressional reform issues; many of the DSG proposals later were implemented in a very significant wave of reform in the early 1970s.

The Congressional Fellowship Program gave me a feel for politics and Congress that no textbook could do.[3] Combined with my academic training and knowledge, the experience inside Congress informed and enhanced my research and analysis. I returned to Ann Arbor in late 1970 to write my Ph.D. dissertation on congressional staffs, based on work I did during my fellowship. Then for 1971–1972, I accepted a job teaching at the Johns Hopkins School of Advanced International Studies in Bologna, Italy, an offer arranged by an undergraduate mentor, Frank Sorauf. After a wonderful year in Bologna, I accepted a tenure track job as an assistant professor at The Catholic University of America in Washington, D.C. Despite the many attractions of Italy, the opportunity to return to Washington was too tempting to refuse.

For many political scientists teaching in Washington, the location was not a major force in their own work. In both teaching and research, they might just as well have been in New York or Des Moines. Not for me. I tried from the beginning to take advantage of Washington, spending time on Capitol Hill with staff and members, developing relationships and contacts with political journalists, and becoming a part of the broader Washington community.

I also began to write occasionally for the *Washington Post*. I started with a review of a book by Congressman Andy Jacobs (D-IN), who wrote an account of his service on a special committee to evaluate the allegations of unethical conduct by Rep. Adam Clayton Powell. The committee's work was ignored by the House, which moved to expel Powell from the House—a result challenged by him all the way to the Supreme Court and ended in the historic decision, *Powell v. McCormack*. I read the book, liked it, dashed off a review and sent it to the *Post*. To my surprise and delight, they accepted it and ran it on the front page of the *Style* section. Soon thereafter, I wrote a piece on House reform efforts, and had that accepted by the Sunday *Outlook* section. I developed relationships with the *Post's* book editor, Bill McPherson and the *Outlook* editor, Al Horne, and was able to write for each of them with some frequency.

Writing 700 to 1,000 word columns for the newspaper required more discipline and focus, by far, than writing articles for journals or chapters for books. To write for a mass audience required clear and understandable language, a meaningful lead, a direct thesis and a related conclusion. It also meant near-instant gratification via quick publication, and over time, some significant increase in my name recognition around town, which in turn meant that my phone calls to lawmakers, policy officials, and journalists were returned more often. Over time, I expanded my occasional writing for non-scholarly publications to include places like the *New York Times, Wall Street Journal, Newsweek, The Atlantic, The New Republic and Foreign Affairs.*

In 1973, I was called by producers at NPACT, the public television operation for public affairs. In the days before cable and C-SPAN, public television was the only place doing serious public affairs coverage, including gavel-to-gavel coverage of such major public events as Watergate hearings. (The networks stepped in for some coverage later on.) They asked if I could come on as an analyst. I did so, was asked back, and began a longtime association with PBS that included regular work with Paul Duke doing analysis of such events as hearings on Nelson Rockefeller's nomination to be vice president, the ethics investigations of figures like Billy Carter and Bert Lance, hearings on Civil Service Reform, various Supreme Court nominations, presidential inaugurations, State of the Union messages, and so forth. I also began a regular association with the McNeil/Lehrer Show in 1976, continuing with it as it moved to an hour as the McNeil/Lehrer NewsHour and then the NewsHour with Jim Lehrer (my involvement has lessened in recent years).

During 1976 to 1977, I took a leave of absence to work in the Senate, on a select committee set up to reorganize the Senate's committee system. I worked with senators like Adlai Stevenson III, Gaylord Nelson, Bill Brock, and Pete Domenici and developed alternative plans for overhauling the system. Each proposed change touched a raw nerve with people in and out of the Senate; careers are built on power centers and jurisdictions, and few things are taken more personally. The year-plus was tough and demanding, but we ended up with some of our recommendations being adopted by the Senate in February 1977, and I finished my tenure as staff director of the committee, along with a deeper sense of how the Senate worked.

During my first five years of teaching at Catholic University, I frequently attended seminars and conferences around town, including many at the two main think tanks, AEI and Brookings, AEI, was newer and smaller than Brookings, and was trying in the early and mid-1970s to establish itself as a serious player in Washington ideas and policy processes. Open, unbureaucratic and entrepreneurial, it focused on lively but scholarly give-and-take, often staging interesting meetings and following up with conference volumes or monographs.

AEI's American politics and public policy area was headed up by one of the country's most distinguished political scientists, Austin Ranney. In mid-1978, Tom Mann and I went to Austin Ranney with an idea. There was no center in Washington, nor any place else, focusing on Congress as an institution and its linkage to policy, tracking change in the institution and relating it to other institutions inside and outside government. We proposed creating such a center at AEI, calling it the Congress Project, and beginning with three initial goals: a book pulling together in one easy source important statistics and trends in Congress from staffing to committees to elections;

a book of essays tracking the important changes that had taken place in Congress during the tumultuous late-1960s and 1970s, and assessing their impact; and a series of dinners with a small group of freshman lawmakers elected in 1978, getting together off-the-record every six months or so to talk about their evolving impressions of Congress.

Ranney and AEI's president, Bill Baroody, agreed to our plan, and in mid-1978, the Congress Project became a reality. We began work on each of our three projects. The first became the book *Vital Statistics on Congress,* which has been published every two years since. The second became the book *The New Congress,* edited by Tom Mann and me. The third resulted in a series of fascinating dinners with seven members of the Class of '78, including Newt Gingrich, Dick Cheney and Geraldine Ferraro, and a book edited by political scientist John Bibby, *Congress Off the Record.*

When we started the Congress Project, Tom Mann was on the staff of the American Political Science Association, and I was an Assistant Professor at CU. Tom began at AEI half time and I began as an adjunct, keeping my teaching job. Gradually, we shifted roles; I moved to half time and Tom to adjunct status as he became Executive Director at APSA. In 1984, I quit teaching at Catholic University and became a full-time resident scholar at AEI. Tom, as his own chapter in this book suggests, ultimately moved to Brookings, but our collaborations have continued and broadened.

My decision to leave teaching and move full time into the think tank world was a natural one, but still quite traumatic. I gave up a tenured full professorship for a more uncertain life, in an institution with no tenure, no contracts, no guarantees, no lavish endowment, and the need to raise a substantial sum of money every year to keep its operations moving along. Soon after I moved, AEI went through a tumultuous period where all of the scholars and fellows found their jobs in jeopardy. Thanks to strong new management, we have moved past any shakiness and are on extraordinarily sound footing. But this is a very different existence than a university life. To me, however, the advantages—including no faculty meetings, no promotion or tenure votes, no university bureaucracy, more intellectual excitement and relevance—vastly outweigh the disadvantages, although I do miss day-to-day contact with students.

There is an underlying theme to my professional life. I believe very strongly in representative, deliberative democracy, which depends on strong and vibrant political institutions. I work to interpret the actions of our institutions for journalists and the public, including providing important context when the institutions are criticized, and to enhance public education about what a representative democracy does. I try to warn against the siren song of direct democracy, which is not democracy at all but which is promoted especially actively in the Internet Age. I am also devoted to maintaining and strengthening our representative institutions like Congress, and to protecting and enhancing a cultural ethos where public service is appreciated and viewed as a positive and desirable option, both for a few years and for a career.

I am very happy with what I do. I have considerable freedom to set my own agenda, a wonderfully interesting group of colleagues, a great staff and terrific collaborators. I have been able to get to know many, even most, of the major political and policy figures in Washington, including presidents and congressional leaders, along with most of the major journalists of our time, and many of the top business leaders. I have tried to define my role as a nonpartisan one, without any strong ideological spin. As a consequence, many lawmakers, journalists, and others see me as an honest broker, and will talk to me openly and candidly. In the process, I am able to learn from the inside about how Washington and our political process work. I recommend what I do highly.

But not every think tank operates as mine does, and not every think tank scholar operates as I do. Many eschew television or writing for newspapers and concentrate more on their scholarly research. Some focus more narrowly on a particular policy area. Some work more directly at shaping policy options, and others aim more broadly at shaping public or elite opinion. These routes can be just as fulfilling and even more effective.

There is no formal slot or set of positions to fill here, and no single path to follow to get here. The good news is that we live in a nation where entrepreneurship now extends to fields like mine, and opportunities are there for people to find their own niches. One key is to begin with a strong educational base; my experiences in college and graduate school, including training in statistics and work on surveys, have been invaluable to me.

Another is to make good and creative use of internships and fellowships. I would not be where I am if it were not for the APSA Congressional Fellowship. There are many other experiences that can serve in comparable ways. Finally, it is vital to develop strong communications skills. Writing for newspapers forced me to abandon jargon and write clearly and colorfully. Doing a lot of public speaking taught me how to use language, humor and eye contact to communicate ideas and connect with people. A third key to success is to seek and find mentors. As this chapter makes clear, at every step along the way in my professional career, I had good mentors, acting as role models and facilitators. Combine these experiences and skills, and you will be able to find a satisfying and fulfilling professional life in an area of public policy research or analysis.

NOTES

1. The distinction AEI makes is that a scholar has come to the institution from a university or academic setting, while a fellow has come from government, business, or another non-academic position. But most of my colleagues, whatever their formal titles or job experiences, have academic backgrounds or a solid grounding in the world of ideas.

2. Our working group included Tom Mann, Michael Malbin, Tony Corrado, and Paul Taylor, with advice from Trevor Potter.

3. I kept up my association with the wonderful Congressional Fellowship Program after my fellowship year. At various times, I served as its director and on its advisory committee, and currently chair the committee.

15

A Foot in Both Camps: Building a Career in Washington and Academe

Thomas E. Mann

Looking back almost forty years on my high schools days, it is possible to detect hints of the unconventional career I was to develop in Washington, D.C. I was active in school politics—elected junior class president and defeated for student council president—and an occasional guest on a local radio news program. My interest in politics was forged at the family dinner table, largely from discussions dominated by my father, who came of age politically during Franklin Roosevelt's New Deal. I recall volunteering in John Kennedy's 1960 presidential campaign and generally keeping abreast of politics and public affairs.

Financial considerations dictated that I put myself through college, which made the University of Florida an attractive choice. (My family had moved in 1957 from Milwaukee to West Palm Beach, where I attended junior high and high school.) I went to Gainesville with an inchoate plan to become a civil engineer, but after only one semester found my way to a more natural home in the political science department. Professors trained in political behavior at Chicago and Michigan whetted my appetite for systematic empirical studies of public opinion, voting behavior, and representation. Nonetheless, like many other political science majors, I intended to go immediately to law school upon graduation. (At that time, with the war in Vietnam intensifying, a hiatus between one's undergraduate degree and graduate or professional school was likely to produce a draft notice.) Only the intervention of two political science professors, who spoke glowingly of the rewards of a life of scholarship, led me to consider graduate school as an alternative. The widespread availability of NDEA and NSF graduate fellowships made that alternative much more feasible than my initial plan. After considering attractive offers from Wisconsin, Northwestern, and Michigan, and following what I considered an extraordinary phone call from Warren Miller to sweeten the financial aid package and make a personal appeal, I set out for Ann Arbor in the fall of 1966, intent on earning my Ph.D. and joining the ranks of academe.

While the University of Michigan was convulsed with social and political turmoil during this period, I found my time and attention almost entirely absorbed with course work and a series of professional apprenticeships. The latter included work on the historical data archive of the Inter-University Consortium for Political and Social Research, research assistance for Donald Stokes on representation in the American Congress and *Political Change in Britain*, and curriculum development and teaching in the summer program in quantitative methods sponsored by the ICPR. These part-time jobs were at least as important as my formal courses, and reinforced my assumption that I would build a career as a political science professor in a research university.

That assumption did not preclude my applying for an APSA Congressional Fellowship, a program designed primarily to enrich the institutional knowledge and experience of students of Congress, thereby improving the quality of research and teaching. I am quite certain that my motivation at the time was to become a better scholar, not to flee the groves of academe, and the impressive scholarly productivity of former Fellows buttresses that recollection. A Michigan graduate student colleague, Norman Ornstein, one year behind me and four years younger, also decided to apply for the program. To our mutual delight, we were both accepted, setting in motion a train of events that was to upset the assumptions both of us had made about our future career paths.

My year in Washington as a Congressional Fellow was an exciting one. Soon after arriving, I recall strolling inadvertently into a cloud of tear gas hovering over Dupont Circle, as the police struggled to contain riots associated with the March on Washington to protest the war in Vietnam. More purposefully, the next day I joined a large contingent of colleagues from around the country in marching behind a banner that somewhat incongruously read: "Political Scientists March for Peace." But my most memorable and lasting experiences were on Capitol Hill. I arranged successive four-month assignments in the offices of Representative James G. O'Hara and Senator Philip A. Hart, both Michigan Democrats. My work for them involved the range of staff activities: legislative research, constituent mail, drafting speeches, newsletters and press releases, and representing the office in meetings with lobbyists, constituents, executive branch officials, and congressional staff. One additional activity stands out: Ornstein (who was working for Rep. Donald Fraser) and I helped prepare and run a campaign seminar for prospective challengers sponsored by the House Democratic Study Group. As part of that effort, we prepared case studies based partly on interviews we conducted with new members about their recent campaigns. We also codified whatever useable knowledge about campaigns and elections that we could find in the political science literature. That experience was for me the first in what would become a lifetime of opportunities to link the worlds of scholarship and public affairs.

While I fully intended to return to Ann Arbor after my year in Washington to write my dissertation, another opportunity intervened. I was offered a staff position at the American Political Science Association, which included directing the Congressional Fellowship Program, conducting studies and building data bases on the profession, and working with a number of association committees to develop new projects on education, scientific communication, research support, and professional development. I was intrigued by the offer and decided to accept, thinking it would delay my return to Ann Arbor by a year or two at most. It was a fateful decision. Without realizing it at the time, I set off on a very different career path than I intended, one that would never include, at least to this point in my life, a full-time academic position.

My years on the association staff were rewarding. I learned how to administer programs, supervise staff, prepare funding proposals, write quickly and clearly, work with an extraordinary range of people in the profession and in the Washington community, and navigate the politics of the association. During this time I developed a strong attachment to and sense of responsibility for the political science profession. I represented the discipline and profession in numerous settings and considered their stewardship a worthy undertaking. I did participate in one modest scholarly research project with two graduate school colleagues during my early years at the association—a study of the Democratic Study Group that was published in 1974 in the *APSR*—but made no attempt to begin, much less complete, my dissertation.

Another professional opportunity stream opened for me in late 1973. Representative O'Hara, who represented Macomb County, an enclave of socially conservative blue collar workers, had barely survived his 1972 reelection contest, dropping a full 25 percentage points from his showing in 1970. George Wallace and George McGovern undoubtedly had much to do with O'Hara's close call, but he began to worry about the changing political complexion of his constituency. Knowing of my training in survey research at the University of Michigan and my work on the DSG campaign seminar while a Congressional Fellow in his office, O'Hara asked me to put together a poll of his district to gauge whether the political storm had passed or if he was likely to encounter continued political difficulties. Given his well-earned reputation for frugality, he was looking for a very low cost—or even better, no cost—poll. I rose to the bait. Given the financial and time constraints under which I was operating, the poll I designed and executed did not meet the high methodological standards of my Michigan mentors. It was a telephone survey and the stratified probability sample I drew was limited to households with listed numbers. I relied on volunteer interviewers, recruited by O'Hara's Michigan staff, who I trained and supervised. I completed the poll during one week in January and shortly thereafter delivered a written report to him.

Hearing of my polling work for O'Hara, Richard Conlon, executive director of the House Democratic Study Group, asked me to help him design and execute a program for providing Democratic challengers and marginal incumbents with an affordable means of gauging public opinion in their districts. By the spring of 1974 we had that program in place. It combined telephone interviewing by volunteers with professional standards in the design, execution, and analysis of the surveys. Initially, that program was little more than me, working evenings and weekends when not otherwise occupied by my full-time job at APSA. For each of the dozen districts in which DSG polls were conducted in 1974, I gathered background information on the race, met with the candidate and campaign staff, designed the questionnaire, drew the sample, arranged for phone banks, produced the necessary materials, trained the interviewers and supervisors, had the pre-coded and edited interviews keypunched, specified the tables to be generated, analyzed and interpreted the data, and prepared a written report for the candidate. It was a fascinating if exhausting experience, one with an extremely steep learning curve for me. In 1976 an additional (and full-time) pollster was recruited and the DSG polling program was expanded to produce eighty-one polls in thirty-four congressional districts.

After the 1976 election I faced an important decision regarding my future career. One option was to move fully into the business of political polling, either by joining an existing firm or by starting my own. Given the proliferation of polling by candidates, parties, media organizations, and interest groups during the intervening years, it now seems likely that such a move would have been financially lucrative. The other option was to take time off to write a dissertation—drawing on the insights and data from my involvement in the DSG polling program—and thereby become a fully credentialed political scientist. My strong identification with the political science profession and the continuing tug of academe led me to opt for the latter. I took leave from the APSA starting in January 1977, completed most of the thesis by early summer when I returned to work, and defended the dissertation in October.

Once again new opportunities presented themselves as a result of the road I had taken. I was invited to participate in a congressional elections research conference that November at the University of Rochester, which gave me an opportunity to link some of my own research findings (e.g., the distinction between name recall and recognition, incumbency as a resource that is exploited more or less successfully, the extent and sources of variability in interelection district swings) with a larger research community. It also launched a longtime association with the National Election Studies, as conference participant, committee member, board member, and eventually chairman of the board of overseers.

About the same time, Austin Ranney and Howard Penniman invited me to revise my dissertation for publication in the election series of the American Enterprise Institute. When *Unsafe At Any Margin: Interpreting Congressional Elections* was published in the summer of 1978, AEI held a press conference, which led to several newspaper columns about the book and its relevance to the upcoming midterm election. One of those columns was read by a booker for the *Today Show*, who saw what she considered a reasonable way to fill some program time on the morning of election day. My interview with Jane Pauley on national television was soon forgotten by everyone except my parents and myself, but it did initiate regular encounters with the press that continue to this day.

The moral of this story is that my decision to write the dissertation some years after completing my graduate course work opened opportunities both in scholarship and public affairs. The two were complementary, even synergistic, not mutually exclusive career alternatives. After the favorable reaction to the book, I joined with Norm Ornstein in late 1978 in proposing to AEI that they establish, under our direction, a Congress Project, designed to use scholarly resources and insights to improve public understanding of Congress. We collaborated on *The New Congress* and the biennial series *Vital Statistics on Congress*, as well as on many other writing projects and public events. In the two decades that followed, Ornstein and I worked together on a wide range of projects and publications, including the Renewing Congress Project in the early 1990s and the Transition to Governing Project that is presently underway.

Another critical career choice confronted me in 1980, when the search for Evron Kirkpatrick's successor as APSA executive director was launched. Having worked on the staff under Kirk for many years, it was natural that I be considered a candidate. My position was strengthened by my more recent emergence as a member of the scholarly community. Yet the APSA position would return me to a full-time administrative post, one that would limit my opportunities for research and writing. Nonetheless, having a strong sense of what needed to be done at the association and viewing the executive directorship as the capstone to my decade of service on the staff, I applied for the job and happily accepted when it was offered to me.

My six years as APSA executive director were personally rewarding and, I believe, productive for the association. My primary focus was managing the association and advancing the interests of the political science profession. Highlights for me include developing the Consortium of Social Science Associations as an effective advocate for social science research funding, starting organized sections, expanding the annual meeting, upgrading the investment strategy for endowed funds, increasing our efforts to improve civic education (largely through projects conceived and executed by Sheilah Mann) and recruiting and working with a strong staff. During this period I retained an affiliation with the AEI Congress Project and managed a modest amount of writing and speaking. I also did some survey research consulting on television captioning for the deaf for the Public Broadcasting System. But I eagerly anticipated my first sabbatical leave, due the seventh year of my appointment as executive director. I arranged a fellowship at the Center for Advanced Study in the Behavioral Sciences for the 1987–88 academic year and began to plan the complicated logistics involved in moving to the West Coast.

Once again, another opportunity presented itself that was to redirect my career path. Bruce MacLaury, the president of the Brookings Institution, asked me to come to Brookings in the summer or early fall of 1987 at the latest as director of the Governmental Studies Program. I initially demurred, largely on the grounds that it would make impossible my planned sabbatical at the center. But the prospect of running a research program at one of the country's premier think tanks, and of devoting a substantial chunk of my day job to research and public education, proved too tempting to resist. After negotiating an understanding with MacLaury that Brookings would provide a comparable sabbatical after three years in my new position (although I didn't take that leave until my eleventh year), I accepted the offer and made plans for a major career shift at age forty-three.

My dozen years as director of Governmental Studies at Brookings was the most stimulating and rewarding period of my professional life. In my final report as director to the Brookings Board of Trustees, I summarized my approach as follows:

From the outset, our strategy has been geared toward providing high quality, timely, and accessible work on important questions of governance. We realize that recruiting and retaining a stable of resident scholars capable of producing first-rate books is essential. But if we are to speak effectively to policy makers and the public as well as to the academic community, we need to diversify our portfolio with short-term projects, nonresident and visiting scholars, and alternative outlets for our findings and recommendations. The challenge is to adjust our research agenda to anticipate the most critical issues, to identify talented individuals who can perform that research with our exacting standards of scholarly excellence, and to package and promote the results in ways that are likely to attract the audiences we seek, all the while persuading potential funders of the importance and impact of our work.

Governmental Studies has responded well to that challenge over the past decade. While impact is always difficult to measure, especially on complex institutions and policies, I believe we have influenced the public debate on critical issues and facilitated solutions to problems. Our resident scholars and nonresident affiliates have written important and influential books, monographs, reports, policy briefs and Op-Eds; garnered substantial visibility through print and broadcast media; offered useable knowledge and recommendations in congressional testimony and meetings with policymakers; and utilized the convening power of Brookings to stimulate discussion among key participants on important questions of policy and governance. And increasingly we have attracted the financial support of foundations that value the focus, quality, visibility, and impact of our work.

My position at Brookings brought together the several streams of professional activity that had engaged me earlier in my career: administration, research and writing, public speaking, press commentary, and regular communication with politicians and policy makers. It allowed me to work in Washington at the intersection of scholarship and public affairs. That means trying to use conceptual frameworks and insights from the discipline to inform public understanding of politics and public policy making—that is, to market political science in the world of public affairs.

It also entails using experiences in the world of politics and policy to shape my own research and that of the broader scholarly community. I am a part of both worlds but not fully a member of either. I often vigorously defend political scientists and politicians but am not reluctant to criticize them either. I derive as much satisfaction speaking to politicians, journalists, business executives, and citizens as I do garnering favorable reviews or citations from my academic colleagues.

Like my longtime friend and collaborator, Norm Ornstein, I have built an unconventional career—a political scientist in Washington. Now that I have set aside my administrative duties at age fifty-five and taken up full-time senior fellow status at Brookings, I expect that double life to continue. Opportunities presented and decisions made over almost four decades make it very likely that I will continue to derive substantial satisfaction from keeping a foot in both camps.

16

The CIA, Defense Department, and Hard Choices

Melvin A. Goodman

I have been a part of the Washington political system for the past thirty-five years, specializing in the analysis of the foreign and national security policies of the former Soviet Union and the Russian Federation. This period includes nearly twenty years as a political analyst at the Central Intelligence Agency and fifteen years as a faculty member at the National War College. During the past several years, I also have been a senior fellow at the Center for International Policy in Washington, D.C. I have served as an intelligence advisor to the Strategic Arms Limitation Talks, as a political officer in the American Embassy in Moscow, and as a visiting or adjunct professor at American University, Johns Hopkins University, the University of Connecticut, and the University of Virginia. I have lectured throughout the United States as well as in Europe and Japan and have testified before many congressional committees. Most of my professional life has been in the intelligence/defense community.

I consider myself fortunate to have held positions in Washington that are close to the policy process; this has provided a wonderful vantage point for observing the political system in the nation's capital. I have witnessed one of the great turning points for American national security, as the uncertainties of the cold war era have turned into the uncertainties of the post–cold war era. The Berlin Wall collapsed, a series of mostly non-violent anti-communist revolutions swept Eastern Europe, Germany was reunified, and the Soviet Union collapsed. I have been able to observe and write about events that members of my generation never even expected to see.

My focus in graduate school had little to do with the Washington political arena. With the help of a Woodrow Wilson Fellowship and a Woodrow Wilson Dissertation Fellowship, I attended the Russian and East European Institute of Indiana University to prepare for a teaching career at the college level. The history and political science faculties at Johns Hopkins University and Indiana University gave me wonderful exposure to the best undergraduate and graduate school teaching; they also offered stimulating environments in which to discuss and debate international relations. But, in 1965, when the choice came down to a teaching position at a small school in the nation's hinterland as opposed to a government position in Washington, I headed for the nation's capital.

My initial interviews were with the Central Intelligence Agency (CIA), the Department of State, and the National Security Agency (NSA); the selection process was easy. The security environment of the NSA was downright oppressive, with security mobiles hanging from ceilings and political posters ("Loose lips sink ships!") facing visitors in every corridor. The foreign service examination of the State Department was rigorous and exciting, but the personnel board of senior foreign service officers displayed no interest in my graduate school training, let alone my doctoral dissertation, and were not prepared to give me an entry waiver in order to complete my research.

I was probably more than somewhat naïve because the CIA struck me as the largest research institution that I had ever encountered in the field of international relations. It contained a wonderful library in my fields of interest, an opportunity for additional language training, and access to the most sensitive secrets of the U.S. government. The directors of the CIA's Office of Current Intelligence were interested in my dissertation on the American diplomatic recognition of the Soviet Union in 1933. More importantly, they offered a one-year waiver to enable me to complete my research at the National Archives, the Library of Congress, and the Roosevelt Library at Hyde Park, New York. Only later did I learn that the security investigation, including an oppressive polygraph test, would take most of that year. The CIA's involvement in the overthrow of the government in Iran in 1953, Guatemala in 1954, and the attempted overthrow of Cuba's Fidel Castro in 1961 were far from my mind.

Actually, the greatest challenge I faced was the negative reaction of my classmates at Indiana University, mostly liberal critics of the war in Vietnam. Some friendships were lost at this point, but this turned out to be good preparation. More friendships were lost in 1991, when I testified before the Senate Select Committee on Intelligence against the nomination of Robert M. Gates, another Indiana alumnus, to be director of the CIA. But I am getting ahead of my story.

My experience as a political analyst at the CIA for the first fifteen years could not have been more rewarding. CIA's Office of Current Intelligence was responsible for tracking political and military confrontations, and it exploited sensitive intelligence to do so. As a specialist on Soviet policy in the Middle East, I had an opportunity to analyze the Six-Day war in 1967, the war of attrition from 1969–1970, the October war in 1973, and the Israeli invasion of Lebanon in 1982. The October war included the largest tank battle since the Second World War, history's first military crossing of the Suez Canal, and the unprovoked U.S. nuclear alert against the Soviet Union at war's end. Israel's invasion of Lebanon has been a controversial issue in Israeli politics for nearly two decades, and the deaths of more than two-hundred U.S. Marines in Lebanon, who were part of a U.S. intervention force, created a great deal of controversy in the United States as well.

Many positions within the intelligence community provide an excellent vantage point for observing and analyzing remarkable events. The October war not only turned out to be a major turning point in Arab–Israeli relations, but Egyptian President Anwar Sadat's strategic surprise totally fooled the analytical community of the CIA and Israel's intelligence organization, Mossad. The October war was Israel's Pearl Harbor, prompting many changes in Israel's political culture. For the CIA, the war challenged assumptions and conventional wisdom and forced an examination of the reasons for intelligence failure. The rational process of intelligence analysis is not well equipped to deal with such seemingly irrational acts as the joint Egyptian–Syrian military invasion of Israel, which had a far superior fighting force.

Although the CIA is not part of the policy process, the agency provides intelligence that can prove embarrassing to high-level policy makers. Our assessment of Israel's preemptive attack that started the six-day war did not go down well with President Lyndon B. Johnson's national security advisor, Walt Rostow, who believed he had assurances from the Israeli ambassador that Israel would not attack first. Rostow refused to accept the CIA's first intelligence briefings, which blamed Israel for starting the war. But CIA director Richard Helms supported his analysts, and there was no slanting of intelligence to satisfy a high-level consumer of intelligence in the White House. Ten years later, there was a different director of CIA and different handling of sensitive intelligence.

There were many exciting debates in the CIA over how far the Soviets would go in support of their Arab clients in the war of attrition, and this is one time when the analysts got it right over the objections of the policy community. Although the CIA failed to anticipate the start of the October war, the agency provided excellent information during the war, including early warning of Moscow's decision to deploy combat air and surface-to-air missile crews in Egypt. But the CIA failed to corroborate the rationale for the Nixon administration's call for a nuclear alert (Defense Condition III) at war's end, and DEFCON III remains one of the major puzzles of the war. Finally, the Israeli invasion of Lebanon provided an example of an irrational Israeli attack against an Arab capital—Beirut—and another example of a seemingly irrational use of military force that was not anticipated by a rational intelligence process. All of these events had important policy consequences, and intelligence officers had the freedom to debate both the issues themselves and the impact of their assessments on policy makers. The internal debates may have been academic and without consequence for policy decisions, but they certainly were exhilarating and particularly rewarding to a professional intelligence officer.

Students who are considering a career in any large organization should be aware that such large organizations tend to reward generalists who are willing to take assignments that create well-rounded staffers who can fill many niches, including those of senior management. On the other hand, expertise in a discrete area, such as political analysis of Soviet or Russian foreign policy, is often considered over-specialization and will not necessarily lead to high-level positions. I was not drawn to the former route, turning down opportunities to serve abroad in an intelligence liaison capacity, to become a staff assistant to the deputy director for intelligence, or to take a tour as a watch officer in the CIA's twenty-four hour operations center. Instead, I took sabbaticals (teaching at the University of Connecticut), professional rotations (working for the Department of State's Bureau of Intelligence and Research), and special missions related to Soviet affairs. These special missions included assignments as an intelligence adviser to the SALT delegation in Vienna, Austria and briefings to the North Atlantic Council (the decisionmaking body of NATO) during the war in Afghanistan. Every one of these assignments enhanced my specialization in the field of Soviet affairs, but they did not lead immediately to management positions or high-level staff jobs. I have never regretted the choices and, by the time I left the agency, I had the opportunity to establish and direct the CIA's first analytical group examining Soviet policy in the Third World.

The headiest experience of all was my assignment to Vienna in 1971 as intelligence advisor to the U.S. delegation at the Strategic Arms Limitation Talks (SALT). The assignment gave me the opportunity to discuss policy and intelligence issues on a regular basis with such American policy makers as Harold Brown, Raymond Garthoff, Paul Nitze, and Gerard Smith, and to discuss arms control issues with Soviet counterparts during the first year of America's rapprochement with China. Moscow clearly understood that the U.S. initiative toward China was essentially an anti-Soviet move that the Soviets fortunately countered with efforts to improve their own relations with the United States. One of the rewards of the so-called strategic triangle between Washington, Moscow, and Beijing was the improved environment at the SALT talks, with the round in Vienna providing the breakthrough for the SALT I treaty and the Anti-Ballistic Missile treaty the following year. It would be difficult to describe the excitement of preparing background papers for the U.S. SALT delegation and then engaging Soviet arms control experts in plenary meetings at the talks for limiting strategic weapons. The experience validated the importance of intelligence to the policy process and provided a front-row seat to the interagency process.

My specialty in Soviet Third World relations, moreover, provided the opportunity to travel to every corner of the globe, giving briefings at U.S. embassies and meeting foreign experts on Soviet foreign policy. I happened to be in India in 1974, when that nation exploded its first nuclear device. I was visiting embassies in the

Middle East only several weeks before Egyptian president Anwar Sadat announced his summit visit to Israel in 1977. And I was traveling in Central and South America in 1982, when Soviet president Leonid Brezhnev died. All of these trips provided firsthand impressions of indigenous attitudes toward key events.

The turning point in my career as an intelligence officer took place in the early 1980s when, for the first time, a president (Ronald Reagan) decided to reward a political crony (William Casey) with the position of director of central intelligence and director of the CIA. Casey clearly had a political agenda that included greater resort to high-risk covert action, an anti-Soviet agenda that eventually corrupted the analysis of Soviet policy, and a system of rewards that benefited intelligence officers who catered to the Casey political agenda. The misuse of covert action led to the excesses of Iran-Contra, and the politicization of intelligence led to the failure to anticipate the weakness and eventual collapse of the Soviet Union. Casey's deputy in all of these matters was Robert Gates, who rapidly climbed the bureaucratic ladder to become deputy director for intelligence, director of the National Intelligence Council and, in 1986, deputy director of the CIA. When Casey died suddenly in 1987, President Reagan nominated Gates to be the director of the agency, but influential members of the Senate intelligence committee made it clear that that they did not believe Gates' claims of non-involvement in Iran-Contra. As a result, Gates withdrew his name from the confirmation process.

The political agenda of Casey and Gates led to more career choices. For fifteen years, I had served as a political analyst at the CIA where analytical conclusions were debated and not dictated. I could justify my position at a controversial agency such as the CIA because intelligence analysis was based on rigorous research and scholarly writing, offering policy makers intelligence on the former Soviet Union with no concern for a political agenda. When I wrote on the October war (1973), I did not have to justify the fact that the Nixon Administration had called for a higher strategic alert during the last stages of the war, although there were no intelligence materials that justified Defense Condition III. When I wrote on the Middle East, I could call attention to the weakness of the Soviet position in Egypt and Syria, although U.S. policy emphasized a Soviet threat that would justify the Nixon Administration's efforts to "expel" Moscow from the region.

The Casey era brought radical change to the CIA and, for the first time, I encountered the tensions between a politicized intelligence agenda and the scholarly independence of an intelligence analyst. As an analyst, I had to choose between a path devoted to scholarship, autonomy, and the often illusive search for truth as opposed to a path of support for an agenda that met the policy goals of Bill Casey and Bob Gates. There were legitimate differences within the intelligence community over Soviet support for international terrorism, Soviet machinations in the Third World, the possibility of a Soviet role in the attempted assassination of Pope John Paul II, the strength of the Soviet military and the Soviet economy, and the Soviet challenge to the interests of the United States. But the Casey–Gates agenda demanded a Soviet Union that was "ten-feet tall," opposed to disarmament, and threatening in such regions as the Middle East and Central America. The intelligence data pointed to a Soviet Union that was becoming increasingly vulnerable in the economic and military areas, was beginning to retreat from the Third World, and had an intense interest in disarmament. The pressures from CIA's leaders, however, allowed decreasing room for differences within the system. It was time for this analyst to move on. Ironically, my unpublished memoranda in the agency provided substantive grist for my first published book on Soviet policy, *Gorbachev's Retreat from the Third World* (Penn State Press, 1990).

By 1986, I already had left the agency twice to recharge my batteries and examine the possibilities for a more permanent career shift, so it was not terribly difficult to consider severing my ties to the CIA. From 1972–1973, I was visiting professor of government at the University of Connecticut. This was a period of heavy student dissent against U.S. involvement in Vietnam, and many professors in the department were strongly opposed to the idea of a CIA analyst holding down a teaching position, even for a year. Fortunately the chairman of the department, Professor Louis Gerson, was a genuine advocate of academic freedom and believed that a different perspective for one year would not be a threat to the academy. The teaching was thoroughly enjoyable, but I missed the immediacy of political analysis in Washington, so I returned at the end of the year. (In 2000, I gave the tenth annual Louis Gerson Foreign Policy Lecture at the University of Connecticut, which is designed to promote careers in Washington that span both policy making and scholarly pursuits in the field of international relations.)

My next assignment out of the agency lasted from 1974–1976, when I crossed the Potomac River to become an analyst with the State Department's Bureau of Intelligence and Research. The job was similar to that of a CIA analyst, requiring memoranda and briefings on Soviet foreign policy. This time, however, the audience was the senior policy making establishment of the State Department and, unlike the CIA, there were ample opportunities for feedback from policy makers and their staffs. The difficulty of generating feedback at the CIA reflected one of the serious weaknesses of the intelligence community in general. With a little energy and imagination, however, it was possible to decipher the issues that were uppermost on the minds of policy makers and gain access to the memoranda of conversations between State Department officials and their foreign counterparts, which were essential to the craft of intelligence analysis.

The State Department afforded other opportunities that the CIA could not provide. During the cold war, the CIA had nearly two hundred political, military, and economic analysts working on cold war issues; INR had less than half that number working on all global issues, with no more than fifteen specialists dealing with Soviet problems. As a result, CIA analysts worked on narrow problems and issues and rarely got an opportunity to look at the big strategic picture; INR specialists had a much bigger piece of the Soviet mosaic to analyze. INR also had the advantage of trying to understand issues in a way that would be important to policy makers and senior foreign service officers. CIA, on the other hand, did not have an obvious constituency in its own building and tried to serve too many masters in the Pentagon, the National Security Council, the State Department, various smaller agencies throughout Washington, and even a foreign policy constituency on Capitol Hill. This often led to analysis that was unfocused and not sufficiently relevant.

At the end of my two-year tour at INR, I was offered the option of taking a full-time position and thus leaving the CIA. This was a difficult decision to make at that time, and one that I have thought about many times. On many levels, INR was the better place to work. As previously noted, INR analysts had a bigger slice of the Soviet pie and therefore were usually better informed than their CIA counterparts. In fact, the small numbers of INR analysts had a great deal of substantive depth and could easily have staffed the history and political science departments of any liberal arts college. And there was access to policy makers, including the seventh floor of the State Department building, which houses the decision-making community of the department, including the office of the Secretary of State. Finally, unlike the CIA, the State Department provided a more benign mailing address.

The two-year tour at State offered me the opportunity to spend a summer at the U.S. Embassy in Moscow as a temporary replacement for a political officer, who happened to be responsible for Soviet policy toward all the countries of Asia, including South Asia and East Asia. With the use of his rolodex, I could call my counterparts at various Soviet ministries, including the foreign ministry, and such Soviet academies as the Institute for the Study of the USA, and schedule appointments with regional specialists. My access to Soviet policy makers was extremely unusual for an intelligence analyst from the CIA, which made me thankful for all of the wonderful language teachers at the Russian and East European Institute at Indiana University. Moreover, the Soviet experience led to substantive exchanges with many IU classmates, including the eventual U.S. ambassador to Russia, the consul general in Leningrad, the former ambassador to Azerbaijan, and even the CIA's director of operations for the Soviet Union.

When I was not in Moscow working at the embassy, I was free to travel around the Soviet Union; during my brief tour, I visited six of the fifteen Soviet republics. During these visits in 1976, I could already see Moscow's incredible economic weakness, the burden it faced in trying to manage the mounting costs of backward economies in the Baltics, the Caucasus, and particularly Central Asia, let alone the burden of the Eastern European economies and some of the most backward economies of the Third World. The CIA's failure to understand the impact of the military burden on the economy contributed to its overall failure to understand the weakness of the Soviet Union and to anticipate its ultimate demise. In actual fact, academic economists and such think tanks as the RAND Corporation did no better in understanding the significant burden of the internal and external empire, but the CIA had more resources and personnel to throw at this problem than any other institution.

The access to policy makers and the opportunity for travel in the Soviet Union were excellent, but if you are not a regular or career foreign service officer in the State Department there is no question that you are a second-class citizen. The department is dedicated to its Foreign Service Officers; they get the best assignments and the fastest promotions. INR, on the other hand, is made up, for the most part, of civil servants and there are fewer opportunities for training and education. It is extremely rare, for example, for a civil servant at the State Department to get a competitive position at the National War College as either a student or a member of the faculty. The State Department bureaucracy is extremely sclerotic and slow-moving; finally, INR is smaller than its CIA counterpart but not necessarily more collegial.

Exactly ten years after returning to the CIA from the State Department, however, I decided to leave the agency because of the politicization of intelligence, turning a temporary assignment at the National War College into a permanent change of career. The original decision to join the agency in the mid-1960s forced me to examine the trade-off between an academic career with total academic freedom and a government position as an intelligence analyst that involved the scholarly pursuit of truth but did not offer total autonomy. Let's face it, no analyst's assessments will always carry the day. I was involved with projects that required negotiations and compromises to reach final conclusions. For the most part, the tensions in this process were healthy ones, and I have rarely had policy and intelligence debates anywhere in Washington that equaled the rigor and intensity of the debates at CIA.

The arrival of Bill Casey as the director of central intelligence and the appointment of Bob Gates as his deputy director for intelligence introduced unhealthy tensions to the system. For the first time, the issue of politicization of intelligence from within the agency became a systemic problem. Previously, there had been external pressures to slant analytical estimates and repress evidence that challenged a particular point of view. In the 1980s, however, there was an institutionalized effort, directed from within the CIA, to slant the intelligence product and support the policy views of Casey and Gates.

So, by 1986, it was time to move on. The fact that I now had twenty years of experience and a doctoral degree from a good graduate school meant that I had more options than most. It was difficult to leave many good colleagues and friends, but the alternative would be to remain and become increasingly cynical about my own work and the legitimate mission of the CIA.

The window of opportunity turned out to be a rotational assignment, occupying one of the two faculty chairs that the CIA maintains at the National War College. One of the positions traditionally was occupied by an analyst from the directorate of intelligence, usually a regional affairs expert who could teach in the core curriculum of the college, direct elective seminars in a particular area of expertise, and lead student trips to key countries. The other position belonged to the directorate of operations, usually a CIA operations officer who had served overseas, had run agents or assets in a foreign country, and had enough experience with covert action to teach an elective on the subject. When I was named to the college faculty in 1986, I joined an operations officer who had actually directed the mining of the harbors in Corinto, Nicaragua. With his training in amphibious warfare and my background in Soviet studies, we formed an odd bureaucratic team. In the summer of 1987, we spent a great deal of time together watching the Iran-Contra hearings, agreeing that if he had not been on the faculty of the War College, I probably would have been watching him testify to the Senate's investigatory committee.

The National War College was officially established in 1946 to give military officers and State Department Foreign Service Officers an opportunity to study grand strategy in times of peace and war in order to prepare for high-level policy, command, and staff responsibilities. Faculty and students are drawn from all of the Armed Services and from civilian agencies and departments concerned with national security policy. The program emphasizes "jointness" in military planning and operations and the interrelationship of domestic, foreign, and defense policies.

The core curriculum is compulsory for all students, consisting of the fundamentals of statecraft, military thought and strategy, the national security policy process, the geostrategic environment, and military strategy and operations. Each semester, in addition to the core curriculum, students take two or three elective seminars, which cover a variety of subjects on military strategy and history, defense policy, international politics and economics, and domestic political institutions and processes. For faculty members, the college combines the best of many worlds: high salaries for teaching positions, a climate of academic freedom in research as well as academic debate in the classroom, and students who represent the best and brightest of their services, agencies, and departments. I spent my first four years at the college on rotation from the CIA; I then converted to a faculty member on the college's staff in 1990, when the congress appropriated sufficient funds to create ten new faculty positions. The decision to leave the CIA and join the faculty of the National War College was an easy one.

Within a year, I faced a major test of my comfortable status at the National War College and my uncomfortable memories of the Casey–Gates era at the CIA. In the spring of 1991, President George Bush nominated Robert Gates to be the director of central intelligence. Gates had been nominated previously in 1987 by President Reagan, but withdrew his nomination when too many members of the Senate Select Committee on Intelligence, particularly Senators Bill Bradley, Howard Metzenbaum, and Arlen Spector, did not believe his claims of having no knowledge of the Iran-Contra operation. Four years later, Bradley and Metzenbaum still opposed the nomination of Gates but the new members of the committee, particularly Senator Warren

Rudman, wanted to put Iran-Contra behind them. No Republican member of the committee challenged the nomination, as President Bush made the vote a test of loyalty to the president. Senator David Boren, the chairman of the Senate Select Committee on Intelligence, supported the White House this time around, and the nomination was clearly Gates' to lose.

The committee hearings began in unspectacular fashion, although the Democrats on the committee were clearly divided over the nomination of Gates. Bradley and Metzenbaum led the opposition and eventually gained support from Senators Earnest Hollings and Dennis DeConcini. Other Democrats on the committee, particularly Senators Sam Nunn, John Glenn, and Allan Cranston were opposed to Gates but had not declared their voting choice. There was enough controversy to prevent a final committee vote in the spring and, after a summer break, the remaining days of the hearings and the final vote were scheduled for early fall.

Late in the summer, I received a call from the director of the majority staff of the committee, George Tenet, who worked directly for Senator Boren. Tenet informed me that the committee had become aware of my knowledge of the politicization of intelligence at the CIA under the deputy director of intelligence, Bob Gates, and invited me to brief the staff members of the committee on my knowledge. I was invited back for two additional visits and eventually spent more than eight hours with various staffers from both parties, including several who subsequently were given high-ranking positions at the CIA. My information was considered compelling and, in September, I was subpoenaed to address the full committee on the issue of Gates' suitability as director of central intelligence.

There was no hesitancy on my part about testifying in closed session before the full committee. Even if I had been hesitant, the arrival of the subpoena afforded no chance for a demurrer on my part. There were pressures associated with the testimony, however, particularly from the commandant of the National War College, who unwisely offered to place the Pentagon's legal staff at my disposal so that I could "get out" of testifying. He was relatively new to the college and was fearful of the fact that a member of his faculty had thrown himself in front of the nomination of the commander-in-chief, President Bush. The commandant failed to understand that even the suggestion of getting me off the hook, once subpoenaed, was illegal. He also failed to understand the importance of academic freedom for his faculty. On balance, the college was very supportive, even presenting me tapes of the televised testimony, and many even seemed proud that one of their own was taking a stand on principle. I am convinced that I suffered no negative consequences from the testimony, and a retired general from the National Defense University offered his support if I suspected the least sign of pressure. Other than the commandant's original intervention, there was none.

Like any opportunity in the field of regional studies and international relations, the faculty position at the National War College provided me with opportunities to lecture and to publish. Just as the CIA offered me the opportunity to serve as an intelligence advisor to the strategic arms control delegation and the State Department offered me the opportunity to go to the U.S. embassy in Moscow as a political officer, the college opened doors to the academic and think tank communities.

I have lectured to universities, think tanks, and World Affairs Councils throughout the United States. As the most senior-level military educational institution in the United States, the college attracts political and military luminaries from all over the world to lecture and exchange views. I have also become a senior fellow at the Center for International Policy in Washington, D.C. and at the Institute for International Affairs in Moscow, Russia. Senior fellow positions, particularly my own at the Center for International Policy, allow analysts and specialists to take their political views to the policy level by lobbying congressional representatives on Capitol Hill or drafting political legislation for congressional committees. It is an excellent facet of Washington's political system, and one that offers a great deal of personal satisfaction.

On balance, there is nothing like a plan that comes together at the end. If there was a pattern, then it was serendipitous. If there was a design, then it was impressionistic. I went into the U.S. Army after high school and began courses at a campus of the University of Maryland in Europe. The courses were in Russian studies, which led to degrees from Johns Hopkins University (B.A.) and Indiana University (M.A. and Ph.D.). The academic work led to career choices between government service and teaching and, eventually, I found a way to do both. A twenty-year career with the CIA and the State Department led to a teaching career, now in its fifteenth year, with the National War College, with adjunct professor stints at American University and my alma mater, Johns Hopkins University. There also have been lecturing stints on behalf of the United States Institute for Peace and various chapters of the World Affairs Council.

In addition to lecturing and testifying, there has been sufficient time to write and publish on such issues as Russian national security, American foreign policy, and the U.S. intelligence community. During the past ten years, I have authored and edited five books on Soviet and Russian policy, including a political biography of former Soviet foreign minister Eduard Shevardnadze, which I co-authored with my wife, Carolyn Ekedahl. I particularly benefited from a sabbatical from the National War College, which allowed me time for research and writing of *The Wars of Eduard Shevardnadze* and interviewing such key officials as former secretaries of state George Shultz and James Baker and President Shevardnadze. My next book, *Lessons Learned from the Cold War*, will examine newly released archival materials from the United States and Russia.

I have contributed numerous chapters to the books of others, most recently *National Insecurity: U.S. Intelligence After the Cold War*, which is being distributed by the Center for International Policy, and "The Phantom Defense," which will be published by Praeger. I have written dozens of articles and Op-Ed pieces for the *New York Times*, *Washington Post*, and *Christian Science Monitor*, and book reviews for such magazines and journals as *Harper's Magazine*, *Bulletin for Atomic Scientists*, and *Washington Monthly*. Computer technology has made me far more productive than I otherwise would have been.

More importantly, I have had wonderful mentors such as Professor Robert H. Ferrell of Indiana University, the late Robert Slusser of Johns Hopkins University, and Ambassador Robert White of the Center for International Policy to provide guidance and counsel. All in all, the most beautiful aspect of this meandering career on the periphery of international relations has been the wonderful people who have guided and tutored me. I cannot think of another profession that offers such collegiality as this one. Students should understand that they can have rewarding and challenging careers in the field of political science, write and do research, and at the same time see one's work have an impact on the political process.

17

Born in a Newsroom:
A Political Scientist on CNN

William Schneider

I was born in a newsroom. Or very nearly so. My mother likes to tell the story of how she broke water in the newsroom of the *Portsmouth Star*, where she was a reporter. A pregnant woman working in those days? Well, it was wartime, and help was hard to get. But she still had to enter the newspaper office through the back door to avoid scandal and embarrassment.

I hasten to add that I remember very little about any of this. But my mother swears I came out yelling, "Extra!"

That must explain the thrill I felt when I first set foot in the newsroom of the *Los Angeles Times* many years later and had the sense of recovering a deep-seated memory. This, I knew instantly, was where I belonged. Which was something I had never truly felt in a library or a computer lab.

I did, however, feel a sense of belonging in the classroom, which is why I got my Ph.D. and embarked on an academic career. I liked teaching for the same reason I like journalism. They're both about communicating, and that is something I believe I have a talent for.

In fact, I know I do. Because the compliment I receive most often, and value most highly, is that I make things clear. Example: Just after the 2000 party conventions, I received an e-mail from a sociologist I do not know, telling me, "I have never known an academic with your ability to speak to a wider audience with such crystal clear clarity." A wonderful compliment! That was my objective as a teacher, and that is my job now as a television political analyst.

That's also the reason why I didn't care for academic research. Academia was about being deep and knowledgeable and profound and complex. But it was rarely about being clear. In the academic world, my zeal for clarity was typically discouraged. I was accused of oversimplifying. And worse, of being a journalist. So that, in a circuitous way, is exactly what I became.

I began writing for newspapers and magazines in the 1970s, while I was still teaching. I.A. ("Bud") Lewis, director of the NBC News election unit and one of the originators of exit polling, gave me access to his data archives. During the 1976 presidential primaries, several newspapers subscribed to the NBC News exit poll in order to report the results the next morning. Since Lewis had no time to brief reporters on the findings, he asked me if I could come to New Hampshire to work with subscribing newspapers on primary night.

My assignment was to explain the New Hampshire exit poll results. It was quite a kick for a young researcher to be right there in the studio on primary night, interpreting data and analyzing the outcome to an audience of seasoned political reporters. I also got the opportunity to meet the future president, Jimmy Carter, who came to the studio that night to claim victory.

I must have been pretty good at it, because I was immediately engaged by the *Los Angeles Times* to work with that newspaper exclusively on subsequent primary nights. Shortly thereafter, the editor of the *Times* Sunday Opinion section asked me if I might be interested in writing for the paper as well. It was then I discovered that my communication skills could reach a wider audience outside the classroom. I began to write regularly for the *L.A. Times* and continue to do so now, twenty-five years later.

I came to Washington in 1979 on a fellowship from the Council on Foreign Relations and began a long and happy association with the American Enterprise Institute. With a lot of help from my friends, I discovered that I could get by—and very nicely, too—outside the university as a writer and consultant. What I was doing was more exciting and fulfilling than academic research, though I continued to miss teaching.

My first love was always politics, not just because of my family background, but also because of geography and generation. I grew up in the segregated South, where I witnessed the civil rights revolution firsthand—a historic social transformation, breathtaking in its scope and, to anyone who grew up in that place and in those times, unimaginable. I was in college and graduate school during the convulsions of the 1960s, and that imprinted even more firmly the centrality of politics in my life. In effect, I got into political science because I loved politics, and I got out of political science because I loved politics. I needed to be part of the events of my time.

Going from academia to journalism may sound like a straightforward transition. After all, it's the same subject—politics. And aren't many of the same skills involved? Actually, no. Different skills are essential to success as a journalist: reporting, communicating, and working on deadline. Training in academic research doesn't particularly prepare you for them.

Reporting is related to research, in the sense that one has to dig for information, but it involves a different kind of temperament—more aggressive than painstaking. Moreover, reporting involves something academics do far too little of, namely, going out and talking to people. I got my first major reporting assignment in 1987, when I was commissioned to do a series of cover stories for the *Atlantic Monthly*. My assignment: to write a "think piece" on the Reagan Revolution and then go out and interview all the major presidential candidates for the 1988 election.

Traveling with campaigns and interviewing political figures was a whole new experience for me, and I had to learn new skills. Not the least of which was the art of listening, so you could figure out what the candidate was telling you and what he was not telling you. My job was not simply to get information, but to probe for ideas and assumptions—to capture each candidate's style of thinking and world view.

I became something of a Great Mentioner as a result of that assignment. An obscure southern governor named Bill Clinton found out that I was writing a piece on the Democratic contenders. He called and asked if we could meet for breakfast. It was pretty clear to me that Clinton was unlikely to run in 1988, but it was also clear that he was a man of enormous ambition who wanted to be mentioned. So I did.

That experience also taught me some of the perils of journalism. I went to Albany to interview Gov. Mario M. Cuomo—always an unnerving experience because you couldn't be sure if you were interviewing him or he was interviewing you. I wrote three thousand words about this fascinating figure, only to see Cuomo pull out of the race the night before the magazine went to press. I had to revise the piece, feverishly, in one night and reassess the field without Cuomo.

Becoming a journalist also involved learning a whole new set of communication skills: writing on deadline, learning to write a lead, using interviews as evidence, feeling confident enough to go with what you know, and expressing your ideas in a clear, concise manner.

The sound bite, you discover, is no small intellectual challenge. It involves taking a complex idea and distilling it to its essence, which is what most of your readers or viewers are interested in. I get real intellectual fulfillment from being able to look at a complicated issue or situation and say, "What's really going on here is this." A good sound bite doesn't cheapen discourse. It communicates.

If you're a weekly columnist, as I have been for *National Journal* for thirteen years, you learn very quickly that anything you have to say can be said in 750 words. It had better be, because your editor will reduce it to that length. And on television, you learn very quickly that you'd better be able to make your point in thirty seconds or less. Because your producer will tell you to "wrap."

Years of experience have taught me that editors and producers really are marvelous people. You have to learn to trust them. Because in the end, they make your copy better. That's one of my biggest complaints about academic discourse: it needs a lot of editing, and no one seems to do that. Effective communication simply isn't valued in the academic world. Which is why too few people pay attention.

Many years ago, when I was still freelancing, I got a call from a booker for a well-known late-night television news program asking me to comment on an issue I really didn't know much about. I gave her the name of a renowned academic expert on the subject. When I watched the show that night, I saw that they had booked someone of far less reputation.

The next day, I asked the booker if she had reached the person I recommended. Yes, she replied, but she decided not to use him. "Why not?" I asked. "Well," she replied, "we found him rather thoughtful." Thoughtful? What could that mean? It meant that he prefaced his answers by saying, "There are four reasons why this is happening." Four reasons? That will never do on television. Your producer will tell you, "Pick one."

I suppose I owe my television career to former Sen. Gary Hart as much as to anyone. Hart's sensational downfall in 1987 created a huge market for political analysis. The media was in uncharted waters, and they needed experts who could explain what was going on. I became what *Newsweek* labeled "the nation's hot new political pundit." When you're hot, you're hot, and I spent several years thereafter as one of the country's most quoted political experts.

In 1990, Cable News Network approached me and asked if I would consider working exclusively for them. Accepting their offer was a pivotal career decision. I was no longer an outside expert. I had turned pro.

When CNN hired me to be a "political analyst," I wondered, what exactly does that mean? I subsequently found out it's different from a correspondent, who goes out and gets the story. It's also different from a commentator, who tells you what he or she thinks. CNN has had many commentators, including Pat Buchanan and Jesse Jackson and Mary Matalin and Michael Kinsley. Their job is to express opinions, from a partisan or ideological perspective: "Here's what happened today, and this is what I think." Commentators appear on talk shows, not on the news. And they almost always appear in pairs, so one opinion is balanced against another.

An analyst is an explainer: "Here's what happened today, and this is what it means." An analyst appears on news broadcasts, usually alone, to offer context and interpretation. Can an analyst express an opinion? Sure. He can say that a politician made a smart move or a foolish move. In fact, for six years now I have been awarding the political "Play of the Week" every Friday on CNN's *Inside Politics*.

But I have to be able to back up my assertions with evidence. Not too much evidence. This is television, after all, not an academic seminar. But the analyst must convince viewers that he can defend what he is saying. In other words, he must communicate authority. Viewers have to trust him.

One way you earn that trust is by being careful not to let partisanship or ideology color your analysis. That's for commentators. And, too often, academics. I take pride in the fact that viewers are often mystified about which way I lean politically. As long as I get letters from both sides complaining that my analysis is biased, I feel comfortable.

My beat is the American people. I was hired, in part, to analyze and interpret the polls, although I am not and have never been a pollster. My job is not simply to report the numbers, but to explain what they mean. CNN decided that was important because public opinion has become a bigger player in American politics. And not just at election time.

My baptism under fire in television news came during the Clarence Thomas confirmation hearings in 1991. When the committee hearings reconvened to consider Anita Hill's sensational testimony, I was put on the air to provide a running analysis of what it all meant. There was only one problem. No one knew what it all meant, especially members of the Senate Judiciary Committee.

As we polled the American public during that amazing event, we found two story lines developing. One was rising consciousness of sexual harassment as a serious matter. Until Anita Hill gave her testimony, men regarded sexual harassment as something of a joke. They simply did not understand women's anger and humiliation.

Anita Hill's testimony turned out to be one of those rare consciousness-raising events in American history. When Anita Hill testified, reluctantly, about her experience of sexual harassment, it had the same effect as Rosa Parks' refusal to give up her bus seat to a white man in Montgomery, Alabama, in 1955. One action released the pent-up anger and frustration of millions. It was the men on the Senate Judiciary Committee who didn't "get it."

The other story line concerned African-Americans. They responded viscerally to Thomas's complaint that he was the victim of a "high-tech lynching" at the hands of his enemies. Our polling showed that most blacks, including black women, supported Thomas's confirmation. Black opinion was absolutely crucial to the outcome. Southern Democrats were the swing voters in the Senate, and they did not want to offend their black constituents.

A few years earlier, blacks had turned against Robert Bork when he was being considered for the Supreme Court, and southern Democratic senators voted accordingly. That finished off Bork. When blacks showed solidarity with Thomas, that cleared the way for his ultimate confirmation. It adds up to a convincing case that the Voting Rights Act has had a profound impact on American politics.

Here's another instance where public opinion turned out to be pivotal: the Monica Lewinsky scandal. The polls saved Clinton. When the scandal broke in January 1998, the punditocracy in Washington declared Clinton's presidency over. They were ready to drive him out of office. His own fellow Democrats felt so betrayed by Clinton's behavior, they refused to step forward and defend him.

Everything changed on the night of Clinton's State of the Union address. What happened? We took a poll. I went on the air to report that the American people had a message for the talking heads in Washington: "Get a grip. Take a deep breath. This presidency isn't over." The president's job rating had just shot up. There were no mass public demonstrations of support for the president. People were embarrassed by what he had done. But they were resolute in their opinion that he should not be forced out of office.

Once the polls came out, conventional wisdom shifted 180 degrees. "Of course the president will survive," the talking heads opined. "People still have confidence in his ability to do the job." Through the year-long impeachment ordeal, I found myself reporting the same poll findings week after week. Two thirds of Americans thought the president was guilty of lying under oath. And two thirds of Americans thought he should not be removed from office. Those results drove Republicans so crazy they became convinced that Republicans were refusing to talk to poll takers. In the end, when President Clinton was finally acquitted by the Senate, he was reported to have remarked, "Thank God for public opinion."

At election time, I approach my job as a political analyst by asking the following question: what do the voters want that they're not getting from the incumbent?

In 1960, after eight years of President Dwight Eisenhower, voters felt the country was slowing down. They feared the U.S. was losing the edge to the Soviet Union in military power and technology, especially after the Soviets launched Sputnik in 1957. Americans were looking for a leader who offered youth, dynamism and vigor. That was John F. Kennedy, who promised to "get the country moving again."

In 1968, the country was being torn apart by racial violence, student protest and the Vietnam War. Americans wanted an experienced professional who could bring order to the country. Richard Nixon won on a promise to "bring us together."

After Watergate, Americans desperately wanted morality. Jimmy Carter shrewdly read the national mood in 1976 and promised, "I will never lie to you." Carter's reputation for integrity remains intact. But by 1980, people wanted something they weren't getting from Carter. As President, he seemed wishy-washy and ineffectual. In 1980, the country yearned for strong and decisive leadership. Enter Ronald Reagan.

Walter Mondale ran against Reagan on "fairness" in 1984. That might have worked in the 1982 recession, but by 1984, when it was "morning in America," it was hard to convince Americans that the system wasn't fair. In 1988, Michael Dukakis ran on "competence." He told the Democratic National Convention, "This election isn't about ideology. It's about competence."

That might have worked if Dukakis were running against Ronald Reagan, a president who didn't seem to know what was going in the White House basement. But Dukakis was running against Vice President George Bush, who had held almost every top job in Washington. In 1988, Bush's competence was not an issue.

By 1992, however, Bush was in deep trouble. The problem wasn't his competence; he had won the Gulf War. The problem was empathy, his seeming inability to understand what ordinary Americans were going through in the recession.

Bush appeared "out of touch." Remember his apparent lack of familiarity with a supermarket scanner? Empathy was Bill Clinton's specialty. He felt your pain.

Clinton also had a weakness—character. As early as 1992, exit polls showed voters had doubts about Clinton's honesty and integrity. They took a gamble that Clinton could get the job done without creating a constitutional crisis. In 1996, the gamble appeared to pay off. Bob Dole tried to run on the character issue. Dole's slogan: "A better man. For a better America." It didn't work. But that was before impeachment.

What voters were looking for in 2000 became clear when I analyzed the biggest story of the campaign—John McCain. What drove the McCain phenomenon? McCain was the un-Clinton. He pledged to "end the big money power of special interests." Bill Clinton broke all records in bringing big money into politics. McCain was a military hero. To many voters, Clinton is a draft dodger.

Remember McCain's bus? It was one of the most effective campaign devices in political history. In fact, after McCain won the New Hampshire primary, I awarded the political Play of the Week to his bus. Why was the bus so effective? Because of its name—"The Straight Talk Express."

President Clinton is a charismatic speaker who always wins his audiences over. But ask Americans to name the most memorable things Clinton has ever said, and they'll probably titter nervously and murmur, "I did not have sexual relations with that woman. . . I didn't inhale. . . It depends on what the meaning of 'is' is." Those statements are exactly the opposite of straight talk.

If there was market for anything in 2000, it was for straight talk. George W. Bush appealed to a lot of voters who see him as a straight shooter, a laid-back, likeable guy who's not driven by politics. It was difficult for voters to see Al Gore—Mr. "No Controlling Legal Authority"—as a straight talker. At least until his acceptance speech at the Democratic National Convention, where the vice president laid out a detailed, straightforward issue agenda with no rhetorical frills or flourishes. That speech got him back into the game.

That, more or less, is what I do as a political analyst. I figure things out. I explain what's going on. The essential skill required is not that of a researcher, but that of a communicator. That's also the skill required of a teacher, a calling I never quite abandoned. During my first five years at CNN, I spent half my time commuting to Boston College, where I held the Speaker Thomas P. O'Neill Jr. Visiting Chair in American Politics. I hope and expect someday to resume teaching. One way or another, I'll still be explaining things.

Part IV

Expanding Access and Influence

18

Roads Taken and Not Taken: My Political Science Career in Washington

Margaret Daly Hayes

My career has focussed on foreign and defense policy and Latin America. With my base in Washington, I have had jobs in academia, policy research, on Capitol Hill, with the private sector as well as international organizations, and with the U.S. government. These many different jobs have given me a uniquely broad and in-depth perspective on my subject area—Latin America. I can talk politics with politicians, business with entrepreneurs, investment with economists, and military issues with the armed forces.

All careers make more sense when viewed in retrospect. I was never really quite sure what I wanted to do for a career besides make a difference. In hindsight, my love of languages (I studied Latin, Spanish, and Russian in high school and German in college) led me to a specialization in foreign areas and influenced how I engaged the political, development, private sector, and military communities with which I have worked. In each case, I have enjoyed learning the "language" of the new community.

As I reflect on what was most important in building this career, six broad principles seem important:

1. Build as strong and broad a knowledge and experience base as possible from the beginning. Interdisciplinary exposure is important. Today's political scientists need to be conversant in economics. To work in the international field, both language and overseas experience give you a better understanding of why other people do not behave like Americans.

2. Build a network and use it. In every activity in which you engage you will find people with whom you interact well. These people are your future network. Stay in touch with them. Use these friends as the editors of what you write. They will want to help you, and your product will be better as a result.

3. Be visible; take risks. Write, speak, take on special assignments—many of which you will have to complete on your own time—so that you can be visible before the different communities in which you move. Other people will see you there and you will become part of their network.

4. Don't be afraid to work in a variety of environments. The broader your experience, the more likely you are to have special insight into why things work as they do.

5. Don't be afraid to leave a position (a) to take on new and additional challenges, or (b) to put behind you an unsatisfactory relationship or one that you have outgrown.

6. Don't compromise on the integrity and quality of your own work. You may not satisfy every boss or client, but you will be recognized by others for being an honest broker. In the end, Laertes' advice to his son, in *Hamlet*, still holds true:

> This above all: to thine own self be true,
> and it must follow, as the night the day,
> thou canst not then be false to any man.

(Hamlet, I, iii, 82–84)

BUILD A STRONG BASE

One has to begin at the beginning. I went to the Medill School of Journalism at Northwestern for my B.A., continued my language studies there, and was fortunate to spend my junior year at the University of Madrid through New York University's Junior Year Abroad Program. The year in Spain set the path for future career developments—I became fascinated with the evolving politics of that country and enjoyed living abroad. I finished my journalism degree and returned to Spain through the NYU master's degree in Spanish literature program.

Next, I applied for a National Defense Foreign Language fellowship to complete my doctorate in political science with a concentration in Latin America. My application argued that my demonstrably good knowledge of Spain and Spanish literature would give me real insight into Latin American politics, thus uniquely qualifying me for this government-supported fellowship. It worked!

Indiana University's Political Science Department was expanding and developing a variety of new fields that represented the "cutting edge" of political science of the day—particularly in the international relations, comparative politics, public choice and quantitative analysis fields of the discipline. The department's young turks were introducing philosophy of science, statistics, and quantitative (and thus presumably rigorously scientific) analyses across the curriculum. Comparative analyses of public spending policies were just beginning in American political studies.

I combined quantitative analysis, American government, and comparative politics and did my outside minor in philosophy of science and logic of inquiry. I also took a smattering of economics. To this day I encourage all graduate political science students to get a thorough grounding in economics and quantitative analysis—the latter for the discipline as much as for the analytical methods. What this potpourri of disciplines provided—in addition to an appreciation for pure science and scientific inquiry—was a grounding in other disciplines that has served me well across my career.

The Indiana faculty opened many doors for me. My first Latin America advisor, Phyllis Peterson, counseled me that, though a lot of male colleagues wondered whether a woman could get anywhere with research in the "macho" Latin American culture, she had not found it a problem and she had often sweet-talked her way into interviews where her male colleagues had failed. "Make sure it doesn't make a difference to you and you will not have a problem," she advised. The faculty encouraged me to publish and offered me a grant to do pre-dissertation research in Brazil in the summer of 1969—my first trip to Latin America. I returned home from my summer project to marry my fellow grad student, Dick Hayes, whom I had met through the political science grad students' Thursday Evening (Drinking) Club, also affectionately known as "Margaret and the boys." When I returned to Brazil to do my dissertation research from August 1971 until the end of 1972, Dick stayed behind to finish his own dissertation. He joined me later, but left again to begin his own first academic job. The one benefit of this separation was that for a good portion of my stay in Brazil I had no one with whom to speak English, and my Portuguese flourished.

ON TO WASHINGTON

By the time I was ready to look for a job, the political science market was in glut. Dick had a good job at the University of Missouri at St. Louis (UMSL). I was offered an early attractive position, but, having spent nearly a year of married life separated while in Brazil, I declined it because there was no opportunity for my husband in the area. No other academic opportunities emerged beyond tentative talk about the two of us splitting a single appointment. We decided to put the word out to Indiana colleagues in large urban areas where we might be more likely to find two jobs for two political scientists, though possibly not both in academia. One of Dick's IR colleagues responded. He had just joined a Washington consulting company that was looking for regional specialists. Would Margaret be interested? By the time we were through with interviews, both of us had offers from CACI, Inc. in Washington, D.C. Thus, in the summer of 1974 we moved to Washington, D.C., to begin two very different policy careers. Mine is shown in the table. As you will see, it is characterized by a job change about every four year (what I finally recognized as my "four-year itch"); a continuing focus on Latin America from a variety of different perspectives, and a lot of research and writing as a vehicle for staying academically active and policy relevant.

1974–1977	CACI International, Inc.	Policy Research Panama Canal Treaty studies
1977–1981	Center for Brazilian Studies, Johns Hopkins University School of Advanced International Studies	Country and Policy Research and *Latin America and the* *U.S. National Interest*
1981–1984	Senate Foreign Relations Committee	Professional Staff—Western Hemisphere policy
1984–1988	Council of the Americas	Director, Washington— private sector concerns in Latin America
1988–1991	Inter-American Development Bank	Office Director—public affairs
1992–1993	Evidence Based Research (EBR), George Mason University and freelance	Research and teaching
1993–1994	Center for Naval Analyses, EBR, and Freelance	Policy Research *Future Naval Cooperation*
1995–1997	Center for Naval Analyses, EBR, and Freelance	Changing civil-military and inter-agency relations*; Air* *Force Engagement*
1997–	Center for Hemispheric Defense Studies National Defense University	Director, build academic program on civil-military and defense issues for Latin American academic, govern- ment, and military personnel

I learned the value of the networking at CACI. The Panama Canal treaties were the most important Latin America foreign policy issue on the U.S. agenda in the mid-1970s and I wanted to play in that arena. To do so, I had to market myself and the CACI Policy Sciences division. Our group had some good talent and a tested decision model that had been demonstrated at the Army War College. Moreover, a team of us had just completed a well-regarded economic study of the economic development potential of OPEC countries for an inter-agency group chaired by the State Department.

Working my network ("trap-line" in CACI parlance) led me to the office of a USAID old timer who had spent years in Panama and reportedly used to go drinking with Omar Torrijos. After listening to my pitch about CACI's skills, he said,

"The people who have money for research are at the Pentagon. Call there." He would tell them to expect my call. (This of course was a fantastic reference.)

The hardest action in telephone marketing is picking up the phone to make the critical call. When I finally dialed the Pentagon office, the colonel answered immediately. He had been waiting for me to call. (Good start!) He was interested; he knew about the decision model. "What did I know about Panama?" (oh-oh) "What was my background?" (Brazil!) "What else did I do?" I responded that I had just gone bonkers over scuba diving. I dive every weekend in a local stone quarry! "Scuba Diving! I love scuba diving! I learned how to in Panama. It's the most fun I've had since sky diving," said the special operations colonel. We agreed on an appointment for the following week, and I sauntered confidently into my boss's office to announce, "The colonel is a scuba diver." Everyone knew what that meant—a perfect ratification of one of CACI's core lessons: "People buy research from people." Thus the importance of working your network.

I learned two other critical skills for playing in the policy world at CACI: how to give a briefing and how to write a point paper. The Pentagon and the State Department teach both of these skills to staff officers from the very beginning of their careers. Our guidelines were that if you want to get your point across to a general officer or senior official, you have to summarize in one paragraph; for a colonel or officer director, you have one page. More than that and you wouldn't be read! This is an important lesson for the policy world aspirant. The academic is not trained to write one paragraph and one page executive summaries of complex research. But no matter how good your academic background, what and how you write is different for the academic and policy communities. You have to be able to tailor your knowledge to the interests and requirements of the community you are addressing.

Because of the Canal Treaty work, my visibility in Washington increased and I received two job offers, one to work as Abraham Lowenthal's deputy in his new Latin American Program at the Smithsonian's Woodrow Wilson Center and a second to work with Riordan Roett to launch the Center for Brazilian Studies at The Johns Hopkins School of Advanced International Studies. I chose to get back into Brazil which, had it not been for Panama, might have been the number-one policy interest in Washington. Brazil's nuclear program, its aggressive conventional arms industry, its space program, and its dynamic development rate all made Brazil especially interesting. And I was a Brazilianist!

The SAIS Brazil program—largely financed with private sector money—expanded my network to the senior leaders of Brazilian and U.S. industry. A World Bank manager spent a year with us studying the Amazon. Scions of Brazilian industry stopped by to address the Washington community on their point of view of U.S.–Brazilian relations. SAIS was the one-stop-shop for everything about Brazil. Riordan Roett gave me tremendous autonomy, encouraged me to get into the SAIS classroom, and gave me the opportunity to work on a project on U.S. security interests in Latin

America, which became my first book. Many of the SAIS contacts would reappear in my network in subsequent jobs.

Despite its success, the Brazil program retained a very small staff—I was number two in a two-person organization—and it became clear after several years (I didn't know then that I was experiencing the four-year itch) that it was time to move on. As luck would have it, in November of 1980, control of the U.S. Senate shifted from the Democrats to the Republicans. Democratic staffers would be replaced on all of the major committees. I submitted my resume to Senator Charles H. Percy, new chairman of the foreign relations committee. I had provided information to Percy's office during the Panama Canal Treaty debates and knew they had been pleased with that assistance. Moreover, I was from Illinois.

As I contemplated taking a job on the Hill, I asked advice (what do I need to know about this job?) from others who had worked there. Perhaps the best holds for any job in the policy world: make sure you are comfortable with the leader's policy position, or you won't be comfortable working for him or her! Other good advice came from former assistant secretary of state for Latin America, William D. Rogers, who counseled me to "keep my eyes and ears open and my mouth shut for the first six months up there." Scott Cohen, the senator's principal personal foreign policy advisor, offered another: "Never tell the senator anything you don't know is absolutely true." On a more practical bent, a seasoned colonel from the Defense Security Assistance Agency, advised us new staffers that the most important thing you can do is to "know the law and its legislative history."

Since both the committee staff and the administration were new, state, defense, USIA and AID and other agency legislative staff liaison had to establish relations quickly. My sorry office, located in Senate Annex, a building that would have been condemned had it not been occupied by the Senate, was visited daily by Legislative Affairs assistants who wanted to get to know me and see whether they could work with me. The committee would be responsible for carrying the new administration's legislative agenda and its membership and its staff were clearly torn in three directions: the now minority Democrats who nevertheless knew both the legislation and floor procedures better than the Republicans because of their long years in leadership; Percy's moderate Republicans and the conservative Republicans who felt themselves the carriers of the Reagan Revolution banner.

El Salvador was the issue of the moment and Congress was "Ground Zero" in the struggle over which policy toward Central American would prevail. I was visited by every possible American and foreign advocate for and against the Salvadoran guerrillas, the opposition and the government, as well as by Nicaraguans—Sandinista and Contra—and Hondurans, Guatemalans of all political persuasions. It was easy to appreciate the saying that "policy and sausage should not be seen in the making."

As a professional staffperson, I understood that I needed to get as smart as I could about all sides of the issue so that I could provide my bosses (the committee) with the best information possible whenever it was needed. I was not an advocate. I listened to everyone and tried to understand where the truth and the most compatible political ground lay. This was tricky, for Senator Percy's office was inundated with anti-administration policy letters (many of them obviously mass produced) from Illinois constituents, while he remained responsible to the administration and to his party for implementing administration policy. On several occasions we had to take strong positions that were frowned upon by the administration. For example, one morning, the *Washington Post* headlines blazed the news of atrocities presumably committed by government forces in Salvador. In the end, the headline exaggerated the event, but Senator Percy needed a strong opening statement for the 10:00 A.M. hearing on funding for El Salvador—one that would respond directly to the challenging headline. I wrote a speech that ended with the words "not one cent for Salvador, if the atrocities don't stop." The press and administration opponents loved it, but the administration was furious. U.S. Ambassador to El Salvador Deane Hinton growled at me: "Sister, the next time, talk to us before you write anything." The day's headline paved the way for the first certification legislation.

During the four years I served on the Senate staff we dealt with El Salvador funding and certification, human rights and the lifting of sanctions against Argentina and Chile; the Falklands/Malvinas conflict; the Contras, the beginning of the Latin American debt crisis, Venezuela's purchase of the F16; the Grenada invasion, Contadora, the Caribbean Basin Trade Initiative and many others. They were fascinating times. For the most part, however, members did not have high interest in Latin American or Caribbean issues. They just wanted those difficult issues off the agenda. As the subject matter turned to economics (debt) and Central America policy moved from the military assistance and aid portfolios to the covert portfolios, one's ability to play diminished. I began to get the four-year itch.

The Council of the Americas, which, under David Rockefeller's leadership, represented U.S. Fortune 500 companies invested in Latin America, invited me to run their Washington office and program. This was an interesting career step because it allowed me to work the issues of the day—debt, trade, and economic reforms—with government and private sector interests. Moreover, it would provide me with some critical management experience.

The council needed visibility with its corporate members. I drew on my research background to develop some policy products that reflected what the private sector knew or perceived about the evolving situation in Latin America. The first council white paper was prompted by a group of Peruvian businessmen who asked the curious question, "What is it that American businesses don't like about the Andean Pact?" We asked the corporate membership to document their answers and we presented the findings to Latin American businesses and governments and to colleagues in the World Bank and International Finance Corporation (IFC) where they were just beginning to try to understand the private sector dynamics as part of their rethinking of the role of the state in economic development. Our second survey focused on the impact of the debt crisis on overseas corporate operations and what would be required to encourage new investments. That survey played a role in shaping the World Bank's change of attitude toward private sector investment as the engine of growth in developing countries and in its definition of effective "enabling environments."

After four years with the council I began to think that I might like to get back to academia and write about some of these experiences. Then one day I received a phone call from a former colleague, a key Hill staffer for a committee responsible for the International Financial Institutions (IFIs). Enrique Iglesias had just been elected president of the Inter-American Development Bank and the bank needed a new Director of External Relations (EXR). The staffer would like to recommend me—he "liked the way I do business."

To a person my friends counseled me against taking the bank job. I ignored their advice. I was intrigued by the bank position because I had never worked in a large, formal, bureaucracy. To be effective in the policy world, you have to appreciate and know how to work in bureaucracy. The bank's international organization salary was also interesting, and considerably more than I was then making in the private sector.

The IDB experience was priceless. The bank was in the midst of deciding whether to embrace structural adjustment lending and market reforms or not. The finance minister was suddenly the most important official in Latin American governments. Enrique Iglesias was brilliant in building consensus for economic reforms and persuading recalcitrant politicians that "this is our idea." Inside the bank's 1300 New York Avenue headquarters one could live the debt crisis and the struggle for a new economic paradigm for Latin American growth from the perspective of the countries of the region.

But external relations was not the right job for me. Contrary to best public communications practices, EXR was not then included in the president's staff meetings and therefore often didn't know what the president was thinking. We undertook a number of new initiatives, but EXR was not expected to have any say in policy issues, and I was used to being a player. When the bank became active in supporting the Bush Administration's Enterprise for the America's Initiative, I was discouraged from seeking a role. I decided to leave. I felt that it would be better to give up the very comfortable salary and benefits for an opportunity to be a player on policy issues I felt were important.

ON MY OWN

The logical source of income was to set myself up as a consultant. I tried it, relatively unsuccessfully, I admit, and the work I got at first was not particularly rewarding. Fortunately my husband had started his own research company, Evidence Based Research Inc., in 1987, so I had a home. Nevertheless, Dick began to worry about me (the only time since graduate school that he worried about my finding a satisfying job) and, unbeknownst to me, was asking friends about "where Margaret should be looking." Out of the blue, one of these questions struck pay dirt. An entrepreneurial executive at the Center for Naval Analyses (CNA) had a request from the Commander in Chief, U.S. Atlantic Fleet (CINCLANTFLT) to give a zero-based assessment of the U.S. Navy's investment in and return on investment from activities with Latin American navies. Could I run this project? Well; I sure didn't know anything about the navy, but I did know Latin America and Latin American policy interests. This project would get me back into serious analysis and right in the midst of U.S. Latin American policy choices in the post–cold war. One of the key questions from my perspective was whether the new democratic governments in the region would provide adequate resources to their armed forces so that they could continue to engage with the United States. I signed on to CNA as a visiting research fellow for one year.

CNA's connection to the U.S. Navy and the mandate from CINCLANTFLT opened doors across the navy and with Latin American navies. I was assigned a rear admiral (ret.), a captain (ret.) and a research assistant right out of college to help me with the project. The two naval officers set about teaching me "Navy" and I loved learning the new language. (The first recommendation was to read Patrick O'Brian's first volume in the Aubrey-Maturin series; I was soon an O'Brian addict.) Their enthusiasm was not matched everywhere. One former deputy U.S. Southern Command asked "why the h... is the navy looking at Latin America and how on earth do they think some female is going to be able to tell them?" I thanked the gent for his time and walked out of his office. But that attitude was a decided rarity—even in Latin America where, following Phyllis Peterson's ancient advice, I just assumed it wouldn't make a different. With CINCLANTFLT's sponsorship, the offices of Fleet Commanders around the region were opened to me and I established friendships with sailors throughout the hemisphere.

Our report, *Future Naval Cooperation with Latin America*, won kudos. My favorite praise came from an officer at the Naval War College who commented to a colleague on my briefing of the study: "That doc ought to be wearing a uniform." And from the Latin American side that "my study explained how we Latin Americans think about what we are doing better than any outsider I have ever read." The chief of naval operations ordered the navy to develop a four-year plan of action to implement the recommendations—an almost unprecedented impact for a piece of policy analysis—and before Theater Engagement Planning had been heard of. I stayed around to do several other studies for CNA and independently undertook a similar effort with the air force which, though well regarded by those working the Latin America issues, did not find an advocate at headquarters and was largely ignored.

The navy and air force engagement research clearly paved the way for my current position as Director of the Center for Hemispheric Defense Studies. I was initially reluctant to look at the job. I wasn't sure that the U.S. government bureaucracy was behind it and my previous venture into a large bureaucracy (the IDB) had been a disappointment. But, I thought again, if it is going to be done, it ought to be done right and I knew the defense portfolio in Latin America. Doubts notwithstanding, I have never regretted the move!

In the above story, I have said little about the challenges of being a female in the Washington environment. I have assiduously followed my early professor's advice: "Make sure it doesn't make a difference to you and you will not have a problem." In fact I have often joked that "I just want to be (treated like) 'one of the boys.'" That approach has served me well. I have never asked for special consideration but rather have gone out of my way to avoid it. On the other hand, I thank the gentlemen who open the door for me.

As half of a two-income family, I have also not encountered insurmountable family problems. My son was born when I was 40 and by then I could afford a full-time nanny—a marvelous Salvadoran woman who shared her experience in raising five boys with me. I was working on the Hill at the time and my boss, Senator Percy, was firm in talking with his staff, that it is important to take time out to be with the family. Today, creating family time is a question of time management, and my husband, the soccer coach, is as hard pressed as I am.

For my generation, perhaps the most disturbing phenomenon of the professional relationship has been the lack of support from female colleagues. Few of my professional friends are female and for the most part, female professional support has either been indifferent or uncooperative. I have heard worse tales from others—but the bottom line is that women have not learned to be team players with other women in my profession and age cohort at least. I hope that this has changed for successor generations. I read with interest (in *Reporting Live*) Lesley Stahl's revelation of monthly meals with other path-breaking female colleagues. In my experience, the political science community hasn't arrived there.

Conventional wisdom suggests that the best way to gain access to the policy world is to acquire a mentor who will see that you get there. I am not quite sure how one goes about identifying and acquiring a mentor, but I have always wished that I had had one. I am sure that my life would have been a lot more orderly. In retrospect, however, I see that I may also have had many mentors—friends or colleagues who took the time to offer good advice at critical decision points in my career. Thanks to them for their friendship and their good counsel.

19

Homem da Lua:
Moving by an Unknown Source

Thomas Orum

The process by which we make professional choices can be, I believe, only characterized as not just unscientific but more properly, serendipitous. As a child my own inclinations were influenced by the people and places I was exposed to as well as an undiagnosed preference for non-conventional interests. I never suffered the angst of my contemporaries about place, a condition that tormented the middle class African American community of my youth. Most of my friends followed the traditional paths of their parents in the professions—medicine, law, or education—or embarked on new occupations—urban planning, architecture, and engineering. None of these options ever appealed to me even at the impressionable age when, one is likely to make an uninformed declaration of professional choice as an adolescent. Unfortunately, and to the embarrassment of my parents, when asked by their friends and acquaintances about my future, I could only reply that I had no idea, but was certainly not inclined to imitate their offspring marching lockstep into something that seemed mundane. The very thought of where or what I was going to be doing at some later stage was personally uncomfortable. I certainly had better ways to waste time than worrying about a future as an adult.

I grew up in Detroit, Michigan where foreigners abounded and I loved to listen to the Polish of Hamtramck, the Spanish of the Mexican community around Clark Park, and the Arabic of the Maronite Christians at Blessed Sacrament Cathedral. Inately curious about people, I devoted time to learning about these groups. Already I was more interested in them than what lay ahead in the future. While most of my friends were bored by the stories of their parents and friends about their lives as children and past experiences, I was fascinated by this recounting of their backgrounds. Most were raised by relatives from the nineteenth century therefore providing a bridge to the past that was more alive than contemporary texts particularly about African American life. However, all were not North Americans, which only augmented my curiosity. An Afro-Cuban doctor was kind enough to listen to my halting Spanish whenever I mustered the courage to accept his standing invitation to come by his office to practice. He in turn treated me to reminiscences of his youth in Cuba that certainly influenced my interest regarding the outside world, particularly of people of African descent elsewhere. One of my friend's father was from British Guiana, today Guyana, and an aunt from Panama all provided unconventional but tantalizing visions of life beyond national boundaries. Trips with my parents to Mexico and constant visits to Canada for shopping and vacations were my introduction to foreign climes by the time I entered high school.

As a child and young adult I enjoyed museums for both the artifacts as well as the paintings and sculpture displayed. These provided a physical link to past societies, which had always fascinated me. One lifelong habit that has served me professionally and personally is the love of books and reading that my mother, a primary school teacher, made an integral part of my existence. I read, perhaps better described devour, everything: classics, mysteries, history, fiction, and magazines. I cannot remember any time when at least several books were not at hand. It was an eighth grade teacher who suggested I read C.W. Ceram's *Gods, Graves, and Scholars*. This opened the door to intellectual interest in the social sciences from whence I never looked back or wavered in academic dedication. Certainly the idea of a black archeologist was unusual in the 1950s, particularly among solid middle-class African Americans who were ambitious but conscious of the social parameters that regulated society. There were enough engineers, classicists, and physicists in my acquaintance whose academic preparation never translated into professional opportunity.

I only survived mathematics and the sciences in secondary school as the result of the tutoring and strenuous efforts of my uncle, a physics major in college, and another neighbor with a Ph.D. in mathematics. The struggle with the sciences tempered my interest in applying to West Point where the son of a friend of my father and the brother of a schoolmate were attending. Certainly the military seemed to be a career where the normal rigors of life could be interesting, however the thought of confronting another round of physics, mathematics and engineering was not just sobering but terrifying.

The years of secondary school did not clarify my professional interests but I maintained an undefined desire to, hopefully, do something without daily routine. The latter was the bane of my existence. What I did recognize was I enjoyed learning about things foreign and foreigners. My first exposure to the world of the foreign service was via the husband of a friend of my mother who had completed two assignments with the Agency for Intentional Development in Africa. In fact we, more precisely me, were left to care for their ex-guard dog, a Rhodisian Ridgeback, when they were transferred. Instantly my knowledge base expanded when I researched the American Kennel Club breed history of this imposing animal. Surprisingly, he had two quirks of which I was instantly made aware while exercising him daily. First, he detested cats of any shape or size. When roaming our backyard he was, despite his bulk, fast enough to catch unwary felines crossing the yard enroute to destinations where they would not arrive. Secondly, he had a serious attitude problem with African Americans, particularly females wearing bandanas or scarves. I learned this on our first walk when I was nearly separated from my arm as he bristled and tried to charge a lady thus attired. Since our neighborhood was almost entirely African American this meant we had to take our walks when there was a minimum of human traffic on the streets. Since this breed was developed to hunt lions, I could understand his aggressiveness toward cats.

All my classmates in college seemingly knew what their designated, appointed or chosen, mission in life was and, as before, I felt slightly out of place. I insured I would at least be able to enter the army as an officer by enrolling in advanced Army ROTC. Many of my fellow history majors were oriented toward law school, an option I evaluated as boring at best. The opportunity to study Byzantine, Russian, Ancient Greek and Roman history with men whose entire focus was on their subject provided an endorsement of my own inclination. Most liberals arts undergraduates in the 1960s were unperturbed by the anxieties contemporary students have about careers. The only certainty for most reasonably healthy males was military service and later some occupation. This pattern, particularly for African American college students, was the norm. The majority of my childhood friends and later acquaintances, followed this path unswervingly.

During my senior year I took an elective course in African politics. Africa to me, as to many African Americans, was an unknown and unappreciated area of the world. Ever since I was a child my father had always counseled me that one day the continent would play an important role in international affairs—advice I certainly could not envision at the time. The course fit my academic style—good lectures, ample reading, and a research paper. When casting about for a topic, I was out of my element until I noted press coverage on the rebellion in Angola, then part of the Portuguese Empire. Since I had a background in Spanish language, like many, I assumed this would be useful in reading Portuguese. My research took me into uncharted waters in which, unbeknownst to me, I would later become completely immersed.

When it was time for officers to submit to branch selection, I opted for a field that seemed to fit my interest in things foreign. Despite having always been cognizant of the limitations for African Americans in career and professional positions, surprisingly, I was assigned to the newly established intelligence branch. The training I received before reporting to my unit was my first exposure to specialized non-academic foreign area instruction.

In the military for the first time in my life at age twenty-two, I assumed responsibility for something other than myself when at times even this was daunting. The forty-man unit I commanded, with an untold amount of equipment, was at first glance a shock to my system. What was even more disturbing was they were all older than me. Certainly having been raised in a culture where age corresponded with position, this seemed to be out of kilter. I became the sounding board and arbiter of family disputes and had to worry about the individual peccadilloes of the members of my unit when few of the answers were certain, even in my own life. My savior was Sergeant Arthur Rivers, an African American from the South Carolina low country who guided me through the thickets of command. Another lurking uncertainty was that a number of my men were white southerners. I'm a native mid-westerner with no previous experience in the deep south, which was in the midst of the civil rights turmoil, so I was thoroughly nonplussed. At this time I was more worried about the Ku Klux Klan than the Russians or the Chinese as real enemies.

For the first time, I had to present unwelcome evaluations and positions to senior officers. These briefings, and the myriad of analytic reports produced, were a form of post-graduate experience. The army provided real-time situations where the work involved cold war policies and politics. Language, geography, and personalities were folded into scenarios to maintain policy and decision makers abreast of status of friend and foe. The time passed rapidly with training and real mission exercises in and out of the United States. The decision to remain in the military or return to civilian life was a crossroad that required thought and planning as to future employment. I was inclined to follow the path of least resistance and stay in the military and apply for the foreign area officer training program. The prospect of a new GI bill to help finance graduate studies proved to be a powerful incentive since by maintaining my commission I could always return to active duty. I wanted to teach history and decided that an advanced degree would be useful in seeking a position at the secondary level.

It was with a combination of trepidation and anxiety that I arrived at the University of Arizona to begin graduate school. I chose Arizona because of family connections and a decision to make Latin America my field of study. Despite initial unease, I found life as a history graduate student exactly what I needed. My confidence increased when I later became first a research, then teaching, assistant in the department. It was personally gratifying at Arizona that no one asked why I had no interest in what was then called Negro history and none of my students appeared perturbed that I was an African American. The program at Arizona gave me sufficient experience to try my luck at earning a Ph.D. Migrating to New York University in search of this final goal my aspirations were now to teach at the university level.

While at Arizona my advisor suggested I might be interested in applying for an opening with the Agency for International Development, but I was not tempted to return to government service at the time. After finishing my course work and passing preliminary examinations, I was awarded a fellowship for dissertation research. In the midst of preparing for these examinations, out of curiosity, I applied to enter the Department of State. One day a classmate in a Brazilian history course informed me he'd had enough of academia and was going to work for the Agency for International Development. This, to me, was almost heresy and I replied—why would you want to do that? He was a master's student in Luso–Brazilian area studies, I noted. We were later to be reunited as colleagues in three different assignments abroad and always laughed when we remembered the incident.

The choice of a dissertation topic helped define my intellectual and personal vision. As a graduate student, I became increasingly interested in the role of African Americans in the Western Hemisphere outside of North America. The civil rights movement had a corollary impact on Afro–North Americans generating a sometimes undiscerning but vigorous quest to know more about the past. The advent of African American studies infused the old Negro history with a new momentum. The experience of writing several seminar papers with Afro-Latin themes convinced me that I wanted to pursue this area. A Brazilian topic at the time was untenable financially and I focused on the growth of an Afro-Cuban post independence political movement that eventually resulted in an armed rebellion in 1912.

Some years later this topic served as a point of reference with the Cuban ambassador in Guinea-Bassau. This, of course, was during an era when the United States and Cuba in the throes of the cold war were not on speaking terms at any level. The ambassador and I had a mutual friend in the government who we both visited. One evening, unexpectedly, we were both at his residence at the same time. Officially, we had never acknowledged one another in public (as demanded by contemporary protocol) and our friend thought it amusing to see us making small talk. I most certainly should have departed but since the ambassador was a young Afro-Cuban, curiosity overcame professional reservations. When he reminded me he was originally from Oriente province I asked about any remaining vestiges of the Partido Independiente de Color. He was taken aback and asked how I was acquatinted with the movement. After explaining this was the topic of my doctoral dissertation he told me his grandfather had been a party member and allegedly a participant in the rebellion. This opened a host of questions from me (archival research left unanswered.) The atmosphere turned from guarded hostility to non-political conversation about the memory of the rebellion and Afro-Cuban life.

The decision to enter the foreign service was challenged by a tempting offer at Tufts University for a one-year appointment to be followed by a tenure track job at State University of New York at Binghamton. The Department of State, after what seemed to be an interminable decision-making process also came forth with a place in the junior officer class of June 1970. In all honesty the deciding factor was the opportunity to go abroad immediately and a substantial salary difference. I had lost out on a teaching fellowship in Venezuela due to a funding shortfall, but completed the major portion of my dissertation research in the ensuing wait. I was ready to go somewhere to apply my knowledge. I reasoned one could always return to academia but not to this job.

The initial career of most new officers is a mix of language training, posting as a consular officer in an embassy, or consulate, then moving into a substantive field, hopefully, of their choice. Over the years the system changed, but the character of this apprenticeship remained relatively constant. I was interested in working in the area of my graduate study but was assigned first to Portugal not Latin America. The first post is like any new endeavor, approached with reservation and high expectations. As fate would have it the officers I worked with were not only a varied and interesting group but professionals from whom I learned the mechanics of the trade. They also formed a core group with whom I would serve more than once because of Portuguese language. Portugal was enmeshed in a war in its overseas territories and also alive with a resident population from Angola, Cape Verde, Mozambique, Sao Tome-Principe, Timor, and Macao. The Indian conquest of Goa had spurred the migration of a substantial number of Goans as well. These people were not only professionally of interest, but personally introduced me to the wide world of the African diaspora, something somewhat ephemeral until rubbing shoulders with them in the course daily life. I also developed an affinity for dealing with the police, an experience that would shape much of my future professional work. Portuguese effectively replaced Spanish as a language of preference and was to be the basis of my assignments for the next decade. The Lusophone world of Africa, Europe, and Brazil was an unrecognized reality within the personnel system, but a cost effective way to move people from post to post.

The Portuguese world, being less culturally fractious than, for example, the Spanish and French, provided the service with not only language proficient officers but individuals whose past professional links could be profitably employed in several places. The African economist I knew who was working in a Portuguese bank and later was my neighbor and president of the National Bank of Guinea-Bassau. Similarly, diplomates from Lisbon turned up in Brasilia at the Portuguese embassy and Brazilians in Guinea-Bassau. It seemed as though there was always someone you knew or a friend of a friend in or out of the circuit. At times it appeared to be a mobile, constantly growing cast or perhaps, better described, a floating card game. Antonio Carreira, the retired Cape Verdean official who lectured at the Casa de Cabo Verde in Lisbon on the history and culture of the islands, and who was a self-trained anthropologist and historian with years of service in the Portuguese administration of Guinea tirelessly explained to me the nuances of both societies. The opportunity to spend several days talking to Luiz da Camara Cascudo, the multi-talented dean of Brazilian anthropology, provided me with a deeper understanding of the people whose actions and activities I was seeking to interpret. Military men, business men, cab drivers, politicians, academics, barbers, all in professional or personal encounters, were conduits of knowledge for an outsider. It takes a while, even for the intelligent, personable individuals attracted to the foreign service, to recognize the importance of a wider vision of life in country—some see it; others, culture bound, ignore these markers. The men I worked for, and most tried to pattern myself after, were what many considered old school. They depended on heavy personal contact and an ear constantly to the ground to detect the faintest seismic political, social, or economical movement. They could tell you why, how, and even when events influence the host country. The kin relationships of those in and out of power and the sources of regional factionalism, present and past, could be spun out at a moments notice to correct or fine tune reports. The United States government and its policy apparatus got more than its money's worth with the solid work and tactile sensitivity employed by these professionals.

By mid-career I decided to follow the path of least resistance and work in anti-terrorism and narcotics. These were, I thought, important issues perceived as ancillary by many. This meant association with police, security forces, and the military—institutions traditional-minded officers shunned or avoided. Meanwhile a tour at West Point as a visiting associate professor and State Department representative in the Sinai Field Mission increased professional breadth. The former only reaffirmed my interest in returning one day to academia. It also made me realize how valuable professional real-world experience added inestimable depth to even advanced academic preparation. The latter provided experience in peacekeeping and maintaining an unusual work regimen in the desert. Working in terrorism and anti-narcotics provided, for a mid-level officer, the opportunity to actually decide and shape plans of action as well as administer and implement programs with independent budgets. This was rewarding and made me feel that I was an important contributor to policy. However, professionally, these jobs still weren't considered mainstream, which caused officers to avoid them and why promotion panels ask why he or she isn't capable of doing something else. It was somewhat personal for me since, unlike many of my fellow officers, I had seen the damage narcotics were beginning to have on United States urban society. It was still too early to convince the policy makers or the general public that this was not just a domestic law enforcement or social problem, but would eventually become a serious consideration in international policy.

All professionals at some point in their careers encounter policies they disagree with or believe are wrong headed. Generally, people do what they can to make an imperfect or poorly concieved plan work as best as possible. The Central Amerian morass and the Contra war was front-page news and a domestic hot potato. Depending on what goals you believed are important, there were, in my estimation, positives and negatives. Our involvement generated consistent high-velocity activity in both the department and the field. The task of keeping the Washington policy apparatus fed with insightful reporting and trying, in turn, to implement decisions from on high was a daunting task. Experience and professionalism were at a premium, and from my vantage point in San Jose, Costa Rica, a heavy, but demanding time.

Seven-day work weeks were not uncommon and long hours the norm. The enthusiasm generated from being in the eye of the storm was the experience many thrived on. To know that Washington was actually reading and heeding field reports, because feedback was at times instantaneous, served as automatic confirmation. The parade of characters generated by the conflict was at times seemingly straight out of a bad "B" movie. Some were useful contacts, others just flotsam of the conflictive environment. It is rare to be associated with a policy for a long time and to observe some form of closure. Somehow Central America was so tied to my destiny that I was a member of the team that negotiated the final draw down of the Contra forces and their return to Nicaragua. This experience was a rare semi-independent action to complement the large scheme of democratizing Nicaragua.

This provided a close-up view of one of the department's senior Latin American specialists, Ambassador Harry Schlaudeman, in the twilight of his career, but exhibiting everything that one presumes an officer should be able to do to accomplish the task. In the face-to-face discussions with the Contras in their camp in Honduras or Sandinista diplomats in New York, he was a paragon of professional demeanor. Once, during a late night watching a brief, Ambassador Schlaudeman told me he was tired and going to bed. I, of course, was perplexed but he said, "You can do it, see you in the morning." After the successful election of President Violeta Chamorro, Ambassador Schlaudeman was called upon again to be the new representative in Managua. This resulted in a long, but temporary, assignment for me to assist in the transition.

The realization, after being passed over for promotion at a certain level, that my career was ending meant that I had to think about a working life in the outside world. My experience, excluding academia, did not seem to have ostensibly prepared me to do much in everyday life. My experience in the foreign service, after constantly adjusting to everything—language, place, task, and people—made me relatively confident in my abilities. The job search was directed toward teaching at the college level. Unfortunately, I entered the market in the throes of academic downsizing and without publications. Fortunately, I maintained, over the years, contact with friends in academia who shared the same vices as foreign service people, a thirst for information, and love of communication. It was this network that passed on the latest news and bibliography to keep me updated. Historians, unlike engineers or doctors, do not have to build bridges or operate to remain proficient, just read. When I was in the United States on leave, by telephone from overseas in the pre–e-mail era, I had the opportunity to follow the twists and turns of the profession. The eventual return to something I loved—teaching—but now with extensive professional experience, I believe, made me a much better professor than if I had gone straight from graduate school to the classroom.

When I was asked to contribute to this compilation, I wondered if I could make anyone understand my peculiar experience with the choices we are all faced with in life and why we make certain decisions. Many people are thoughtful, introspective, calculating, and carefully weigh the pros and cons of selecting something as important as a profession. These were the very people I always felt uncomfortable with since childhood. To my surprise many of my colleagues in the foreign service saw life as I did. There is a Portuguese expression about people with this rather undirected trajectory. They are described as *da lua* or moved by an unknown force, most likely extraterrestrial. The number of my fellow officers who had not focused on a career in the service and, like me, simply backed in from something else or decided to take the examination on a whim, was legion. This, I believe, explains the flexibility and collegiality that made even difficult situations manageable. Perhaps one of the most interesting phenomena for an African American serving abroad is that your phenotype does not immediately flag you as a foreigner. In fact several times people refused to believe I was a North American, let alone a diplomat. Maybe subconsciously I selected places where anonymity was an option when I cared to exercise it. Walking out the embassy door opened a world available for personal exploration without being identified as an outsider. I can never forget the confusion of the North Korean Ambassador in Guinea-Bassau, who spoke neither Portuguese nor French, always greeting me at official functions until one day someone must have informed him who I was and thereafter treated me as if I had an active case of the plague; or the confounded Brazilian marine guard in Rio de Janeiro where I was enroute to visit a friend on the Ilha das Cobras, unable to comprehend that the North American diplomatic passport I showed him really did belong to me. It took the officer a day to sort out the confusion; the understanding waiters from Mozambique and Sao Tome of the Libson restaurant I frequented, who, even when a North American tourist was choking on her meal, left me in peace; the curious and observant waiter who once asked me in Lisbon to explain why I spoke Portuguese but wore a class ring like many North Americans.

Hopefully, an African American official be will no longer be unrecognized by the government representatives sent to greet him at the airport because of the stereotype of what a North American is supposed to look like. The Brazilian local employee in our consulate who told me, before I could present myself as the temporarily assigned officer, to have a seat and wait to talk to the consul was embarrassed when I finally explained who I was. I discovered in these experiences that my humor and curiosity as to what the reaction would be once people knew the truth has always superceded any anger. Indeed, I convinced a Rio cab driver that I was a Portuguese veteran of the war in Angola visiting relatives in Brazil and received a free ride.

Foreigners were not the only individuals abroad to make these errors. It was not unusual, particularly in consular work, to be commended by a fellow United States citizen on my excellent command of English or ask to see the person in charge and be surprised when I identified myself as the one they sought.

Historians seek to understand the lives of the past; the life of a foreign service officer makes it possible on a daily basis if you are so inclined.

20

Bridging Two Cultures, Straddling Two Disciplines

Alfred G. Cuzán

I was a boy when Fidel Castro rode triumphantly into Havana, an event that would eventually lead me to study political science. That January 1959, we went wild about the man everyone credited with having driven out dictator Fulgencio Batista. For several months we listened, enraptured, for hours on end, to Castro's manly, eloquent voice, as he deceived us into thinking that the revolution was, as one of his early slogans put it, "as green as Cuba's palm trees." His image saturated the country. It was an exhilarating time.

The following year ushered in a cataclysmic change in the political climate. In February, Soviet Deputy Premier Anastas Mikoyan arrived. It was as if the specter of communism was stalking the Island, presaging the coming darkness at noon. Joy turned into terror, hope into desperation. Family members and friends who never before would have contemplated emigrating stampeded for the exits, desperate to get out of the country via any avenue available, before the Iron Curtain clamped shut. In April 1961 we (that is, my parents, three younger brothers, and myself) boarded a Spanish-flag ocean liner bound for Veracruz, Mexico. As the ship sailed out of Havana harbor, half of our extended family, some never to be seen again, waved goodbye with their handkerchiefs. It was only a few days before the Bay of Pigs landing. One of my favorite uncles, my father's older brother, a member of the expedition, was taken prisoner. Supported in Mexico City by my mother's godfather for several months, we applied and were granted resident visas to the United States. In September we made our way to Miami, then (as now) the capital of Cuban exiles.

Exile turned into permanent expatriation. My father, a lawyer, had a difficult time of it. He never fully recovered from the loss of his country and his profession. For some time I, too, had difficulty adapting. English did not come easy to me. In Cuba I had hated the weekly lessons, telling myself, "Why do I have to study this? I'll never use it." In Miami, upon entering the eighth grade, like many of my peers I was placed in an English-as-a-second-language program for half the school day, and the other half, in classes it was believed I could handle, including math, music, and physical education. However, outside school I continued to resist learning English, obstinately clinging to my native language.[1] I loved the sounds of Spanish poetry, above all the *Rimas* of Gustavo Adolfo Bequer. It wasn't until the family relocated to Kansas City (we were there for only seven months, after which we returned to Miami) that I read my first full-length book in English, Melville's *Billy Bud*. Not until high school did I begin extensively to read English literature. I don't remember anything dramatic forcing me to make the switch. I think it was a natural evolution arising from necessity. In any case, read I did. *Pride and Prejudice, Silas Marner, The Caine Mutiny, A Summer Place, The Citadel, Good-Bye Mr. Chips, Cheaper by the Dozen, Tales of the South Pacific,* and the Dobbie Gillis series are some of the titles of the many novels and collections of short stories I enjoyed.

Reading outside of school improved the quality of my composition, and it was on the strength of my writing that I was placed in college-prep English in my senior year. The teacher, after reading one of my essays, a satire, said to me, "I hope you don't take offense, but when I read your essay, I couldn't believe it was you." Far from offending me, her remark flattered my vanity. But her confusion was understandable. I spoke with a heavy accent, my pronunciation and enunciation leaving much to be desired. This was partly for lack of practice. Just about all my friends were Cuban-born and we conversed in Spanish among ourselves. The asymmetry between my written and my spoken English continued for many years, indeed, to this day.

I graduated from high school and earned a B.A. in government and economics from the University of Miami, all the while working part time at various jobs, in grocery stores, restaurants, a bank, and finally at the campus library, and as assistant to a member of the faculty in the Department of Government, Bernie Schechterman. As a child, I had assumed I would follow my father's footsteps to the law (a path two of my younger brothers took), although in my adolescence I fantasized about becoming a popular writer—a novelist, playwright, or lyricist. But no sooner did I arrive on campus than the prospect of spending my life reading, lecturing, and writing on matters of historical import captivated me. I debated whether to pursue a doctorate in political science or economics (which I took up at my father's suggestion), finally deciding in favor of the former, for two reasons. One was practical, based on realistic self-knowledge: I didn't think I could master the mathematics that was increasingly required to excel in the latter. The other was idealistic:

I thought economics had solved its basic problems but political science had not. Nevertheless, I was attracted to both, and envisioned using economic tools to analyze political phenomena. With the help of collaborators I have accomplished that goal, although only time will tell whether this work, unconventional in its assumptions and going against the grain in its conclusions, constitutes a real contribution to the discipline.[2]

By the time graduate school loomed ahead, I was ready to break out of the Cuban environment. It didn't even occur to me to apply to a Florida school, as I wanted to venture deeper into America, penetrating its geography and culture. I applied to several schools: Harvard, Wisconsin, North Carolina, Indiana. All accepted me but it was IU that made me an offer I could not refuse: a three-year NDEA fellowship. I had picked Indiana because Bernie Schechterman had gone there. In September 1969, one month shy of my twenty-first birthday, I arrived in Bloomington. This was my first time outside the family hearth and in an all-English environment. I fell in love with the place. That first fall was a wondrous experience—I had never seen leaves turn before. It was at that time, too, that I began dating the woman who became my wife, a native of Baltimore. She was working toward an M.A. in French. Fittingly, we got married in Bloomington, our families meeting for the first time the day before the wedding. To this day we visit our alma mater every three years or so.

My graduate education, like my interests then and now, was eclectic. In my first interview with the graduate advisor, Alfred Diamant, I told him I was not interested in studying Latin America. Indeed, I was not; neither did I care to be pigeonholed. Later, though, looking for a third field in which to take my "comps," I changed my mind. It helped that David Collier, a new professor fresh from the University of Chicago had joined the faculty. Moreover, adding Latin American politics to my repertoire was a sensible choice, since competence in Spanish gave me a comparative advantage. All the while, though, I took courses from several political science professors while minoring in economics. Via the Ostroms, I encountered the work of Gordon Tullock and other contributors to the public choice school. Years later I would write Gordon who, even as he relentlessly criticizes my work, has encouraged me ever since.

Among the books that made a lasting impression were Anthony Downs' *An Economic Theory of Democracy*, James Buchanan and Gordon Tullock's *The Calculus of Consent*, and Gordon Tullock's *The Politics of Bureaucracy*, Friedrich Hayek's *The Road to Serfdom,* Jane Jacobs' *The Death and Life of Great American Cities*, Vincent Ostrom's *The Intellectual Crisis in American Public Administration* (which I read in draft form, as it was being written at the time), Charles W. Anderson's *Politics and Economic Change in Latin America*, Alexis de Tocqueville's *The Old Regime and the French Revolution*, and W. Ross Ashby's *Design for a Brain*. The last book, a fascinating discussion on the attributes of a stable system, was in Vincent Ostrom's reading list.

Also at IU, it was with shock and consternation that I discovered that Fidel Castro's stock among Latin Americanists was high and rising. This seemed to confirm the assessment I had made as an undergraduate, that political science had yet to solve its basic problems.[3] If interpretations of the Castro regime could be so wide off the mark, the discipline had a long way to go. In the 1980s, simmering indignation turned to outrage when Latin Americanists embraced Nicaragua's Sandinistas with the same fervor many of us had greeted Castro in 1959. I had had enough. In a series of guest columns published over a period of several years in *The Times of the Americas* (now defunct), I challenged their interpretation of the Nicaraguan revolution and the war in El Salvador, ridiculing their sophomoric infatuation with the Sandinistas and their Salvadoran counterparts. Many of these essays were translated into Spanish and distributed throughout Latin America by FIRMAS Press.

When it came time to pick a dissertation topic, my concerns about the state of Latin American studies led me to propose a comparative study of Costa Rica and El Salvador. I had become interested in Costa Rica at UM, when I read a chapter on that country by James L. Busey in Martin Needler's *Latin American Political Systems*. Noting that it was an island of democratic stability in a sea of political storms, I wondered why. Looking for a contrasting case, I settled on El Salvador, about which I had also read a chapter in the Needler reader, by Charles W. Anderson. However, although intrigued with Costa Rica, and getting to know it became an end in itself, I chose it primarily because I wanted to evaluate a hypothesis I had come up with about a three-way relation between the structure of government, the scope of government, and its stability. To maintain stability, I thought, there has to be a balance between centralization and scope—if one goes up the other must fall. I fancied that some day this might become known as "the law of centralization and scope," and conjectured that the key to understanding Costa Rica's stability was that, unlike its neighbors, it had decentralized as the scope of its government had widened. Long on theoretical speculation, I was rather vague about methodology, but anticipated it would be in the traditions of participant observation and case studies.

I applied to several standard sources of funding for field research, but I can't remember how I hit upon applying, as well, to the National Institute of Mental Health, a most unconventional sponsor for the type of work I was planning to do. But it was the only one that came through, granting me a two-year fellowship. So in February 1973, in the middle of our winter but their *verano* (summer, by which they designate their dry season) my wife of less than two years and I boarded a LACSA flight out of Miami for San José. We spent a year in Costa Rica and five months in El Salvador, returning to Miami in June 1974 with boxes of books, newspaper clippings, and about a dozen or so thick notebooks recording my observations and interviews with local officials and citizen activists in cities and towns across both countries.

Parenthetically, before leaving for Central America I wrote to both Jim Busey and Charlie Anderson, asking them to comment on my dissertation prospectus. Both kindly answered me. This was the beginning of a long-running correspondence with the Buseys (his wife Marian adds observations to his letters now and then). Jim continues to comment on everything I send him, always generous with praise and encouragement. We've met only twice in all these years, although occasionally I telephone. As for Charlie, two years ago I found out that, having retired from Wisconsin, he spends the winter in Pensacola, where as well as writing books he is active in the Leisure and Learning Society. I attend his lectures to that group, and over occasional extended lunches we carry on wide-ranging discussions on anything that pertains to the life of the mind, to borrow a phrase from the title of one of his recent books (*Prescribing the Life of the Mind*).

Rather than return to Bloomington, we decided to stay in Miami while I wrote the dissertation under the long-distance direction of David Collier (now at UC Berkeley). David was extremely helpful and kind. On the one hand, he was indulgent, allowing me to develop and evaluate my hypothesis pretty much as I wanted. On the other, he was strict in holding me to deadlines for turning in drafts of chapters, as well as the complete product. He would read every line with care, expertly editing the manuscript and critiquing my arguments and evidence, which consisted in a series of case studies. His mentoring was exceptional, and to this day I read and evaluate my own students' term papers and theses in the same manner. Although the dissertation did not and could not accomplish anywhere near what I had initially imagined it would do, (i.e., establish a "law of centralization and scope") it did compare the two regimes in terms of their performance in responding to public demands, and it was approved. I had yet to find a teaching position, however. The next six months were difficult, full of fears that the job for which I had prepared for so long would never materialize. I even began to entertain the possibility of pursuing alternative careers, interviewing with the Miami-Dade County metropolitan government for a position as an analyst. But life as a local bureaucrat did not appeal to me, so it was just as well that I was not hired.

Fortunately, my anxieties were over in the spring of 1976, when I interviewed and received an offer from New Mexico State University. On the telephone, the chairman told me that I would be expected to contribute to the MPA program and teach the introductory course in American politics, but that there would be no opportunity in the Latin America field, it being already occupied by two other faculty. Between my interview and the written offer from New Mexico I received a call from The University of the Pacific. They were looking for someone who would teach public administration in Spanish. I was intrigued by this possibility, but was deterred from pursuing it for two reasons. One was the condition for the interview: if I flew there and either accepted an offer or one was not made, the cost was on them. However, if I turned them down, then I would be expected to pay half the fare. It was not an attractive bargain. The other reason was that, with both our families residing on the East Coast, we thought that going to New Mexico was far enough.

I spent four years at NMSU before wearing out my welcome. Several years ago I read a wonderful novel by Bernard Malamud, *A New Life*, about a Jewish man from New York who takes a job teaching composition at an agricultural college in the Northwest. That novel, better than anything else I know, depicts the kind of environment I encountered at NMSU. This is not to say that I bore no responsibility for our parting of the ways. For one thing, about halfway through my stay I became smitten with libertarianism, along the lines of Murray Rothbard's *For a New Liberty*. Theories of anarchism, and the way I expressed them, did not sit well. The libertarian spell was soon broken: in rapid succession, the Sandinista seizure of Nicaragua, the Soviet invasion of Afghanistan, the war in El Salvador, and the crackdown on solidarity in Poland had the effect of sobering me up. Libertarianism, I concluded, had nothing to offer by way of effective counters to communist threats around the globe. But the damage had been done. An aggravating circumstance is that, twenty-eight years old at the time of arrival, I was a young man in a hurry who did not wish to be subordinated to any hierarchy other than one based on superior knowledge, which in my presumption I fancied was not to be found among those who wrote my annual evaluations.

Nevertheless, my time at NMSU was by no means a net loss. For one thing, being shut out of teaching Latin American politics turned out to be beneficial in unanticipated ways. Drawing on my economics background, I developed a graduate course in budgeting and an undergraduate one in political economy. This enabled—indeed, required—me to read more economics. Also, I became interested in natural resources. Actually, one of the case studies included in my dissertation was an analysis of Costa Rica's national aqueducts agency. Never having lived in a dry climate before, I began to read about water policies in America's Southwest. In pursuit of that interest, I attended a Chautauqua workshop held in Austin, Texas. There I met Richard J. Heggen, then an assistant professor of civil engineering at the University of New Mexico. On the return flight we coincidentally happened to sit next to each other. To pass the time I showed him a model I had developed to account for political violence in Central America. He observed that it was similar to microeconomic models used in engineering. Subsequently, we pursued the discussion by telephone and letter, eventually writing two articles based on the initial model.[4] Then we developed a different, but related model to study American presidential elections. Recently, after a long hiatus, we have resumed our collaboration. Also at NMSU, I met two wonderful people, Cal and Janet Clark (now at Auburn and West Georgia, respectively) who have been friends ever since. An expert on methodology, Cal taught me a lot while collaborating on two conference papers. From him I learned to appreciate the value of statistics in testing political hypotheses, something I had been unreasonably skeptical about in graduate school.

On the strength of my natural resources work, I was offered a position in the public administration side of the coastal zone studies program at The University of West Florida. In contrast to NMSU, just about everything fell into place. I struck a collaborative relationship with Mike Bundrick, a mathematician and statistician who has been indispensable in the continuing progress of my work on American presidential elections. My chairman, Jim Witt, was in his own way as indulgent with me as David Collier had been. When the department's Latin Americanist left, he allowed me to take over her courses. And when another colleague moved into university administration, a shift of faculty left a hole in political theory, and he allowed me to fill that, too. So, step by step, I left public administration behind. In retrospect, I was not made for it. My guess is that anyone steeped in economics would have a hard time fitting into the field. The philosophical or, if you prefer, the ideological foundations of the two disciplines are not compatible. To put it as simply and neutrally as possible: economics is biased toward the market, and public administration against it.

Looking to make new acquaintances, I joined the Florida Political Science Association. At my first meeting, I spotted Bernie, whom I had not seen in many years. With his characteristic enthusiasm he had become founding editor of the association's journal, *The Political Chronicle*. Ever the mentor, Bernie lost no time inviting me to join the journal's board of editors, and nominating me for the executive council. Eventually, I was elected president. I still see Bernie (who after retiring from UM found a new career as an expert witness in immigration cases) and his wife Joyce, either at FPSA meetings or on our way to or from Miami.

I am now completing my second decade at UWF. For the last eight years I have been privileged to serve as chairman, having been elected a year after promotion to full professor. When I assumed the position, the department was a small conglomerate that included, in addition to political science and international studies, criminal justice, legal administration (which educates would-be paralegals), and public administration. I had long advocated allowing the more applied programs to go their own way. Fortunately, most of their faculty were of the same mind. Although at first the administration, for budgetary reasons, was reluctant to do so, in the end the dean decided to make the move. Since the split, we have had several years of departmental tranquility. On the downside, we were left with a skewed age distribution: at fifty-one, I am the youngest member of the group. It is nothing less than melancholy that most of my colleagues are at or near retirement and will be phasing out in the next three years. For consolation, if I continue to chair it, I will have the opportunity to help shape the department for some time to come.

As I said, I am fifty-one, and would like to think that I am not much more than halfway through my career. At this point, the question is, what next? The obvious options are few. One, the most likely, is the default option. That is, to stay at UWF, continuing to pursue scholarly interests wherever they may lead, always with publication in mind. Another possibility is to pursue a career in academic administration.

For a while I flirted with this option, even sending letters of application to several openings for deanships. Nothing materialized. And during a sabbatical in the fall of 1997, immersed in research, I lost interest in climbing the ladder of academic administration. A third path would lead to another institution, one with a larger graduate program that offers the Ph.D. That would have its attractions, but I realize that at my age it is mainly the stars of the discipline who enjoy much upward institutional mobility. But I could do a lot worse than stay where I am. UWF has been good to me, giving me the freedom and resources to pursue my interests, both in teaching and research, and rewarding me for doing so.

To those contemplating an academic life in political science, I offer the following advice. First, pursue your interests. Be inner-, not other-directed. Let your researches be guided by what intrigues you, not necessarily by what others think is important. Find mentors who will assist in the exploration of ideas that excite you. Never compromise your intellectual integrity. Neither should you fear going against the grain, nor playing role of the Socratic gadfly, if that's where your reason takes you. That's what academic freedom is for. Use it. Also, at every stage of your academic life, write to scholars whose work you admire. Ask them to comment on your latest paper or article. Don't hesitate to criticize their work where warranted, although of course this has to be done tactfully. Although you won't hear from a few, most will respond, and out of these several long-term relationships, and even friendships, may grow. These are extremely valuable. I do not mean in the narrow careerist sense, although it is true that such contacts can ease your way to forums where your ideas can receive a hearing, write letters of recommendation, and otherwise help promote your work. All that is important. But the critical thing is that private communication with like-minded academics is indispensable, like oxygen to a diver. It is a fact of university life that faculty are so distributed across space that most of your colleagues, even your friends, will not share your interests. They are busy in their own fields. Most of the time, then, you'll be working alone. For intellectual feedback and fellowship born of shared assumptions, the sine qua non of a true meeting of minds, you need a lifeline from without.

For the foreign-born would-be political scientist, I have additional advice. Do not allow yourself to be stereotyped or pigeonholed. Whatever your country of origin, it will always be with you. Because you were born into it, you have a comparative advantage when it comes to comprehending it or the broader cultural region of which it is a part. Moreover, you may have a strong sense of duty to your compatriots, and therefore may wish to foster a better grasp of their politics and society among U.S. policy makers or the public at large. At the same time, you need to pursue broader comparative interests. Above all, you need to study the United States. Bear in mind that some of the most insightful commentaries about this country have been made by foreigners, Alexis de Tocqueville deservedly being the most renowned. But note that, in *Democracy in America*, de Tocqueville analyzes the United States through implicit and explicit comparisons with France (as well as

England), and vice-versa. It was by bridging the two cultures that he was able to improve his understanding of both. Being *in* the United States but not fully *of* it has its liabilities, to be sure. But it also affords you a valuable vantage point that those who were born and raised here do not have. Make the most of it.

NOTES

1. My struggles with English have some parallels with those in *Hunger of Memory. The Education of Richard Rodriguez,* by Richard Rodriguez (Boston: D.R. Godine, 1981).

2. See Alfred G. Cuzán and Richard J. Heggen, "A Fiscal Model of Presidential Elections in the United States, 1880–1980," XIV *Presidential Studies Quarterly,* 1 (1984) 98–108 and Alfred G. Cuzán and Charles M. Bundrick, "Fiscal Policy and Presidential Elections: Update and Extension," in 2 *Presidential Studies Quarterly* 30 (2000) 275–287.

3. In *Reflections on a Ravaged Century* (New York: W.W. Norton, 2000), Robert Conquest remarks on the "mental incapacitation" and moral obtuseness that blinded countless Western intellectuals, including many academics, to the true nature of Stalinism. When it comes to Castroism, a similar disability appears to have crippled the judgment of all too many Latin Americanists. See my "The Latin American Studies Association vs. The United States: The Verdict of History," 7 *Academic Questions,* 3 (1994) 40–55 *and Dictatorships and Double-Standards: The Latin American Studies Association on Cuba,* Miami, FL: Endowment for Cuban-American Studies, Paper #13, 1995. For my own interpretation of the Castro regime, see *Is Fidel Castro a Machiavellian Prince?,* Miami, FL: Endowment for Cuban-American Studies, 2000 and "Fidel Castro: A Machiavellian Prince?" in *Cuba in Transition,* Papers and Proceedings of the Ninth Annual Meeting of the Association for the Study of the Cuban Economy (ASCE), Miami, Florida, August 11–13 (1999) 178–191. This paper is available online at the following Web address: http://lanic.utexas.edu/la/cb/cuba/asce/cuba9/cuzan.pdf.

4. Richard J. Heggen and Alfred G. Cuzán, "Legitimacy, Coercion, and Scope: An Expansion-Path Analysis Applied to Five Central American Countries and Cuba," 26 *Behavioral Science,* 2, (1981) 143–152, and Alfred G. Cuzán and Richard J. Heggen, "A Micro-Political Explanation of the 1979 Nicaraguan Revolution," XVII *Latin American Research Review,* 2, (1982), 156–170.

Part V

Conclusions

21

How to Be a Public Policy Manager in Washington: The Pi Sigma Alpha Lecture to the American Political Science Association

Donna E. Shalala

It is a pleasure to join so many friends and colleagues from the American Political Science Association.

You call this a lecture.

But I prefer to think of it as an opportunity to share knowledge—because Pi Sigma Alpha represents the collected wisdom of each generation's brightest young political scientists. The president told me he was a member of Pi Sigma Alpha when he was at Georgetown.

As you know, I spent many years studying and teaching political science and public policy. But I must admit that what I learned didn't fully prepare me for the mysterious ways of our nation's capital. So, I've tried to combine my knowledge of political theory with practical experience in managing the Department of Health and Human Services.

Thinking about a large organization like HHS reminds me of the movie *Sunset Boulevard,* in which Joe Gibbs says to aging actress Norma Desmond, "You used to be in silent pictures. You used to be big." To which Norma replies, "I am big! It's the pictures that got small."

I quote this bit of movie trivia to illustrate that there are many big things Americans like: cars, open spaces, movies. But we don't like big bureaucracies. Americans think that large government organizations are too complex, too impersonal, too inefficient, and cost too much.

And without doubt, they're partly right.

This was very much on my mind in 1993 when President Clinton asked me to become CEO of one of the largest government organizations in the world.

As many of you know, I had already served in the Carter Administration and two leading public universities. But I knew that taking over the leadership of HHS—a department whose budget, at that time, consumed 40 percent of federal spending—would be unlike anything I ever did before.

Because of its size and complexity, HHS is one of the most difficult jobs in the world for a public official. It is also a department whose policies touch the lives of every American. We have not accomplished everything we wanted to. All of us have taken some wrong turns, and endured the hard lessons of that great teacher: Experience.

Let me start by knocking down two myths. The first, described by Hargrove and Glidewill, is that my job—and others like it—are simply impossible. Too many difficult clients. Too many internal conflicts. Too little public confidence.

It's not true. Managing a large organization is the art of the possible. And, as I'll describe shortly, with some common sense lessons, it can be done.

The second myth goes back to the theories of Frederick Taylor.

That organizations are essentially machines. Pull the right levers in the right way, and you'll get the right result.

Were it only that easy.

In complex organizations there will be failures for any number of reasons: poor communication; impractical or unclear goals; lack of public or congressional support; lack of sufficient expertise or resources; too much—or too little—oversight. And too much work.

Between these two extremes—that nothing works or that everything can be made to work—lies some basic truths about large modem organizations.

SO, IN THE SPIRIT OF DAVID LETTERMAN, BUT WITHOUT THE DRUM ROLL, I OFFER YOU DONNA SHALALA'S TOP TEN LESSONS FOR MANAGING A LARGE, COMPLEX BUREAUCRACY.

Some of these lessons are well-established norms for administering large public and political organizations. You've read about them. You've written about them. And some of you may have even practiced them. Others are borrowed from recent scholarship, such as Doig and Hargrove's analysis of what makes an innovative and successful leader in government. And some of the lessons are from two decades of experience as a sub-cabinet official in the Carter Administration; as a student of government and politics; and as a leader of large public universities. Finally, some of these lessons are well known. Others less so. But I believe they are all applicable to large public organizations.

Number one: Know the Cultures of Your Organization.

I said *cultures*, not culture.

Organizations are usually made up of many smaller units—each with its own history, needs, culture, and constituencies—but working toward a larger objective. That is certainly the case at major research universities. The goal is the same: well-educated students and quality research. But different colleges, schools, and departments often take very different roads to reach that goal.

So, Levin and Sanger are right when they emphasize the importance of understanding these cultures and constituencies. National Institutes of Health (NIH) is a good example.

Have you ever tried to apply standard personnel rules to hiring scientists? I can tell you right now: they don't work. Scientists have their own language and traditions. And their own measures for assessing merit.

When I became secretary, personnel managers in the Office of the Secretary had overall responsibility for hiring scientists for NIH. These personnel officers were highly skilled, but they weren't used to hiring first-rank scientists in a competitive market place. I thought the scientists at NIH were best able to judge scientific competency and credentials.

There are also times when it's actually helpful for an organization to have more than one identity.

When NIH, CDC, FDA, and the U.S. Public Health Service all line up in favor of a particular policy, say, banning the marketing of tobacco to children, that policy will more likely be accepted by Congress, the public—and, we hope—the courts.

Unique cultures within a department can also increase credibility.

That's why a cabinet secretary is not always the best salesperson for a departmental policy. In criminal investigations, the FBI is usually called on to speak on behalf of the justice department. If there's a major fire, the local fire commissioner may have more credibility than the mayor.

And at HHS, I like to let the experts—especially physicians and scientists—speak directly to the public, because the great scientific agencies—CDC, FDA, NIH, NCI, and the Public Health Service—are institutions trusted by the American people. The physician-scientists who head them, while appointed by a president, have enormous credibility. They must be the reassuring voice—and face—explaining the Hanta virus outbreak; food borne illnesses; AIDS transmission; and the age women should start having annual mammograms.

Finally, the press provides its own cultures and traditions.

That's why there is no substitute for a public affairs staff with Washington experience. And I've had the best.

Number two: Make Sure the Right Hand Knows
What the Left Hand Is Doing.

There's a scene in the movie *Ben Hur*, where Ben Hur is trying, without success, to get his four new chariot horses to run. The bedouin who owns the horses tells him that each horse has its own personality, and they must be harnessed together in a way that allows them to run as a team.

The same holds true for any large organization. The sum has to be greater than the parts.

The different agendas of smaller units have to be melded or modified—and a belief in the larger team built. What can an administrator do to promote teamwork and a corporate identity?

When I first became secretary, I encouraged my top appointees to distinguish the HHS forest from their particular tree by asking each of them to participate in each other's budget hearings—and to prepare a budget for the entire department. In other words, to look at the department from my perspective.

When they took a look at the big picture, some senior administrators recommended cuts in their own budget requests. We are still using that process.

There are, of course, other ways to share information, build cooperation, and keep an organization the size of HHS speaking with one voice. One, described by Roger Porter as "centralized planning," has been rejected by most leaders, even very forceful ones like Richard Darman. A second, which Porter calls "multiple advocacy," lies between centralized planning and ad hoc decision making, and generally uses existing systems, some of which, in the case of HHS, I've been fine tuning.

For almost any public organization, the primary system for melding a team and an agenda is the budget process, which is increasingly important in an era when money is tight and budgets have to be balanced. In fact, in this new era, the budget process has the potential of being divisive and competitive—instead of a road to team building and unity.

But at HHS, and other public agencies, there are other ways to build a team.

At HHS, the executive secretariat controls the enormous paper flow.

But more important, exec. sec. is the honest broker. It ensures that ideas are considered throughout the department—and that everyone is brought to the table. That way, I get the benefit of every viewpoint. And when a decision is made, every participant owns it.

The assistant secretary for policy and evaluation runs the numbers, evaluates the likely consequences of a proposed policy, and makes recommendations to the secretary.

And there are some units within the office of the secretary that are designed to coordinate what the entire department does, especially in an emergency.

When Mad Cow Disease was discovered in England, we wanted to avoid panic by getting out accurate information about the steps that had been taken to protect American beef—years before.

The assistant secretary for health did that. Overseeing the work, and the public statements, of the FDA, NIH, CDC, and the Public Health Service—and coordinating with the Department of Agriculture.

Number three: Don't Overlook the Needs and Abilities of the Career Public Service.

My first day of work started with many top jobs in the department unfilled. And it stayed that way for some time. So what did we do? We ran the department with the top civil servants—the people who are responsible for most of our day to day leadership. It was fun.

Hugh Heclo, in his 1977 book, *A Government of Strangers* wrote this: "If democratic government did not require bureaucrats and political leaders to need each other, it might not matter so much when in practice they discover they do not."

I don't agree. The two sides do need each other.

I also don't share Heclo's belief that career civil servants resist the leadership and policy turns of political leaders.

I think the relationship is reciprocal. That both institutional and political guidance are needed. And that trust can be built by using the experience and institutional memories of career civil servants. In fact, when I became secretary, I wanted to send a very strong message to the civil service—that they were important. That we were going to be a team. So my first appointment was from the senior executive service—a career person of both great competence and experience. We need to make sure we respect the integrity of the civil service in words and action. In fact, relying on career professionals is especially important in the age of downsizing.

Today, political staffs are doing more work, with less help, and in less time. This is an open invitation for policy mistakes and failure. But many of these potential mistakes and failures can be avoided by using the career civil service to identify hidden minefields from the past—and to help plan, not just implement, policies for the future.

Which brings me to number four: Choose the Best and Let Them Do Their Jobs.

The days of political appointments as a spoils system are over.

A large organization is complex; its programs difficult to manage; and their purpose almost always vital to the well-being of the American people. That's why political appointees must be experts in their fields—and skillful leaders and managers.

They must be adept at both policy and politics.

Otherwise they will not get the respect and cooperation they need from career staff. So, while we've worked to create a team, I believe that the most important thing any public administrator can do is choose the right top management.

At HHS, the president nominated many leading experts in their field. They were Democrats—and our party was ten deep in talent for each position.

Some even compared our team to the incomparable 1927 Yankees: Phil Lee and Jo Boufford at Public Health; Mary Jo Bane at Children and Families; Harold Varmus, Rick Klausner, and Ruth Kirschstein at NIH; David Satcher at CDC; David Ellwood at Planning and Evaluation; Bruce Vladeck at HCFA; Melissa Skolfield at Public Affairs; Harriet Rabb as General Counsel; June Gibbs Brown as Inspector General and we retained David Kessler at FDA and brought Claudia Cooley from OPM to the executive secretariat.

Each of these leaders had years of academic and—or—professional experience in their areas of expertise—not to mention a deep sense of mission. But we also worried about the next generation. I always try to remember that we are replaced by those we recruit.

Which brings me to number five: Stitch Together a Loyal Team.

I've always thought that you need to instill loyalty in both professional and personal ways. We worked hard to make everyone feel a part of a team. That they are listened to.

I talked about how proud I am of our appointments—and their diversity of skills and experience. But that core team showed up with different agendas, different approaches to achieving their agendas—and often without knowing much about their new colleagues.

So I encouraged a healthy debate in private, but made it clear that I didn't want arguments in public. I can't say we were always successful. But for the most part we put together a loyal and cooperative team of very nice people who liked each other. And I encouraged that by creating events for my top staff where they could get to know each other better.

At Hunter College, the top administrators and faculty once did a play with the students. Although Hunter is a big commuter school, the play bonded us for years.

Which brings me to number six: Stand up and Fight for the People Who Work for You.

People behave in large organizations pretty much the way they behave outside of work. They are motivated by friendship, support, and loyalty. That's why showing the people who work for you that you really care about them pays dividends.

I had a unique opportunity to do that during the government shutdown. The shutdown actually strengthened HHS because it gave people a renewed sense of loyalty to each other and the department. I sent everyone a letter saying: We're fighting for you. And to show my support, I was very visible—making the case in the media about the devastating impact of the shutdown.

Then we did something almost no other agency thought of.

During the shutdown, pay checks were supposed to be half the normal amount. We found a legal way not to cut pay so drastically. We put off taking out deductions in our employees checks until after Christmas. So they were made whole—and they appreciated our caring.

We also managed our budget with considerable skill to avoid RIFS—the entire department held vacancies and helped to absorb cutbacks.

Number seven: Set Firm Goals and Priorities—
and Stick with Them.

The old saying is still true: To govern is to choose.

But in a large organization, with a limitless number of decisions to make—and a very limited time with which to make them—how do you choose?

Let me start by saying that Larry Lynn was correct when he wrote, "Public executives need a frame of reference to aid them in skillfully allocating their time, attention, and political influence." But they also need a reality check.

Managing is not the same as coming up with a wish list. And if you try to do everything, you'll accomplish nothing. You need to set priorities.

I have six secretarial initiatives.

And I have asked all the agencies within HHS to not only focus on those initiatives—but to do crosscuts. Share information. Pool money and other resources. Work in teams. Don't duplicate efforts.

Setting priorities doesn't mean choosing only what's easily achievable.

When President Clinton first came to office, we set a goal of increasing child immunizations. We established targets, and as the president recently announced, we met them.

But at least some of my six initiatives will be more difficult. For example, reducing teen pregnancy.

One reason is—and this is another reality check—the roots and solutions are often beyond any government's control. Which means whether you work for a mayor, a governor, or a president, you need to set ambitious—yet realistic goals; figure out your role in meeting them; and then team up with partners outside of government to accomplish them.

The reverse side of goal setting is delegating responsibility and demanding accountability—from both political appointees and career staff. You have to show confidence in the people who work for you—and at the same time have a system for obtaining timely information and measuring results.

One caveat: Delegation is not the same as abdication.

When I became secretary, there was a move to delegate all departmental regulations to the individual agencies. Literally hundreds every year. I didn't want to go that far. So I set up four criteria.

If a regulation fell under any one of them, for example, it's impact on the economy was one hundred million dollars or more, that regulation would have to be approved by the secretary.

Which brings me to number eight: Don't Forget Politics Is Always Part of Policymaking.

There is no way to succeed in the world of government without paying attention to that other world: politics.

For HHS, that means primarily the White House and Congress.

None of us, whether we're political or career, can operate in a vacuum. All of these external pressures—from the economy to the press, from the governor's office to, yes, regulators in Washington—affect government decisions and raise questions for which there are no simple answers.

I have two rules of thumb in politics. One, be fiercely loyal to the president on policy and appointments. Two, be skillfully bipartisan in the administration of the department.

When I go up to Capitol Hill to testify before Congress, I present the administration's case as vigorously as I can. When I return to the department, it doesn't matter to me if a Medicaid waiver request, or any other request, comes from a Republican governor or a Democrat governor. They get the same professional consideration.

And when there is a threat to the public health in a particular state, the politics of that state never makes a difference in how HHS responds.

Which brings me to number nine: Look for Allies Where You Don't Expect to Find Them.

To manage a large organization in this age of instantaneous communication, it always helps to look beyond the usual borders—and to reach out to nontraditional allies. That's why I believe in being nice to Republicans—and spending time speaking to newspapers like the *Washington Times* and the *Wall Street Journal*—two papers not exactly known for supporting Democratic causes.

That's why we work hard to make friends out of adversaries; to cooperate with the leadership of both parties; to disagree without rancor; and to build on areas of agreement. And that's why if it will help me communicate better, I enlist help from people who don't expect me to come knocking on their door.

Number ten: Be Flexible. Be Realistic. And Don't Expect to Win Every Time.

Perhaps the biggest mistake the manager of a large organization can make is to stand in one place for too long. Change comes. And as NASA's Jim Webb once noted, these changes come from both inside and outside the organization.

That doesn't mean there shouldn't be a strategic plan and systems in place for carrying out the operations of a large organization. But it does mean that governing is as much art as it is science.

We must expect the unexpected. And be nimble enough to change course—even in mid-sentence—if that's what it takes. In other words, keep moving.

In 1994, we lost on universal health care—in part because the other side organized quickly and framed the debate. By 1996 we were flexible enough to find a slower, more incremental—and successful—approach. Last year we passed Kassebaum–Kennedy. This year we passed a budget that will provide up to five million uninsured children with coverage. A great victory.

The unexpected can also mean having something removed from your plate. In 1993, the Social Security Administration was part of HHS. It no longer is. Downsizing in the federal government—unheard of in 1993—became the norm in 1994 and 1995.

The unexpected can mean a changing economy. Low unemployment is helping to lower the welfare rolls.

But with unexpected change comes unexpected opportunity. The opportunity to be creative. To find more efficient and less costly ways to deliver services. To find new partners and break new ground. To be—in the words of Mark Moore—an "explorer commissioned by society to search for public value."

I've certainly felt like an explorer since becoming a member of a remarkable president's cabinet.

This trip of discovery—although risky, difficult, and once in a while disappointing—has been the trip of a lifetime. I wish I had time to tell you how much fun public service is most of the time. My dream is that a young member of Pi Sigma Alpha who today is preparing for a career in the academy will have similar opportunities to spend some time in government.

I also believe that the disciplines of political science and public administration will be enriched as more students of government have a chance to be practitioners.

Thank you.

22

Conclusion and Recommendations

Howard J. Wiarda

We've now completed our survey of various careers in public policy. Not all careers or all types of persons are represented, of course; that would take far more space than we have available. But we do have a good sample and a good diversity; most of the main career patterns are represented here: law, foreign policy, think tanks, media, lobbying, staff aide, academia, and others. It remains for us to sum up the main lessons learned.

GENERAL CONCLUSIONS

First, it is striking how many of our contributors are, on balance, happy and satisfied with their public policy careers. Serving in a public policy position obviously has its ups and downs, its highs and lows, its uncertainties, doubts, and sometimes mixed feelings. But almost all of our contributors believe they were greatly enriched by their public policy careers, that they were enhanced by the experience, that they contributed to the public good while also having a rich and exciting job. It is impressive how many of our authors conclude, without any prodding, that they wouldn't trade their public policy experiences for any other life. Serving in a public policy position proved to be a grand adventure, often an exciting one, the high point of a career.

A second striking conclusion is how many of our contributors attribute their public policy careers to luck, good fortune, or serendipity. There is, in many of these essays, a sense of wonder, even awe, that a person from a small town, often of an immigrant family, usually lacking establishment political connections, can, on the basis of intelligence and hard work, rise high in the policy-making hierarchy. Perhaps we can say,

"Only in America!" But it is true that few of our contributors came from wealthy or well-connected families. Rather, they made it on their own.

Third, many of them also had mentors who helped along the way: mainly teachers who recognized their abilities, sometimes colleagues or superiors. So while, on the one hand, our contributors point to luck as a factor, they also, virtually all point to a person, emphasize the need to be well prepared, to be in the right place at the right time, and to be prepared to take advantage of the opportunities offered. It turns out that luck plays a role but, when lightning strikes and the job offer opens or the invitation comes, you also have to have the background, abilities, experience, and talents to be able to take advantage of it.

A fourth general conclusion that comes through from all our authors is the importance of a good education. An education in the liberal arts, one that gives you a broad and comprehensive background, that teaches you analytic skills and how to write well, facility in oral as well as written expression, a background not just in political science but in history, economics, sociology, philosophy, computer skills, and, if you're interested in foreign affairs, international relations, area studies, and foreign languages. Technical skills and particular specialization may also be useful but among our contributors there seems to be no substitute for a good, solid liberal arts education.

That may not necessarily involve getting a Ph.D., however. The consensus nowadays is that a master's degree (M.A.–master of arts, M.P.A.–master of public administration, M.P.P.–master of public policy) is almost an entry-level degree in Washington policy making, particularly in such areas as diplomacy, economics, administration, budgeting, and public policy. It is still possible for a person with just a bachelor's degree to enter the Washington public policy arena and, on that basis, to enjoy an interesting career. But jobs for persons with only a B.A. are increasingly harder to get; in addition, after the first few years, one discovers there is a glass ceiling above which, with only the bachelor's, you cannot rise. So you ought to get that master's degree either before entering public policy or soon after getting that first job.

That leaves open the question of whether you go on and work for a Ph.D. or whether you opt for a law degree. The answer is: it depends. Strikingly, several of our authors conclude that, for the jobs they do—in the Congress, the executive branch, the UN, and so forth—they didn't need a Ph.D. On the other hand, if you're an "in'n'outer" and want to have a varied career in teaching, research, *and* government, or in the think tanks or such agencies as the Legislative Reference Service, then you ought—if you have the abilities—to think seriously about a Ph.D. As for the Ph.D. versus law degree debate, both options have their advantages. Lawyers in Washington are often thought of as pragmatic problem solvers—able to do almost all jobs well—but the specialized knowledge and training that go with a Ph.D. are also highly valued, depending on the job you fill and what you want to do with your career.

Fifth, all our contributors advise flexibility. You need to be prepared for a variety of possibilities. You may need to move several times from one job to another, even from one agency or one career to another. Administrations come and go; congressmen come and go; and Washington policy making is both partisan and fickle. The job you have one day may not be there the next; tenure and permanence are not always possible in Washington policy making. So you need to be flexible and to be prepared to change jobs several times in your career and often on short notice. Uncertainty is sometimes hard on individuals and families but that is the nature of Washington policy making and you, therefore, need to be flexible in case a sudden change is called for.

A sixth general conclusion is how hard all of our contributors worked to get where they are today. These are definitely not laggards or goof-offs. Our contributors are usually too modest to say so but all of them worked tremendously hard in school, got good grades, and *earned* the scholarships and fellowships that got them through graduate school. Recall how many of them in analyzing their careers pointed to serendipity and being in the right place at the right time, but it was *hard work* and *getting to* the right place at the right time that enabled them to be tapped. Luck played a role but you also have to be very well prepared so that, when and if luck does strike, you're in a position to take advantage of it.

A seventh conclusion is the importance of internships and early training in public policy. Go to Washington while still in college, go to the state legislature or to local or county government, get an internship for a summer semester, or year, with a private interest group or think tank. Do almost anything to get yourself into the public policy arena. Not only will this give you wonderful experience, but it will also give you mentors to help your future career; it gives you an advantage when you next apply for a public policy position; and often temporary internships in an office or agency have a way, if you do a good job, of turning into permanent positions. All our authors agree: internships are the key.

It is clear, too, that getting to Washington early in your career, serving in an internship or two, is critically important. Even for those of our contributors who waited to come to Washington until mid-career, they also started early, interned, and made good contacts. What's valuable about an internship is not just that you work in an interesting job but you also learn how Washington works, the give and take of politics, and how to function in an office: to get along with people, to fit in, to function as a budding politician as well as a political scientist. For students interested in foreign policy, a year, semester, or summer abroad is especially valuable, especially if combined with language and foreign culture studies. It is striking how many of our policy wonks got their own first starts as interns, how highly they recommend internships, and how many of them say they learned as much or more in their internships as in their classroom work. Get to know your boss—and his friends as well.

Good grades, a good academic record, and useful extracurricular activities are similarly helpful in securing that first Washington job or internship. You need to have a good, solid record but not always at the genius level, and you can often compensate for your less-than-perfect GPA with communication skills and extracurricular activities that look good on your resume. It is striking how many of our contributors had double majors, put together interesting combinations of majors and minors, earned interdisciplinary certificates to go along with their degrees, studied language or business or economics or journalism along with political science. At the same time it is equally impressive how many of our contributors sharpened their skills by volunteering in election campaigns, participating in student government, writing for the campus newspaper, or doing volunteer work with underprivileged children. Not only do these activities help to compensate for less-than-stellar grades, but they look awfully good on your resume to prospective employers.

Few of our contributors were wallflowers, but that doesn't mean they were pushy. All of them worked hard as undergraduates. They strove to get ahead. They had ambition and wanted to succeed as policy works. If you just sit around and wait for the world to come to you, nothing will ever happen. At some point you've got to sit down with yourself (or friends or family) and decide on a major, on what you want to do in life. These are big decisions but you've got to face them—and before graduation. You've got to match your interests with your abilities (note how many of our contributors started off in engineering before figuring out they didn't have the talent). Then you've got to go after what you want, take the right courses, send in those internship or grad school applications. Because, if you don't take the initiative, no one else will. Fortune plays a role, of course, as our authors have pointed out, but most lucky breaks happen only because someone started the process. So when the call or letter or offer comes, you've got to be prepared for it.

SPECIFIC RECOMMENDATIONS

In this section we turn from general conclusions and advice to the specific recommendations offered by our individual contributors.

Our first contributor is Carolyn Blackwell who graduated from Wheaton College, came to Washington with only a bachelor's degree, and then agonized over where, when, and in what field to return to graduate school. Ms. Blackwell's advice is: if you don't know what your career goals are, don't use graduate school as a place to experiment. Rather, she says, get some work experience first, sort out where your interests and talents lie, try to get a job in your field, and then return to graduate school when you're mature and clear enough about your goals to profit from it. She also demonstrates how by energy and creativity she was able, even with only a bachelor's degree, to take on added responsibilities, that early career choices are important but don't lock you in, that she eventually reached a "glass ceiling" in her area of interest beyond which, without more education, she was unable to go, and that her decision to return to graduate school was based on careful prepared deliberation.

Our second contribution is by Janine Perfit. Ms. Perfit also came to Washington directly out of college but, knowing clearly what her field of specialization would be, enrolled immediately in Georgetown University's School of Foreign Service and earned a master's degree. She began her public policy career in the think tank world but over time move up to a position of program director at the International Republican Institute and the Inter-American Development Bank. Her advice to prospective policy wonks is: do even boring tasks well; keep up with the issues; get to know your boss *and his contacts* (they'll help you someday); Don't make enemies; show a passion for your field and issue; be perseverant; and learn to take advantage of opportune moments. Recall her final admonition: Stir gently, let rise, warm, and enjoy!

Next comes a fascinating chapter by Steven Bosacker. Mr. Bosacker began his political career while still an undergraduate in Minnesota by working for a congressional campaign, went to Washington when his candidate won the election, and eventually rose to the position of legislature assistant. Strongly committed to public service, he eventually returned to graduate school and earned a master of public administration (M.P.A.). He then went to work for the University of Minnesota Board of Regents and was later tapped to be chief of staff to the reform party governor, Jesse Ventura. Mr. Bosacker's chapter stresses timing, preparedness, and taking advantage of opportunities. He urges would-be policy makers to go to Washington early, get an internship, throw yourself enthusiastically into your work. Be hungry but not too hungry, he advises; good manners, civility, and a willingness to compromise are important. Use your education; decide carefully where and when and in what field to return to graduate school; and be proud of your work for the public and on public policy issues.

The next section of the book includes people who decided not to stop at the bachelor's or master's level but to go on directly for a law degree or Ph.D. Our first contribution is by Prof. John Brigham. Prof. Brigham grew up in the Berkeley Free Speech and Anti-War movements; he has been, for most of his career, a leading academic in the field of public law while at the same time retaining his social and political activism. Prof. Brigham suggests that, not only are universities nice places to be and to work, but also that he can have an impact on policy through his students and his writing. He has been especially successful in placing his students in good law schools and graduate programs and influencing policy and courts through them. His published work on public law and policy has also attracted wide attention.

In contrast, Lowell Fleischer also earned a Ph.D. but then immediately joined the Foreign Service after graduation and spent most of his career in the Department of State. He has had an exciting career and been stationed in virtually all areas of the globe; his assignments have also included stints in Washington, D.C. Dr. Fleischer's advice for students is to work in student government or on the student newspaper and develop skills in clear expression, good writing, and meeting deadlines. His chapter reflects the agonizing decisions that many would-be policy wonks face:

law vs. graduate school, State Department vs. writing and teaching, making the right moves within one's career. Interestingly, he concludes by not recommending a career within the Foreign Service (foreign policy has changed), nor does he believe having a doctorate helped (it may have hurt) his foreign policy career.

Our next contribution is by Joseph Nye, a writer of major foreign policy texts and a professor of government at Harvard. Along with several of our contributors, Joe Nye is known as an "in'n'outer." That is, he has an academic career, then on the basis of his ideas and writing he is called into government service, next after serving a couple of years he returns to his academic position (where his teaching and research are enriched by his policy experience), later he returns to government again at a higher level, and so on back and forth. Several of our contributors think of this as the best of all possible worlds because it enables one to influence policy while, at the same time, avoiding being tied to a single bureaucratic career and also giving one the opportunity to teach, write, and do research. If you enjoy the latter as well as the policy world, then the "in'n'outer" career may be for you. More on this below.

Susan Kaufman Purcell provides the next perspective, from the point of view of a woman who has had a career in academia, government, and the private sector. Ms. Purcell began her career as a professor at UCLA, was then called to Washington to work in the administration of President Jimmy Carter, and, though working in various capacities, has been over the last two decades one of the country's leading foreign policy influentials. Throughout her career, and recognizing the need particularly for women to balance marriage, family, and career, Ms. Purcell has looked for jobs that have flexible work rules and hours. She has found those possibilities and the potential to combine work with family obligations best served in teaching, research, and the think tank worlds. Ms. Purcell also advises would-be policy advisers to work hard, achieve good grades, be proactive, and take the initiative.

The final contribution in this section is by attorney William Rogers. Bill Rogers has had a marvelous career as a lawyer and government official and is often thought of as a consummate Washington wheeler-dealer, in the tradition of Clark Clifford, Robert Strauss, or Vernon Jordan. Mr. Rogers reports that, while he chose a career in law, the rest was pure accident. Humorously, he argues that a career in public service is like that of a priest, pastor, or rabbi: you have to love the calling and be prepared to take vows of poverty, charity, and self-denial. But, like almost all our contributors, he has loved every minute of it, serving in one capacity or another with every government since Eisenhower. Mr. Rogers is also an "in'n'outer" and has gone from law to public service and back again on three different occasions. He reports on the frustrations of the policy maker in pushing against bureaucratic inertia as compared with the joys of getting things done. And, while arguing that chance and serendipity are decisive in landing an interesting policy job, Mr. Rogers argues that one needs to be well prepared, to learn languages, and have a good writing background, to go to Washington early, and to be *in the way* should the lightning of a policy opportunity strike. To put this in political science terms, career opportunities and career shifts are the dependent variable; one's reputation, abilities, and preparation are the independent variables.

The discussion now moves from career goals, opportunities, and educational decisions to life as a policy wonk. What is it actually like to work for the CIA, in a think tank, in state or local government, for the UN, the defense department, the media, the Congress, and other institutions? What are the opportunities as well as uncertainties and frustrations that go with being a policy activist? Can you have a rewarding career this way, live a life, have a family, fulfill your own plans, dreams, and expectations? Some of our earlier authors have already partially addressed these issues; here we discuss them head on. And, as we said in the introduction, these are the questions that only rarely can college counselors, parents, relatives, or peers adequately answer.

We begin with an essay by Steve Boilard. It would have been useful in this volume if we could have had separate essays analyzing policy opportunities at the local level, in urban areas, in suburbia, and at the state as well as national levels. But space considerations ruled that out so we settled on a single essay, entitled "Close to Home," that covers most of the issues involved. For the facts are that many political science majors and M.P.A. graduates (like Steve Bosacker) will work mainly at the local, municipality, county, or state levels before, if ever, going to often higher-paying and more prestigious jobs at the federal level.

Mr. Boilard studied political science as an undergraduate in the California State University system, lined up an internship with one of the party caucuses of the California Senate, and parlayed that into a *paid* (rare) internship in Washington, D.C., working for a U.S. congressman. But he was repeatedly drawn back to California, first as campaign coordinator for a (losing) state senate campaign, later, after graduate school and a teaching career in the Midwest, to the professional staff of the California Legislative Analyst's Office (LAO). The LAO provides nonpartisan budget and policy advice to the state legislature, and Boilard tells some amusing tales of his life as a professional civil servant, his dealings with the bureaucracy, and the excruciatingly difficult effort in his job to balance politics and nonpartisanship. Boilard's essay is wide-ranging and may be especially valuable to budding policy wonks who prefer to have policy careers "close to home" at the local or state level.

Next comes a sparkling essay by Elizabeth Gibbons who, in contrast to the previous chapter, has the whole world as her stage and who describe the joys and agonies of her work for the United Nations in the field of economic and social development. Ms. Gibbons stressed the importance of good education, language training, and solid analytical skills. She began her international career as a volunteer with Lutheran World Relief, later got more education and was hired by the United Nations Children's Fund (UNICEF). She has lived in six countries, visited over fifty, and held twelve different international positions. It sounds like and is an interesting career, in difficult countries, with important, even life-and-death responsibilities. But Ms. Gibbons's essay also makes clear that her career path, while fascinating and sometimes glamorous, exacts a toll on one's personal and family life. Her essay intends not to discourage young people from following her career path but to make them aware of both the advantages *and* the costs involved.

In the following chapter the editor of this volume provides a survey of the main Washington think tanks and what it's like to work in these prestigious organizations. He is an exception to many of the stories recounted in this volume in that he had an academic career first, came to Washington at middle age (forty), and continues to divide his time between university teaching and research *and* a policy role in the think tank world. The author shows how think tanks function, how they influence policy, and how they bridge the worlds of academia and policy. He paints a glamorous picture of the Washington think tanks but also indicates the perils of a think tank career and why, after serving in a policy capacity, it's also a good idea to step back from Washington, gain perspective, and do other things. An ideal position, he argues, is to combine university, think tank, and policy roles.

Next came a chapter by K. Larry Storrs who has spent most of his career working for the Congressional Reference Service (CRS). CRS is a division of the Library of Congress; its employees do nonpartisan research work for members of Congress. Mr. Storrs recommends that those interested in a policy career such as his gain, not only a good academic background, but experience in debate, student government, or the college newspaper as well. He has enjoyed his Washington career because it brings together people from all over the country, gives him a chance to do the research and writing that he enjoys, and provides an opportunity to influence congressional decision making. Storrs does part-time teaching at Washington universities as well as working full time at CRS, and it is clear from his comments that he has thoroughly enjoyed his career and found both stability and personal satisfaction in it.

Victor Johnson is another contributor who found great satisfaction in working for Congress. And while K. Larry Storrs first lived abroad and learned international affairs as a young missionary for his church, Vic Johnson cut his teeth on foreign policy as a young Peace Corps volunteer. Johnson went on to earn advanced degrees in political science and international relations, but like Lowell Fleischer in the State Department he is not sure that he needed a Ph.D. to have a successful congressional career. Like other of our authors, Johnson stresses being in the right place at the right time: in his case he was tapped by a rising congressman to be chief of staff of an important subcommittee on a red-hot issue. Johnson discovered that he was "born" for that position and flourished there. Later he had a career as an administrator in the agency that was his first love, the Peace Corps, and as an academic dean. But the congressional experience remained the high point of his career. He advises: be prepared, seize opportunities, cultivate your political connections, learn on the job, and forge your own career path.

The next chapter is by Norman Ornstein. Norm Ornstein has become a fixture on television and in the print media, quoted so often that he became known as "Washington's Leading Quotemeister." But he is also a serious researcher, a specialist on Congress, and, over the last twenty years, a leading think tank scholar. Ornstein is one of those who has made the transition from academic writing to policy writing (clear, straightforward, no jargon), who prides himself on his nonpartisan commentary, and who is especially strong in communicating. His chapter in our book stresses the importance of finding good faculty mentors who can guide your career, choosing a good graduate school, and coming to Washington at an early age. To advance your own career, he—like so many in the book—stresses good writing skills, the importance of early internships as a way to get your foot in the door, perseverance, and flexibility.

Ornstein's chapter finds a nice complement in that by Thomas Mann—not least because the two went to graduate school together, came to Washington together, and vie yearly for the title of "most quoted" even while remaining good friends. And, like Ornstein and many of the people brought together in this volume, Mann has long operated at the intersection where scholarship and public policy, the public and the private domains, come together. The former executive director of the American Political Science Association and the recent director of studies at the Brookings Institution, Mann is well known for his policy writings, his administrative abilities, and his level-headed television commentary. His advice, which in this book is now starting to sound like a refrain: a good political science background, good writing and communication skills, good mentors and apprenticeships, early internships, be prepared when the opportunity arises.

While Ornstein and Mann focus on American politics, the next chapter by Melvin Goodman looks more at foreign policy. Goodman is like Lowell Fleischer: he earned a Ph.D. early in his career but, instead of going into university teaching, joined the government, specifically the Central Intelligence Agency (CIA), immediately out of graduate school and had a marvelous career there and as a civilian in the Department of Defense doing analyses of his area of specialization, the Soviet Union. Goodman has been involved in some of the major events and controversies of the cold war, including wars in the Middle East, arms reduction talks, and the collapse of the Soviet Union. In this volume Goodman is especially concerned with explicating the difference between pure, unadulterated research that the scholar and policy analyst may do, and the politicized use of that research by policy makers. It is a fascinating chapter by a person who has been able to combine a career in teaching, research, and influencing policy, and it serves as a warning that Washington policy making is not all fun and advancement but involves hard political and moral choices as well.

Finally in this section we have a chapter by William Schneider. Although principally known to the public for his political commentary on CNN, Bill Schneider has had a long career as a teacher, scholar, and think tank denizen. What he has done particularly well on CNN—and for which he is widely admired—is to take complex political science concepts, research findings, and poll data, and analyze and put them in terms that the mass public can understand. Bill Schneider's career shows that political scientists can also become "stars of stage and screen." His advice: be well prepared, know your stuff, learn to write and communicate well, be quick on your feet, stay flexible.

In the next section we deal explicitly with the issue of expanding access and career opportunities to those historically excluded or treated marginally in public policy discussion. Here we focus specifically on women, African Americans, and the foreign-born. Obviously there are other marginalized groups in American society but, again, we ran into space considerations, cannot cover all contingencies, and determined to focus attention only on these three important and illustrative groups. The book had hinted at a number of these themes before but in this section we deal quite explicitly with how such marginalized groups have sought to accommodate themselves to the American public policy-making process and how they feel about it.

The first essay in this section is by Margaret Daly Hayes who dealt with the subject of women and careers in public policy. Dr. Hayes has worked in many policy positions in Washington (university, think tank, Congress, consultant, lobbyist, defense department); she tells us that every four or five years she gets the "itch" to move to a new position. She has also not let the fact of being female get in the way: though occasionally finding prejudice against women, she has successfully managed both career and family. Her advice as a woman: don't get hung up on the issue, go forward with your career, become "one of the boys." She also advises: build a strong knowledge and experience base, build a network and use it, be visible and take risks, try a variety of jobs, don't be afraid to leave a position if it's not working out or to seek new challenges, and, above all, don't compromise the quality and integrity of your work.

The second essay is by Thomas Orum who deals with issues of race and careers in public policy, specifically the State Department. Dr. Orum served abroad for many years, mainly in the Portuguese-speaking world: Brazil, Angola, and Portugal itself. He tells some wonderful (and other not wonderful) stories of his adventures abroad as an African American representing the United States government. Always interested in comparative race relations, Dr. Orum wrote his doctoral dissertation on an Afro-Cuban political movement, and at various stages in his career he has taught at the United States Military Academy (West Point) as well as various universities. From his point of view, humor and curiosity have served to supersede the anger he has sometimes felt in his career.

The third essay is by Alfred Cuzán a Cuban-American whose family and personal life were indelibly shaped by the experience of forced, permanent, political exile. For a time the Cuzán's were people without a country, poor and struggling, until they found refuge in the United States. Young Alfredo reported (without feeling sorry for himself) how he struggled to learn English, how he was held back in school, how he adapted to American ways even while not discarding his Cuban identity. He also needed to adjust to American academic life, to the field of political science with its distinctive approaches and methodologies, and to the politics and sociology of exile communities. But like many of our contributors, he made it on the basis of intelligence, hard work, and the development of his own skills. He urges students to find good mentors and teachers, to immerse themselves in the best books, and follow their own interests, Most importantly, he urges students *not* to get stereo-typed or pigeonholed as Cuban Americans (or Greek Americans or Hispanic Americans or African Americans) and only specialize or take jobs in the narrow niche that society assigns them. Instead, Cuzán argues, since we already have a kind of native-born specialization in our own country, culture, and language, we should branch out, study other countries and cultures, and we will find that not only will we become a more knowledgeable and better-rounded people but that our understanding of our own native country and culture will be enriched in the process as well. Interestingly, Cuzán's recommendations from an Hispanic perspective run remarkably parallel to Orum's comments as presented by an African American.

The book concludes with a wonderful essay based upon a speech she gave, by Donna E. Shalala, who was President Clinton's Secretary of Health and Human Services and is now president of the University of Miami. Secretary Shalala had earlier served in the Carter Administration and as president or provost of two leading public universities. It is less well known that she is also a political scientist of note and was widely considered one of the best appointments and administrators of the Clinton Administration. Secretary Shalala's essay, which began as a lecture to Phi Sigma Alpha, the political science honorary, tells us something about her early career but mainly focuses on her Top Ten Lessons for Managing a Large, Complex Bureaucracy. Obviously, this advice is not necessarily meant for the beginning student but her comments are so challenging, provocative, and worthwhile for all policy wonks to absorb that they need to be reiterated here:

1. Know the cultures of your organization.
2. Make sure the right hand knows what the left is doing.
3. Don't overlook the needs and abilities of the career public service.
4. Choose the best and let them do their jobs.
5. Stitch together a loyal team.
6. Stand up and fight for the people who work for you.
7. Set firm goals and priorities—and stick with them.
8. Don't forget politics is always part of policy making.
9. Look for allies where you don't expect to find them.
10. Be flexible, realistic, and don't expect to win every time.

There you have it. No better advice could be given to all present and aspiring policy wonks. Good luck with your own career!

How to Find Jobs in Washington: An Annotated Bibliography

Compiled by Rebecca Root

Alternative Careers for Political Scientists. (Washington, D.C.: American Political Science Association, 1984.) Careers in business, journalism, government, interest groups, politics as well as academics.

Anderson, Sandy. *Women in Career and Life Transitions.* (Indianapolis, IN: JIST, 2000.) Career and life decisions at different stages.

Barkley, Nella. *Taking Charge of Your Career.* (New York: Workman, 1995.) Useful for general career choices.

Basalla, Susan and Maggie Debelius. *So What Are You Going To Do With That? A Guide to Career Changing for M.A.'s and Ph.D's.* (New York: Farrar, Strauss, and Giroux, 2001.)

Baxter, Neale J. *Government Careers.* (Lincolnwood, IL: McGraw Hill, 2001.) Extremely helpful.

Bell, Arthur H. *Great Jobs Abroad.* (New York: McGraw Hill, 1997.) Useful but not specifically political science.

Boldt, Laurence. *How to Find the Work You Love.* (New York: Penguin, 1996.) A popular how-to-do-it.

Bolles, Richard Wilson. *Job Hunting on the Internet*, 3rd ed. (Berkeley, CA: Ten Speed, 2001.) As the title suggests.

Campbell, Beth. *Washington Jobs: How to Find and Get the Job You Want in the Washington Area.* (Arlington, VA: Vandamere, 1992.) Very helpful.

A Career in the Foreign Service. (Washington, DC: Department of State, n.d.) Useful information about working for the Department of State, Department of Commerce, and the U.S. Information Agency.

Career Encounters: Political Science. (Washington, D.C.: American Political Science Association, n.d.) Useful, from the APSA.

Careers and the Study of Political Science, 6th ed. (Washington, D.C.: American Political Science Association, 2001.) A discussion of alternative careers open to political science majors.

Careers in the Department of Defense. (Washington, D.C.: Department of Defense, n.d.) A useful brochure, but getting through the DOD phone answering system to get information about careers is difficult.

Central Intelligence Agency Jobs. www.odci.gov/cia/employment/ciaindex.htm. Getting jobs on the internet.

Damp, Dennis V. *Book of U.S. Government Jobs*, 4th ed. (Coraopolis, PA: D-Amp Publications, 1991.) Where they are, what's available, and how to get one.

DC Jobs. www.eih.com/dc.jobs/

Donovan, Craig P. and Jim Garnett. *Internships for Dummies.* (New York: Hungry Minds, 2001.) Good, useful.

Earning a Ph.D. in Political Science. (Washington, D.C.: American Political Science Association, n.d.) Very useful in providing answers to questions undergraduates have about grad school.

Edwards, Paul and Sarah. *Finding Your Perfect Work.* (New York: Penguin, 1996.) A popular account.

Figler, Howard. *Complete Job Search Handbook*, 3rd ed. (New York: Holt, 1999.) A big handbook.

For Starters: Federal Government Jobs. (Washington, D.C.: U.S. Office of Personnel Management, 1979.) Old but good.

Forty Plus of Greater Washington. www.fp.org. Good for finding NGO jobs in the D.C. area.

Frantzich, Stephen E. *Storming Washington: An Intern's Guide to National Government*, 4th ed. (Washington, D.C.: American Political Science Association, 1994.) Much useful information about internships and living in Washington, D.C.

Frommer's Washington, D.C. (New York: Hungry Minds, 2002.) How to tour and live cheaply in D.C.

Gale, Linda. *Discover What You're Best At.* (New York: Simon and Schuster, 1998.) Making up your mind.

Giordano, Philip and Greg Diefenbach. *Jobs in Washington D.C.: 1001 Great Opportunities for College Graduates.* (Manassas Park, VA: Impact, 1992.) A useful handbook.

Graduate Faculty and Programs in Political Science. (Washington, D.C.: American Political Science Association, 1995.) A helpful compilation of faculty and programs.

Grow, Michael. *Scholar's Guide to Washington, D.C.*, 2nd ed. (Washington, D.C.: Woodrow Wilson International Center for Scholars and the Johns Hopkins UP, 1992.) Part of a series of scholars' guides that cover all major geographic areas; also available as part of the series are audio resources, a film and video collection, and cartography and remote sensing imagery.

Hispanic Yearbook, 15th ed. (McLean, VA: TIYM, 2001.) Valuable information about Hispanics in the U.S., plus, for everyone, important guidelines for career and business opportunities, careers in the Department of Defense, international careers, and careers in education, health, and media.

Hollings, Robert. *Nonprofit Public Policy Research Organizations: A Sourcebook on Think Tanks in Government.* (New York: Garland, 1993.) Useful on this growing field.

Insider's Guide to Washington Internships. (Washington, D.C.: National Internships, 1997.) Good for internships.

Intern in Washington, D.C. (Washington, D.C.: Washington Center for Internships and Academic Seminars, n.d.) A brochure put out by one of Washington's better internship programs.

Internships 2002, 22nd ed. (Lawrenceville, NJ: Peterson's, 2002.) More of the same.

Jacci, Duncan. *Washington for Women.* (Lanham, MD: Madison Brooks, 1997.) A guide to working and living in the Washington area.

Killingstad, Kay. *Mastering D.C.: A Newcomer's Guide to Living in the Washington, D.C. Area.* (Arlington, VA: Adventures, 2000.) As the title suggests.

Krannich, Ronald. *Directory of Federal Jobs and Employers.* (Manassas Park, VA: Impact, 1996.) A useful directory, not specialized.

Lauber, Daniel. *Complete Guide to Finding Jobs in Government.* (River Forest, IL: Planning Communications, 1989.) Where and how to find professional and non-professional positions in local, state, and federal government in the U.S., Canada, and overseas.

Maxwell, Bruce. *Insider's Guide to Finding a Job in Washington.* (Congressional Quarterly, 1999.) Contacts and strategies to build your career in public policy.

McAdam, Terry. *Doing Well by Doing Good: The Complete Guide to Careers in the Nonprofit Sector.* (Rockville, MD: Fundraising Institute, 1986.) The Washington motto: do well (for yourself) by doing good.

Metropolitan Washington, D.C. Job Bank. (Holbrook, MA: Adams Media, 2000.) Good, useful.

Opportunities in Public Affairs. www.brubach.com/opamain.html

Phillips, David A. *Careers in Secret Operation: How To Be a Federal Intelligence Officer.* (Frederick, MD: University Publishers of America, 1984.) Useful information for careers in intelligence.

Pitz, Mary Elizabeth. *Careers in Government.* (Lincolnwood, IL: NTC Publishing Group, 1994.) Part of a series; useful.

Political Science: An Ideal Liberal Arts Major. (Washington, D.C.: American Political Science Association, n.d.) A useful brochure outlining careers for political science majors.

Rowh, Mark. *Great Jobs for Political Science Majors.* (Lincolnwood, IL: NTC/Contemporary, 1999.) Very helpful.

Schwartz, Lester and Irv Brechner. *Career Finder.* (New York: Random House, 1982.) Making up your mind.

Selden, Annette, ed. *VGM's Handbook of Government & Public Service Careers.* (Lincolnwood, IL: VGM, 1994.) Very helpful.

Seymore, Bruce and Matthew Higham, eds. *ACCESS Guide to International Affairs Internships.* (Washington, D.C.: Access, 1996.) One of the few publication focusing on international careers.

Sheehy, Gail. *New Passages: Mapping Your Life Across Time.* (New York: Random House, 1996.) One of the inspirations for this book.

——. *Passages: Predictable Crises of Adult Life.* (New York: Dutton, 1976.)

Smith, Paul I. S. *Think Tanks and Problem Solving.* (London: Business Books, 1971.) What think tanks do.

Studying in Washington. (Washington, D.C.: American Political Science Association, 2002.) Very useful.

Summer Jobs: Opportunities in the Federal Government. (Washington, D.C.: United States Civil Service Commission annual report.) Good for summer, temporary employment.

Total Guide to Careers in International Affairs. (Poolesville, MD: Jeffries and Associates, 1987.) Dated but still helpful.

Trattner, John. *2000 Prune Book: How to Succeed in Washington's Top Jobs.* (Washington, D.C.: Brookings, 2000.) At a higher level.

Warner, Jack and Beverly Sweatman. *Federal Jobs in Law Enforcement.* (Lawrenceville, NJ: Peterson's, 2002.) Helpful in that field.

Washington, D.C. for Dummies. (New York: IDG Books, 2001.) How to get along and get settled.

Wiarda, Howard J. *American Foreign Policy: Actors and Processes.* (New York: Harper Collins, 1996.) Contains useful chapters on think tanks, interest groups, Congress, the executive agencies, including what they do and hints about jobs there.

Win, David. *International Careers: An Insider's Guide on Where to Find Them, How to Build Them.* (Charlotte, VT: Williamson, 1987.) OK, but of limited use to political scientists.

Wood, Patricia. *Applying for Federal Jobs: A Guide to Writing Successful Applications and Resumes for the Job You Want in Government.* (Moon Township, PA: Bookhaven, 1995.) The art of making yourself look good, a useful art in Washington.

Index

About the Editor and Contributors

HOWARD J. WIARDA, the editor of this book, spent the first fifteen years of his career as an academic political scientist at the University of Massachusetts Amherst, then moved to Washington as a resident scholar and program director at one of the country's leading think tanks, and continues to divide his time between Amherst and Washington, between teaching, research, and policy.

CAROLYN BLACKWELL is a recent graduate of Wheaton College in Massachusetts. She worked for the Montgomery County, Maryland, Conservation Commission, worked previously at the Center for Strategic and International Studies (CSIS) in Washington, D.C., and is currently finishing a master's degree in urban planning.

STEVE D. BOILARD taught political science and is the author of a best-selling text on Russia; he is presently a Legislative Analyst for the California Assembly in Sacramento.

STEVEN BOSACKER had a career as legislative assistant in Congress and is chief of staff for Minnesota Governor Jesse Ventura.

JOHN BRIGHAM is professor of political science at the University of Massachusetts, a superb teacher, and author of some of the most original, stimulating, and thought-provoking books in the field of public law.

ALFRED G. CUZÁN is professor of political science at the University of West Florida and a distinguished scholar, teacher, and author.

LOWELL R. FLEISCHER earned his Ph.D. at the University of Connecticut, immediately joined the Foreign Service, and has had a distinguished State Department career serving in Africa, Latin America, Europe, and Asia.

ELIZABETH D. GIBBONS received her B.A. from Smith, an M.A. from Columbia, and then joined the United Nations Development Office. She served in Africa for eight years and is currently director of UN relief services for Central America.

MELVIN A. GOODMAN is professor of national security affairs at the National War College and a former policy analyst at the Central Intelligence Agency.

MARGARET DALY HAYES received her Ph.D. in political science from Indiana University. She worked for the Senate Foreign Relations Committee, the Center for Naval Analysis, and is currently director of the Center for Hemispheric Defense Studies of the Department of Defense.

VICTOR C. JOHNSON has worked for both the House Foreign Affairs and Senate Foreign Relations committees as well as in the executive branch and for the Peace Corps. He is currently senior director for public affairs at the Association of International Educators.

THOMAS E. MANN was executive director of the American Political Science Association and was director of studies for the Brookings Institution; he is a frequent commentator on American politics for national television programs and the press.

JOSEPH S. NYE, JR. has had a distinguished academic career at Harvard University; he also served as assistant secretary of state for international organizational affairs in the Carter Administration and was deputy assistant secretary of defense and chaired the National Intelligence Council in the Clinton Administration. He is currently dean of the Kennedy School of Government at Harvard.

NORMAN ORNSTEIN is a resident scholar at the American Enterprise Institute for Public Policy Research (AEI) in Washington, D.C. A frequent media and television commentator on national politics, he is one of the most oft-quoted pundits in American public life.

THOMAS ORUM received bachelor's, master's, and doctoral degrees and had a distinguished career with the Department of State. He continues to divide his time between the private and public sectors.

JANINE T. PERFIT began her professional career at the American Enterprise Institute for Public Policy Research (AEI) in Washington, D.C., then worked at the International Republican Institute for International Affairs, and is presently program director at the Inter-American Development Bank.

SUSAN KAUFMAN PURCELL began her career as professor of political science at UCLA and was then called to Washington by President Carter to serve as deputy assistant secretary of state. More recently she has worked as director of studies for the Americas Society in New York.

WILLIAM D. ROGERS is one of Washington's most distinguished lawyers and a partner in the leading law firm of Arnold & Porter. He has had an incredible career as a private attorney, lobbyist, assistant secretary of State, policy influential, and adviser to the last seven presidents.

REBECCA ROOT is a graduate student in political science at University of Massachusetts.

WILLIAM SCHNEIDER is an academic political scientist by training but a journalist by profession. A columnist and commentator, he is a political analyst for CNN.

DONNA E. SHALALA, a political scientist, was provost at the University of Wisconsin/Madison before being tapped by President Clinton to be secretary of the Department of Health and Human Services, where she has been an activist, outspoken secretary. She is president of the University of Miami.

K. LARRY STORRS, a specialist in foreign policy, came to Washington as a young man out of graduate school; he is a foreign policy analyst at the Congressional Research Service (CRS).